INSIDE

INSIDE

Life Behind Bars in America

Michael G. Santos

St. Martin's Griffin

New York

www.stmartins.com

Library of Congress Cataloging-in-Publication Data

Santos, Michael, 1964–
    Inside : life behind bars in America / Michael G. Santos.
       p. cm.
    ISBN-13: 978-0-312-34350-7
    ISBN-10: 0-312-34350-7
    1. Prisons—United States. 2. Imprisonment—United States. I. Title.

HV9471.S35 2006
365'.973—dc22

                                             2006041122

First St. Martin's Griffin Edition: July 2007

10 9 8 7 6 5 4 3 2 1

With gratitude and loving memories
I dedicate this book to my friend, my teacher,
my mentor, Dr. R. Bruce McPherson.
He was a great man whose goodness, generosity,
and compassion I strive to emulate.

Acknowledgments

I thank God for opening all of my opportunities to grow. I thank my grandparents, my parents, my sisters, my brothers-in-law, my nieces, and my nephew. Their loving embrace eases my life, and from their support I draw strength.

I thank all of the teachers and mentors who guide me through these decades. They are friends and role models. I am grateful that each accepts me as being more than a prisoner. In particular, I thank Jon Axelrod, Tristan Axelrod, Zachary Axelrod, Peter Benekos, Tony Bisceglie, Mary Bosworth, Patricia Brieschke, Robert Brennan, Tom Cappa, Todd Clear, George Cole, Francis Cullen, John DiIulio, Seth Ferranti, Tara Gray, Colin Harris, Michael Hamden, Nichole Hinesley, Sabra Horne, Tom Jones, Nick Karis, Nancy Karis, Dennis Luther, Chris Mackey, Silvia McCollum, Carolyn McPherson, Phil McPherson, Marilyn McShane, Norval Morris, Joe Reddick, Geoffery Richstone, Maya Silva, Jonathon Solovy, Sam Torres, Howard Kieffer, Jim Sutton, Tom Tompkins, Michael Vitez, Diane Young, and Carol Zachary.

I especially thank Dr. James Schiavone, the literary agent who agreed to represent my work, and Ben Sevier, the editor at St. Martin's Press who opened this publishing opportunity for me. His guidance not only strengthened this book, it makes an indelible contribution to my ongoing education. I also thank Adam Goldberger, the copy editor whose diligence and attention to detail make this book easier to read.

I thank those with whom I share space inside these boundaries. With all of the years that I have served, space does not permit a list of names. These individuals contribute to my development and understanding of life's journey. I hope they find this work worthy of the trust they have placed in me to tell these stories we live.

Finally, with a full heart I thank my beloved wife, Carole. She is my inspiration. Her loving devotion makes all things possible in my life, and for it I pledge all of my tomorrows.

Author's Note

The characters and episodes that I describe in this book are real, although I have frequently changed their names or other identifying characteristics. I began collecting information about prison life in 1987, when my time inside began. Since then I have passed a continuous string of years in prisons of every security level. The tale of my own adjustment and efforts to reconcile with society runs through this book, but this is not one man's story. It is intended as an honest description of life in prison. I introduce readers to over one hundred characters, and through these real-life characters I hope to bring readers inside the walls of the nation's correctional facilities.

To bring readers with me into this abnormal world, I describe the realities of everyday life inside, including countless crimes and violations of prison rules. I have obtained this information from the men I have lived with throughout my eighteen-plus years in prison. Some of the men are gang leaders, murderers, drug barons, and mob leaders. Still others are white-collar offenders. Many of the people I present never expect to leave prison. Others are on their way out.

While gathering information from these men in countless conversations and interviews, I described my intention to write for publication. My goals are no secret inside. This is my fourth book on various aspects of prisons, the people they hold, and strategies for growing through confinement. Just as an author cannot describe all about any culture with a single book, I write continuously to help others understand our prison system and how people proceed through it. Some men agreed to share their stories with me on condition that I do not reveal their identities; others want their stories told whether or not their identities are revealed. I remain true to the promises of confidentiality I made; consistent with those promises I provide details about my various sources of information in the endnotes section of this book.

There is a reason that my fellow prisoners speak candidly with me. I am not an outsider. I am one of them. They know that I have never sought my own release through the punishment of another. No one has ever faced a court of law or a prison disciplinary board as a consequence of anything I have said or written. And no one will ever suffer as a consequence of my work. On the contrary, I strive to illuminate the shadows in which prisoners live.

My fellow prisoners know that I do not write to alleviate my own exposure to the time I must serve. I write to help others understand this growing American subculture that prison administrators have effectively closed off from wide scrutiny. To that end I tell this story raw, without sugarcoating or holding back tough details about the prison environment. I describe the blood that I have seen spilled when acquaintances of mine have plunged knives into the flesh of others. I describe how prisoners manufacture and conceal lethal weapons. I describe the ways that people I know smuggle drugs into prisons, and how those drugs fuel an underground economy inside. Through this story readers will learn how prisoners manipulate staff into consensual sexual relationships. I'll show how some prison gang leaders use manipulation, greed, and intimidation to turn correctional officers into prostitutes. I'll provide the lurid details of prison rape.

This book brings readers into the minds of men who pass decades in cages. It strives to show the motivations and values that drive their behavior. Perhaps more important, I hope to help outside readers understand the environment that exists in these cages. With that information, readers may form conclusions on why our nation suffers from such high recidivism rates. They may grasp why relatively few prisoners manage to grow in positive ways through the adversity of the American correctional system.

Rather than using sociological jargon, I present this story in a narrative form. I base dialogue on the recollections of the participants from whom I've heard firsthand accounts of the various stories I tell. In order to remain true to assurances about protecting identities, I have disguised certain details to protect some of my sources. Although this is a nonfiction accounting, I have used storytelling techniques to write some portions of the narrative in order to bring audiences inside with me; I detail instances in which I've used these techniques in the endnotes section of the book.

Although I do not want my work to serve as the basis for the prosecution of others, nor do I intend for any staff members to lose their jobs, I do not want to leave any doubt about the veracity of what I present. Because I am a long-term prisoner who has been convicted of a crime, some readers may consider me prone to prevarication or exaggeration; that's a risk I take every day in my writing. Just as few would have believed the stories that came out of the Abu Ghraib prison scandal had they been presented by a prisoner, I expect that many will overlook my academic credentials and experience and question this narrative. Some of the stories and details in this book may seem surreal, or even a bit fantastic, to those uninitiated into the world in which I live.

In anticipation of such objections I have included as many details about my methods as are practical in the endnotes section. It is my hope that this transparency will serve to validate my work. When appropriate, those endnotes provide citations of published case law to document that the problems with sex, violence, drugs, and weapons that I describe are true to life. I am confident that anyone who has served time in our penitentiary system will corroborate what I have written. It is important to me that I leave audiences with an accurate image of the sixty-billion-dollar industry, subsidized by American tax dollars, that our correctional system represents. The endnote citations are meant to assure readers that the picture of prison I paint is 100 percent real.

—Michael G. Santos
March 1, 2006
www.MichaelSantos.net

Introduction

As an American, I feel a great sense of both honor and pride to live as a citizen of the United States. Besides the many ways in which our country leads and contributes to the world, we also embody the virtues of kindness, compassion, and forgiveness. Someday, I hope, leaders will extend those same Judeo-Christian values to the millions of people our land of second chances locks inside prison cages.

A branch of the United States Department of Justice predicts that 6.6 percent of American residents will find themselves in a state or federal prison at some point during their lifetime. Although the rate of incarceration in the United States is much higher for members of minority groups, the broad numbers published by the year 2000 census indicate that our country's population approaches three hundred million people. Of this population, our government expects that nearly twenty million people will serve time in prison. That amounts to nearly one in every fifteen people. Many more will experience confinement through the nation's jails and probation system.

Government statistics indicate that 13.5 million people spend time in some form of confinement each year. Ninety-five percent of those we incarcerate return to their communities after serving their sentences. Further, nearly eight hundred thousand people work inside prisons and jails as guards, counselors, administrators, and psychologists, among many other positions. Whether we recognize it or not, the jail and prison system touches everyone in our land of the free.

I know what it is like inside.

Almost two decades have passed since Judge Jack Tanner, from the Western District of Washington, sentenced me to serve a forty-five-year prison term. That was way back in 1987, when I was twenty-three. Ronald Reagan was enjoying high approval ratings in his second presidential term. His war on anyone affiliated with illegal drugs was just blasting off, benefiting from wide public support.

I was not a drug abuser, just a kid from an affluent suburb in north Seattle. That didn't stop me from orchestrating a distribution scheme responsible for supplying hundreds of thousands of doses of cocaine. Our group did not use guns or the threat of violence. The clientele to whom we sold was from similar suburban backgrounds. Our purchasers were consenting adults, people who were not ready to embrace government admonitions that they should "just say no."

Cavalierly, I perceived myself as a late-twentieth-century swash-buckler, but government prosecutors did not view me in such an innocuous light. They frowned upon the lifestyle I had been leading. With no legitimate source of income, I drove Porsches and Ferraris. I lived in an oceanfront penthouse condominium on Key Biscayne, just off the coast of Miami. From that gated community I directed others to distribute cocaine in cities from coast to coast.

Arrogantly, I lived as if I had impunity from the law, blowing tens of thousands of dollars in cash each week as if I were a rock star. I dressed in expensive, tailor-made clothing, wore gold watches with diamond bezels made by Piaget, Cartier, and Rolex. My offshore race boat was christened *The Outlaw,* and that is how law-enforcement officers rightly perceived me.

When the bust came down, agents arrested scores of people in cities from Seattle to Miami. I had just returned from Marbella, on

Spain's Costa del Sol, where I had leased some property on the coast-
line and was setting myself up to establish a new life as an expatriate.
I had been trafficking in cocaine for less than two years. During that
time I had accumulated enough money to live off a small business I
planned to put together, or I thought perhaps I would educate myself by enrolling in college. My hopes at that time were to leave any
prospective legal problems behind me, on this side of the Atlantic.
The criminal justice system put an end to the fantasy life I had been
leading.

Because I had had little if any direct contact with the cocaine
itself, I deluded myself into believing that no jury would convict
me. My high-priced criminal attorneys helped foster those foolish
thoughts, of course. Such lines as "There is a big difference between
an indictment and a conviction" and "With the right amount of
money you can win" gave me the false sense of confidence to think I
could skate through my troubles. Knowing I stood guilty of every
charge against me did not then influence my conscience. Remorse
failed to register with me until after the jury convicted me on every
count, until after the judge had imposed the forty-five-year sentence
that would control and constrict what seemed like the rest of my life.

Scores of other people, my associates and co-conspirators, were
related to my case. The government had charged us, under multiple
indictments, with distributing cocaine worth several million dollars.
My case was big news in mid-1980s Seattle, a time when *Scarface* and
Miami Vice were establishing a romantic image of drug traffickers in
popular culture.

Just as legislators during Prohibition had been committed to
eliminating the poison of alcohol, public officials in the early eight-
ies were increasingly determined to stomp out the scourge of drug
abuse. Those lawmakers demanded sentences for drug offenders like
me that would exceed the sentences judges impose on many murderers, rapists, child abusers, and armed robbers.

Because of the way the system was and is set up, the only way for a drug offender to lower a potential prison term is to cooperate with the government in the prosecution of others. Most of the people who had been involved with me in the scheme chose such a route. Rather than serve decades of imprisonment, they chose to mitigate their sentences by pleading guilty, providing testimony against me and assisting in the prosecution of others.

I understand the choices they made. I feel no anger toward them or anyone else. Like me, they had been reared in suburban backgrounds, where the concept of having to live in prison was about as incomprehensible as living with leprosy. When prosecutors gave them an easier way out, they took it.

My frame of mind was different from theirs. It was not that I had any more allegiance to a criminal code, or any code at all. As my behavior and values suggested, my character was weak. I lived under the delusion that because law-enforcement officers had never caught me with any cocaine, because I knew there were no tape recordings of my voice or videos of me engaged in illegal activity, a jury would never convict me. The testimony of others, I thought, would not be enough. I was wrong. After my conviction, our country's interpretation of justice demanded that I be sentenced accordingly. It is for those reasons that I have served virtually my entire adult life as a federal prisoner.

I blame no one but myself.

When I began the term, our nation confined about five hundred thousand people. Other than those associated with my case, I was not acquainted with anyone who had served time. In fact, I think that prior to my ill-advised foray into cocaine trafficking, I hadn't known a single person who had been arrested. I certainly did not know anything about prison.

Now, of course, I know the criminal justice system intimately, and

I know prison as well as I know my own skin. After two decades of continuous confinement, it feels as if the world of prison and prisoners is all I know. I continue to live through a period of explosive growth in America's prison system. Population levels inside have rocketed by a factor of four. With 2.2 million people serving time in confinement on any given day, I expect that nearly every citizen now knows someone whose life has been disrupted as a consequence of confinement. That was not the case when I came in.

We have celebrity athletes and entertainers who battle through the criminal justice system. Superstar corporate executives like Michael Milken, Bernie Ebbers, and Martha Stewart have served time alongside gang members and felons who live without hope or interest in contributing to society as responsible citizens upon their release.

In August of 2003, Supreme Court associate justice Anthony M. Kennedy delivered a powerful speech to the members of the American Bar Association. Recognizing that it costs American taxpayers over sixty billion dollars per year to house, feed, and care for the 2.2 million people serving time in our nation's jails and prisons, Justice Kennedy suggested that it is our responsibility as citizens to know what happens after the prisoner is taken away. With both a personal interest in the topic and a unique perspective from which to view the system of confinement in this country, I am the person to tell that story.

Prison has become mainstream, touching the lives of tens of millions of Americans. It is a closed society, almost secret in its operations. My own life has been a long odyssey through confinement, one that I expect will require several more years before I can anticipate release. The journey has brought me into contact with tens of thousands of other felons; I am well prepared to describe this world.

I have served time in maximum-security, medium-security, low-security, and minimum-security institutions. I have held a job assignment in the federal prison system's only supermaximum-security prison, where terrorists, both foreign and domestic, serve their time. I live under the same rules and regulations, eat food from the same menus, share the same toilets and showers, as murderers, rapists, tax evaders, and corporate criminals. I listen to the stories of these men, observe their behavior, and witness the values by which they live their lives.

Ever since my prison term began, I have worked to redeem the criminal actions of my early twenties which led to my confinement. It has been integral to my adjustment to work toward reconciliation with my community. Others have not been so eager—for reasons this book will explain—to embrace the values of law-abiding Americans.

One of the choices I have made is to participate in independent personal development programs that have resulted in bona fide academic credentials. I have earned an undergraduate and a graduate degree from within prison walls, and I work with several universities to contribute to the education of others. Despite the lengthy sentence I serve, God blesses me with a calming peace.

Discipline and action have helped me build and nurture an extensive and supportive network of friends and mentors who continue to enrich my life. They help me focus on achieving the goals I set. Many other prisoners have different values, and as such, they make decisions differently than I.

This book seeks to expose readers to the adjustment patterns of the full range of prisoners, some of whom allow rage, hatred, and bitterness to consume them. It describes how the prison experience influences their behavior as well as the preparations they make for the rest of their lives; it explores any expectations they may have for release. I ask men to describe the thoughts that zip through their mind as they participate in bloodshed, as they acquire and use weapons, or as they engage in criminal rackets within prison walls.

The men whom I have chosen to help me describe America's prison system come from various backgrounds. I have selected people who represent prison populations from across America. Some of the men serve sentences of less than one year, while others have no release dates. Some of the men have served numerous previous terms and hail from urban ghettos, while others have never been confined before and come from the sheltered life of suburbia. Some of the prisoners struggle with literacy, while a small minority hold advanced university degrees.

Prison, to a somewhat limited extent, is a microcosm of the larger world. Its population may be, on average, darker of skin color, more volatile, and cruder than people in most typical American communities. But all prison populations draw from each and every class of society.

It has been my intention to provide readers with an authentic taste of prison life, and so readers may cringe as I expose the language and describe the violently charged atmosphere. To help others grasp how this panoply of personalities adjusts to what amounts to a shared life inside these restricted communities, I frequently portray the prisoners in their own words, complete with their individual argot, profanities, vulgarities, and racial epithets. Through these vignettes and stories, readers may gain an understanding of how prisoners respond to the myriad complexities that accompany a life in confinement, and why different men make the choices they do.

I have not always identified the racial or ethnic backgrounds of the characters I present, and I hope that readers will not take umbrage at such offensive terms as "nigga," "nigger," "muthafucka," "motherfucker," "pussy-ass bitch," "cocksucker," "cunt," "Uncle Tom," "cracker," "spic," and the like. This racist and sexist language is common inside the American subculture of felons. It is not restricted to the prisoners or particular racial groups. Staff members, too, use such vulgarities in conversation, regardless of whether they are speaking to a colleague or a prisoner. These are crass communities, and in order to bring the readers inside, I have written this story using the authentic language of the prison environment.

Besides speaking with actual prisoners, I have also pulled information from published legal cases that explain or further illuminate various aspects of prison life. Readers may remember the deplorable pictures of American troops humiliating Iraqi prisoners at the notorious Abu Ghraib prison. As some passages in this book will make clear, humiliation by prison guards is far from the worst thing American prisoners have to fear.

I have made every effort to provide a comprehensive description of this growing American subculture that exists at taxpayer expense. As ugly as it may be, it is a picture of American prisons in the early twenty-first century.

Because I am a prisoner, I have not been eligible to interview or speak candidly with those who set the policies of and staff America's prison system. I have made numerous formal attempts to present my work to those who work at executive levels in the corrections profession. I hope to learn through discussions with them, and broaden the perspective from which I write, but my written efforts go unanswered or are rebuffed. Indeed, I was formally reprimanded for sending one of my earlier published books to a warden. The executive staff member required that I sign a paper acknowledging that she had warned me, and ordered that I never attempt to provide anything of value to a staff member again.

Over the years I have had informal opportunities to speak with countless staff members of lower pay grades. My understanding that their career prohibits them from speaking with me in an official capacity, however, tempers the conversations I have with them. It is a shame that the perspectives of corrections professionals cannot therefore be included in any representative capacity in this book. I only hope that my work leads to a more comprehensive evaluation of the prison environment and perhaps to some kind of forum in which these men and women can present their own viewpoints.

I am certain that all sides would benefit from an open debate on the motives that stand behind the punitive policies of today's prison system, a debate that should include those who administer the nation's prison system, those whom the system confines, and taxpayers whom the prison system ostensibly represents. My choice of language is deliberate; I say the system "ostensibly represents" because those who choose careers in corrections have zero accountability to taxpayers in relation to either "corrections" or rates of recidivism among prisoners. Prison workers may face demotion or termination if prisoners escape, or if institutions run over budget. For such failures, they are regularly held accountable. Clearly the objective is to lock people in caged communities for the duration of the sentences imposed.

No one measures the so-called corrections profession, however, by how many offenders it prepares to live as law-abiding, contributing citizens upon release. Although her statement contradicts the literature published by corrections administrators, one of my former unit managers, who now supervises a prison education department, told me, "We don't care anything about the preparations you're making for release or what you do when you get out. The only thing we care about is the security of the institution."

The reason she doesn't care, of course, is because to her I am a prisoner and not a human being. There is no relationship between her success as a corrections professional and her efforts to help people succeed upon release. It is my considered opinion that instead of providing a bridge to society, prisons erect barriers to reentry in the community. Instead of inspiring corrections, they inspire continual failure. The corrections machine has never been held accountable by the taxpayers who fund it for its ineffectiveness at preparing people for law-abiding lives upon release.

As *The New York Times* reports, our nation's prison population has grown more than tenfold over the last thirty years. It now confines people at eight times the rate of France and six times the rate of Canada. And, of course, prisoners in America serve longer sentences than in any other Western nation. Still, American taxpayers know very little about what goes on inside these closed communities. I am convinced administrators want to keep it that way. What is worse, as prisoners move deeper into their lengthy sentences, they often forget the purpose of imprisonment and adapt to the twisted world in which they live.

As Justice Kennedy observed in his groundbreaking speech, prisons are closed societies. Administrators go to great lengths to design policies that not only physically isolate offenders from society, but also confine their thoughts and restrict their interactions with those outside of these barbed-wire bureaucracies. Prisoners have no access to the Internet, to e-mail, or even to basic word processors. Prisoner telephone access in the federal system is limited to an average of only minutes each day, and those privileges are routinely taken away for offenses as trivial as a three-way phone call with family.

In federal prison, administrators prohibit many from visiting with people in the community whom they did not know prior to confinement. For example, Dr. Sam Torres, who chairs the Criminology Department at California State University, Long Beach, wants to visit me as a consequence of contributions I make to classes he teaches in corrections. Besides leading his distinguished department, Dr. Torres also is retired from an earlier career as a senior United States parole officer. In that position, he met prisoners locked in federal prisons of every security level. When he requested to visit me at a minimum-security camp, however, the warden denied Dr. Torres permission because we do not have a relationship that precedes my confinement. This system of "corrections" hinders my ability to build mentor relationships with law-abiding citizens who can help my transition to society. As future chapters show, policies and practices discourage prisoners from preparing themselves for even legitimate careers they want to pursue upon release.

Those of us in prison live as the pariahs of society, and it is only through extraordinary efforts that some men are able to cultivate networks of support that will help them overcome the obstacles certain to follow confinement. I question whether such policies can help prisoners prepare to lead contributing, law-abiding lives upon release. It would seem that such isolationist policies are more likely to contribute to America's surging prison population levels through increased recidivism. Indeed, those high recidivism rates suggest that serving time in today's prison system makes it increasingly unlikely that a man can function successfully upon return to his community.

My goal throughout this book is to help readers understand what happens to the prisoner after he is taken away. My hope is that it will inspire a debate on steps legislators and administrators can take to increase the effectiveness of this sixty-billion-dollar investment of public funds.

If the end goal is to warehouse human beings, then the American prison system is a costly but effective design. On the other hand, if the goal is to prepare people to live as law-abiding, contributing citizens, then objective data suggest that our prison system is a stellar example of failure, ripe for reconsideration.

Prologue

Minutes after I finished the draft of this manuscript, an officer announced an order over the loudspeaker at the federal prison camp. He wanted me to report to the control center. Expecting bad news of some kind, I addressed and stamped an envelope. Then I sealed my manuscript pages inside and dropped the package into the outgoing mailbox before reporting. It was a good move, because soon after I presented myself, officers locked me in steel cuffs for placement in solitary confinement. As a long-term prisoner who writes about the prison system, I am not surprised when administrators take steps to silence me.

"What did you do?" the officer cuffing my wrists asked me. He wanted to know the reason for my removal from the general population.

"I didn't do anything that I know about," I said. "Living in the unknown is just part of being a prisoner. Isn't it?"

"Well, you must have pissed someone off," the officer said while driving me across the street and into an adjacent prison complex. "A lieutenant told me to come lock you up immediately."

Despite serving years of confinement, prior to that morning I had never been locked in segregation for disciplinary reasons. I did not then know what was going on. When we arrived at the segregated housing unit, an officer with whom I'd had no previous interaction unlocked the steel door and spoke to the officer escorting me. "Why's this asshole here?"

"Don't know. Lieutenant ordered me to lock him up. No reason given."

"Strip down," the SHU officer told me. "Take everything off and throw it in the corner."

I removed my shoes and all of my clothing as directed and stood naked before the two officers.

"Take your wedding ring off too. I don't want you taking nothin' into my hole."

"What do you mean take my wedding ring off? It's just a silver band, and the policy authorizes me to keep it on my finger as long as it has no stones. I don't want to remove it."

"I don't give a fuck what you want, asshole. And don't tell me about no policy. This is my hole and I'm running it." The officer stood before me in a challenging position, as if he wanted to fight. "Now are you going to take the fuckin' ring off or am I?"

"I'm not resisting you," I said while holding my open hands out to my sides. "I'm just asking you to show me where the policy concerning wedding rings has changed."

"Turn around and face the wall!" The officer barked the order as if he were a drill sergeant.

I complied and stood naked, nose to the wall. The officer grabbed the wrist of my right arm and yanked it behind my back, bending it up at the elbow toward my shoulder. "When I give you an order you fucking follow. Got it? I've enough problems in here and don't need no fuckin' scum bags questionin' my authority. Now are you going to take the ring off or am I?"

I contemplated challenging the officer further, then realized this is a small battle in the longer war of surviving a lengthy prison term. I removed the ring and handed it to him. He then issued me an orange jumpsuit and locked me into a tiny cell designed to hold two prisoners. Two men were lying on their steel racks and another was stretched out on the floor. With no room in the cell, I slid the mat that a guard had handed me onto the concrete beneath the rack, my head near the toilet. It left no walking room in the filthy space.

During the fifteen hours I spent in the cell, no officer came to explain my change in status. Although I would have welcomed an explanation, it wasn't necessary. I surmised that the administration was taking steps to remove me from the population because of publishing efforts I make to help others understand the prison system. They don't like such information leaving prison perimeters.

At three the following morning, my suspicions were confirmed. That is when officers unlocked the cell door and ordered me into chains. They marched me onto a bus that drove me to an airport in a neighboring community. In small steps because of the chains binding my ankles, I boarded an airplane full of convicts. We began a long flight that would keep me in transit for six weeks.

After stops for prisoner exchanges in Montana and Seattle, the plane landed at a federal transit center. I hobbled off and waited in a large holding cell with more than a hundred other prisoners of every security level. Administrators began processing us into the facility. By midnight I learned that I was being transferred to the minimum-security camp in Lompoc, California.

This was good news. Although I am from Seattle, administrators had locked me in prisons far away from home throughout the course of my imprisonment. It felt good to leave the old prison camp, where the warden had interfered with my mail and opportunities to receive visitors. He was particularly sensitive to my work and did not want me connecting with the world beyond prison boundaries.

After fingerprinting, photographs, and pages of admittance forms, a guard escorted me to a pod on the third floor of the facility. He locked me into cell number 412, where another prisoner lay on the lower bunk. My cellmate's body and limbs, I noticed immediately, were tacked out in gang-style tattoos.

"What's up, holmes," I said, using the vernacular of hard-core convicts. My adjustment has taught me that using a common language with the men around me can help defuse potentially volatile situations.

"What's up," he said. "Where you headed?"

Virtually every prisoner in the facility is in transit. I am reluctant to tell the new prisoner that I am on my way to a minimum-security camp, as I know that those in higher security resent campers. "I've been in a long time," I said. It was a transparent effort to let him know that I was not new to confinement. "On my way out to Lompoc now. Where you headed?"

"I just left USP Pollock last February," he said, confirming my assumption that he had been held in high security. It is a badge of honor among hardened criminals to be locked inside a United States penitentiary. "I'm back on a parole violation. Heading out to Otisville, in New York."

"It's a good joint," I said, letting him know that I was familiar with the federal prison system. "One of the best in the East from what I hear. You from New York?"

"I'm from the Southwest. They got me down as a confirmed gang member, so I can't serve time out here."

My cellmate told me his name was "Funalito," a nickname that he translated for me as John Doe. He was in his late twenties, and as we spent time talking, I learned that he had begun serving time in correctional institutions during his early teens. Infatuated with gangsters and criminals, he had led a violent life. His current conviction stemmed from a drug-trafficking offense that brought a sentence of less than five years.

Funalito's criminal history required him to begin serving his term at a medium-security facility in Oklahoma. Within a few weeks of his arrival at the federal correctional institution El Reno, he said, a prisoner disrespected him in a card game. Funalito sought permission from the shot callers of his gang, the notorious Barrios Aztecas. Permission granted, Funalito lured his target into a card room, then began pummeling him with a steel padlock that he had clenched inside his closed fist. When the man fell to the ground, Funalito began stabbing his mark profusely with an icepick-like weapon.

"I was trying to kill the motherfucker," he said. "But the cops rushed in and I had to bust out runnin from the card room. They caught me a few weeks later. After confirming me as a gang member, they sent me out to the new pen in Pollock. That's where I served my time."

More than a decade had passed since my security level dropped, removing me from the constant presence of penitentiary perils. One of the things I hated about being in transit was that during the precarious status prisoners endure while being transported from one prison to another, administrators herd predators together with prey. The atmosphere is tense. It is like filling a tank with rattlesnakes and rabbits, wolves and sheep. A prisoner must remain alert to avoid altercations.

I spent thirty nights locked inside that cell with Funalito. During that time he described the values that drove his life and the reasons behind the choices he made. I listened to his justifications for committing his life to a prison gang; he was willing to kill people he didn't even know if it was for the gang's cause. Funalito would read the Bible at night, but had no compunction about describing how he spilled the blood of many other people on both sides of prison fences. I listened to him describe which gangs were at war in the prison system and thanked God that I would soon return to a minimum-security camp, where such barbaric behavior does not exist.

Besides Funalito, I met and interacted with several other high-security prisoners during the month I passed in Oklahoma. Several of the men were serving multiple life sentences. Just as in the pen, some of those in transit engaged in the predictable prison scams of manufacturing alcohol out of orange juice and sugar. Others were hoarding food. A few openly pursued homosexual relationships. I kept myself busy doing push-ups all day, and pacing along the tier of the fully enclosed unit. With some difficulty, I tried to keep my eyes from staring and interpreting the demonic tattoos inked on so many arms, necks, faces, and foreheads.

After a few false starts, guards locked me in chains, and I joined another group of prisoners for a flight from Oklahoma to California. We stopped first in Sacramento for a prisoner exchange, then traveled on to Victorville, California. I was called off the plane and marched into a line of several prisoners. Guards assigned us to board one of the many buses operated by various law-enforcement agencies. A deputy ordered me onto a bus heading for the Metropolitan Detention Center in downtown Los Angeles. The bus was transporting mentally deranged prisoners. I felt as if I were the only sane man on the bus. One prisoner sat behind me conversing with the evil spirits in his head.

"I'm a kill you, muthafucka," he kept saying. "I'm a fuck you up." When I looked back I didn't know to whom the man was speaking. His eyes were glassy and looked as if they were staring into space. As the bus began to move, he simulated a grip on an imaginary machine gun. He acted as if he were blasting at cars along the road. "Die, you bitch muthafucka!" he would yell between vicious laughs as he imagined himself a sniper.

Seated directly across from me was another gem of a human being. Despite his wrists being cuffed together and fastened to a chain around his waist, the man managed to slide his hands into his pants. He began masturbating in plain view. The prisoner was oblivious of the others on the bus as he focused his gaze on any females he could see through the window. In prison, such nutcases are known as "gunslingers."

Once we arrived at MDC Los Angeles, officers realized that I had been boarded onto the wrong bus. They removed me from the tank with the deranged prisoners and marched me back onto a bus headed for the San Bernardino County Jail. "Bullet" was one of the other prisoners who accompanied me for the journey. He had been serving time in USP Victorville. As a consequence of his plunging a fiberglass shank into the stomach of a chow hall guard who had reprimanded him for taking three pieces of toast, he was sent to court in Los Angeles for prosecution. Following his legal proceedings, Bullet joined me for the bus ride back to the jail, where he would be held until his return transport to the penitentiary.

Bullet's neck had large, solid block letters in blue-green ink that identified him as a Bulldog. The Bulldogs are a prison gang based out of Fresno, California. Besides the marking on his neck, Bullet's arms were sleeved out with prison ink. He had daggers printed on each of his cheeks and a tribal design that extended across the bridge of his nose and down and around his chin. His forehead had horn drawings, and he had a bulldog graphic inked on the back of his bald skull. The man looks scary.

Whereas I had positioned myself in the back of the bus for the ride to San Bernardino, Bullet parked himself on one of the middle benches. While the deputy was locking the cage that separated the prisoners from the driver, he ordered Bullet to move to the back of the bus.

"Fuck you, bitch," the convict responded. "I'm a sit wherever the fuck I want. What, is you scared?"

"I'm giving you a direct order to move to the back of the bus," the deputy responded.

"And I'm telling you to suck my dick, motherfucker. Now what you gonna do with your bitch ass? You can stand there giving orders or come back here and do something about it. It's on you."

"Oh, you're one of those," the deputy said. "I'll see you back at the jail." The deputy turned around and retreated toward the driver's seat.

"That's what I thought, punk. You ain't got the stones to fuck with no real man. We'll see what you and your fifty cops can do."

"You know what?" The deputy turned around. "We got those fifty cops. They stand ready to kick the shit out of punks like you."

"Fuck you," Bullet said, completely resistant to authority.

When we finally returned to the jail, about a dozen officers were present to welcome the bus. They escorted Bullet off first and marched him to a cell by himself. Officers then locked me and other prisoners in an adjacent cell; they removed all of our cuffs and chains. In the cell next to me, Bullet reached inside his pants and defecated into his hands. He smeared the excrement across his chest, his arms, his neck. After covering himself, he began taunting the guards.

"You motherfuckers want some of me? Come on and get it. I've got all you can handle." He yelled invectives at every uniform that passed. In time, a group of guards rushed him. After subduing him, they carried Bullet out of the cell horizontally. The last time I saw him, his arms, legs, and body were strapped in a chair like a barber's that was bolted to the floor in the center of a locked cell.

After processing me into the San Bernardino County Jail, a deputy directed me to cell 5 of the B-south range. A total of ten inmates were crammed into the small cell. I remained there for five days before guards called me out to chain me up with twenty-eight other prisoners for the final leg of our journey to Lompoc. After making the six-hour drive, and going through the lengthy admittance procedures, I walked onto the camp compound just before seven in the evening on July 13, 2005.

Like in every other federal prison, prisoners at Lompoc camp are crowded into tight quarters. We have two large dormitories here, each holding more than 150 men in rows upon rows of bunk beds.

I am assigned to the top bunk, above "Leroy," a totally blind inmate who makes his way around with a tapping stick. If I stretch my arms out I touch the men who sleep in the bunks beside me; when I sleep, my head is less than twelve inches from the man who sleeps in the bunk behind me. The space is so crowded that I do not have access to a personal locker; I keep my toiletries and clothes in duffel bags beneath my bunk. There is no room for a writing desk, or even a chair in the housing unit. We wait in line to use the bathroom.

The minimum-security camp at Lompoc requires all inmates to work full-time jobs. There is a dairy where inmates work on a farm, a slaughterhouse where inmates tend to cattle and ranching duties. There are construction projects and maintenance crews. Having been here for only five days, I have been assigned to pick up debris and sort through garbage on a recycle crew while I await my permanent job assignment. I expect administrators to assign me a job that will require me to work forty hours each week, as that is one way to slow my writing.

Most prisoners who transfer from one minimum-security camp to another minimum-security camp come via unescorted furlough. Despite my having minimum-security points, as a writer, such privileges are denied me. That is why my transfer took six weeks. It is more difficult on my wife than anyone, as she will now uproot her life in Colorado to reestablish herself here in Lompoc.

This is the life of a prisoner. It is the life I live because of the bad decisions of my youth. Through this book I describe what it is like to live inside.

INSIDE

1

In 1982 I graduated from Shorecrest High School in Seattle. I was a teenager who was driven by such status symbols as Calvin Klein jeans and Armani sweaters—part of the in crowd, but only a mediocre student. I didn't concern myself much with academics.

Like most of my friends, I had parents who were business owners. As a spoiled adolescent, neither advancing my education nor developing a social conscience held much interest for me. For the first three years out of high school, I followed the script and worked for my father. Then, at twenty-one, tired of responsibility and lured by excitement, I joined with like-minded friends in a scheme to enrich us all through cocaine distribution.

Because everyone involved was of similar age and opinion, we did not listen to those wanting to steer us clear of the folly we were about to embark upon; I failed to grasp the seriousness of my criminal wrongdoing. As idiotic and shortsighted as it sounds, neither my friends nor I then considered that our actions could actually lead us into the vise grip of the criminal justice machine. We knew that distributing cocaine was against the law, but our self-indulged minds could not bring us to accept that we were criminals.

The subject of jail or prison was not one that my friends or I identified with or thought about. It was a matter that may have concerned others, but not me. I did not even understand the difference between the two categories of confinement. Then, in 1987, five years after high school, I was arrested. Trapped.

As much as they would have liked to help, my parents had no influence to absolve me from the troubles I had created, or from the shame I had brought our family. I have been incarcerated ever since that arrest, and now, in my early forties, I know very well that there is a difference between jails and prisons. Although society uses both as a response to crime, I now know firsthand that each serves a different purpose in confining people.

The popular media and perhaps my imagination shaped my perceptions of incarceration prior to my arrest. Like many Americans, I suffered from the misconception that all people who serve time live in barren cells and have little freedom of movement. I pictured long corridors of concrete and steel, and men confined to three-walled cells separated from the hallway by evenly spaced steel bars. I assumed that guards locked prisoners in their cells for the duration of their terms, that the men slept on steel racks bolted to concrete walls. Guards, I presumed, were always close by to observe and direct those who were serving time.

In those days I had no idea that living experiences could vary so dramatically from one place of confinement to the next. In one jail, a man may sleep soundly and without worry for his safety. Then, without warning, guards may transfer him to another. The new spot may require the prisoner to remain alert to the constant threat and inescapable presence of predators, sexual and otherwise. He must know not only how to live among violent men who have no hope for a better life, whose concepts of self are rooted in their ability to instill fear in others, but also how to strip naked and share shower space with them.

As I moved deeper into my lengthy journey through the criminal justice system, I learned to live in jails of every kind. And although I am of average height and build, I have learned to live and grow in prisons of every security level without once having had to use a weapon, to spill or draw blood. Others have not been so blessed.

After the arrest at my residence on Key Biscayne, marshals transported me to stand trial in Seattle. It is the city in which I was reared and where I faced a criminal indictment exposing me to the possibility of life imprisonment. With such serious criminal charges, the judge declined to issue me the possibility of bailing out of jail by posting a bond. Because I was a cocaine trafficker, the government rightfully had reason to consider me a flight risk.

Being transported cross-country as a prisoner is a horribly dehumanizing experience, but it is one that I have come to know well over the decades I have served. The United States Marshal Service accepts the responsibility of transporting prisoners across state lines. To ensure security, they lock each prisoner's ankles in manacles that make walking difficult. Then the marshals wrap a heavy steel chain, the kind that children use to secure their bicycles, around each prisoner's waist. Following that, the marshals lock wrists into handcuffs that weave through the waist chain. These security measures effectively restrict the movement of legs, arms, and hands.

Over the years, I've spent much time chained up for transport, but it was never more difficult than on that first road trip on my way to Seattle. I hadn't yet grown used to my new status as a federal prisoner. The worst part, for me, was neither the chains nor the crippling restrictions on my movement. It was fighting the demons tormenting my mind about what my future held, that and having to live in the constant company of other prisoners, other people in chains whose history I didn't know and whose behavior I could not predict.

We traveled on buses and airplanes authorities reserve for prisoners. Traveling days begin around three in the morning, when a guard comes by the room and unlocks the door. The politically correct term for guard is "correctional officer," but at that time I had not seen any "correcting" taking place. The guard uses his flashlight to

wake the prisoners for transport. If the prisoner doesn't respond to
the beam of light in his eyes, then the guard may whack the steel rack
of the bed with his heavy flashlight, or use his steel-toed boot to kick
it. Prisoners are simply cogs in the machine, and guards have the responsibility to keep that machine moving on schedule.

Progressing through each phase of the criminal justice process is
very impersonal. During the transport, guards herd hundreds of
prisoners together. Other than the fact that each of the prisoners in
custody has at least been charged with breaking the law, neither the
guards nor the marshals know much about the people they transport. The very nature of their job requires the officers to treat all
prisoners as inanimate objects rather than fellow human beings.
Their primary concern is security.

The officers do not know who among the prisoners are dangerous
terrorists and who are being transported to face charges of failing to
report a portion of their income on a tax form. Accordingly, the people wearing law-enforcement uniforms, with their heavy leather
belts on which they attach an arsenal of handcuffs, flashlights, canis-
ters of Mace, and other weapons, regard all prisoners as a threat. The
job may not be anything personal to the officers, but for the incoming prisoner, the process is intensely invasive and dehumanizing.
Perhaps that is the point.

My trip to Seattle from Miami took about a week. We had to stop
in several cities along the way to load and unload scores of prisoners.
When I finally arrived in Seattle, the marshals locked me into a small
county jail as a pretrial inmate. The federal government did not then
have its own holding facility in the region. Marshals confined people
being held without bail for charges in federal court, like me, in one of
many surrounding city or county jails. The marshals initially elected
to place me in the city jail of Kent, Washington.

Kent is a suburb southeast of Seattle. When I was confined there in
1987, its jail was relatively new. With a capacity for perhaps two hun-

dred people, it is tiny compared with other places where I have been held, and it is as clean as a well-run medical clinic. I was there only during the initial months of my confinement. After it became clear to prosecutors that I was not going to plead guilty or participate in the prosecution of others, the kid gloves came off and they transferred me into the mayhem of large county jails, which I will describe later. Looking back, I now suspect that the relatively tranquil Kent City Jail was an inducement to cooperate, but I did not recognize it at that time.

The facility itself is designed in the shape of a geometric dough-nut, more like an octagon than round. The perimeter sides of the gray concrete-block building contain either small living units for the prisoners, or administrative and support offices. The living units themselves hold fewer than thirty single-man rooms, and a dayroom with tables where prisoners take meals or play cards and board games when they are authorized to be outside of their rooms.

Guards are not stationed in the living units themselves. Each area of the jail is equipped with a sophisticated electronic surveillance system that allows a centrally located staff member in the control center to monitor the goings-on throughout the entire facility. Fur-ther, the walls separating the living units from the building's interior corridors have large windows. Staff members make continuous rounds walking the corridor, relying upon each other to patrol the living units. The center of the building holds an open-sky courtyard, a concrete recreation square enclosed by the jail's interior walls. The ceiling of the courtyard is of steel mesh, designed to discourage es-cape attempts. Through it prisoners catch rare glimpses of blue and, much more often in the Pacific Northwest, the ubiquitous clouds above. The courtyard provides the only opportunity a prisoner in Kent has to breathe fresh air. I spent as much time as I was allowed walking in loops around that confined space.

The city built that small facility to confine prisoners for relatively brief periods. Most of the men the jail confines await release on bail, serve sentences of less than a year, or are prisoners in a holdover status as they conclude legal proceedings and await release or transfer to a more permanent facility, like state or federal prison. At any given time, the jail confines its share of prisoners who serve sentences of a few weeks or months for offenses like domestic violence, driving while intoxicated, disorderly behavior, and so forth. Other prisoners, however, expect to serve several months in the jail, and perhaps several years or decades in a prison after that.

Administrators in the Kent jail use a carefully designed series of incentives to induce good behavior and compliance with jail policies. The physical structure of the jail itself seems designed to enhance the staff's ability to manage the population in this way. After prisoners are fingerprinted and processed into the Kent City Jail, guards ordinarily issue them a jail jumpsuit and a sleeping mat. Then the guards assign the men to an area of the dayroom's floor in Living Unit C. Unit C is not the lowest of the graduated living units, as guards lock recalcitrant, troublesome prisoners in isolation cells. The dayroom floor of Unit C, however, is the first step for incoming prisoners at the Kent City Jail and represents the bottom rung on the jail's graduated living standard.

Through the surveillance equipment, staff members can monitor not only telephone conversations, but conversations inside the living units as well. On a weekend, when city officers make more frequent arrests requiring jail time, the dayroom of Unit C, designed to hold thirty people, might become home to an additional fifteen people sleeping on the floor. Guards do not allow profanity. They do not allow smoking. Nor do guards allow rudeness or talking in loud voices. Some prisoners refuse to embrace the control of such rigid rules and do not advance their living situations through compliance. But for those prisoners who do comply with the Kent City Jail's strict code of conduct, graduation from assignment on the floor of the dayroom to one of the single-man rooms in the initial housing unit is a sweet reward.

Other than providing a semblance of privacy, the rooms in the initial housing unit are not special. Each has a steel rack for a sleeping mat, and a steel desktop with a steel stool. Each room is equipped with a stainless-steel toilet bowl. The steel sink is attached to the toilet. Rather than faucet handles, the sink has push buttons to regulate the flow of water. The walls and floors are of bare concrete, and each room has a nonopening window that is too narrow for a human body to pass through. Despite the spartan nature of the room, most prisoners try to behave without incident in order to get out of the dayroom and into a much more comfortable single cell.

Staff members hold daily inspections of the living quarters. Those inmates found to be unsanitary or in breach of some other jail regulation are demoted to a lower housing status. Some men move back to the dayroom floor from the single-man room, while guards transfer those found guilty of more serious rule violations to segregation. Segregation, also known as "the hole," means the prisoner remains locked in his closet-sized cell for twenty-three hours a day; he also lives with additional restrictions. The prisoners who comply with the rules of the jail for a sustained period of time, on the other hand, earn privileges and advance to better living accommodations. A measure of hope is thus available.

Whereas prisoners in Unit C live in a transientlike atmosphere, with new bodies appearing each morning, sprawled on sleeping mats across the dayroom's concrete floor, those prisoners who graduate to Unit B live in a more relaxed atmosphere. In Unit B, each prisoner has demonstrated his willingness to comply with the jail's rules while assigned to Unit C.

In the higher-ranked unit, there are no transients sleeping on the floor. With carpeting on the common floors, and oak doors rather than steel, Unit B is much quieter. The single-man rooms in Unit B

have oak bed frames with springs and mattresses rather than steel
racks and mats. They have porcelain bathroom appliances with
faucets instead of stainless-steel fixtures with buttons. And square
tiles rather than unfinished concrete cover the Unit B room floors.
What is more, guards grant those assigned to Unit B more out-of-
cell time than the prisoners assigned to Unit C. They may use those
extra hours of free time to talk on the telephone, play table games
with others, watch television, or sign up for recreation in the courtyard. Each evening, the prisoners in Unit B receive an extra snack.

Those prisoners who remain in the Kent City Jail long enough,
and who maintain a record free of any disciplinary infractions,
graduate to Unit A, which is reserved for jail trustees. The trustee
unit resembles the softer Unit B in appearance, but trustees hold
their own key to the wooden doors separating their cell from the
open area of the living unit, and the only time guards require them
to remain locked in their rooms is at night. The cell is more like a
bedroom. In addition, each room has the special advantage of a
small television equipped with cable access that the prisoner is free
to watch while lying in bed.

Those prisoners whose behavior merits advancement to the
trustee unit earn their privileges not only through rule compliance,
but also through work they perform in the jail itself. They sweep,
mop, wax, and buff the ceramic tile floors to a high gloss. Trustees
cook the meals and deliver them, under staff supervision, to each living unit. Trustees clean the windows and maintain the jail's grounds.
Some work as clerks, helping jail officers to manage inventory and
order supplies. Recognizing that the promise of rewards is better at
shaping behavior than the threat of punishments, administrators
encourage the prisoners to abide by the rules and defer to the policies of the Kent City Jail in exchange for potential privileges.

I served my time relatively easily during those months when I was
held in Kent. I never saw a single fight, never saw an effort by

prisoners to subvert staff authority. There were no weapons, no gangs, no rapes or escapes. All the prisoners were eager to take advantage of the incentives offered, to move into better conditions. It is clear to the prisoners of Kent that jailers cannot influence release dates, but through their use of incentives, the jailers have the power to determine each prisoner's living accommodations. And more important, by behaving well, so do the prisoners themselves.

I minded my behavior and graduated from the entry unit to the intermediary housing unit. Finally, I moved into the trustee unit. The space gave me room to think, to contemplate what I would do with the many years I would have to serve if a jury were to return a guilty verdict. Since the court would not consider releasing me on bond, I would have liked to remain in Kent during my entire pretrial period. Though I knew how I could improve my living situation through good behavior while in the Kent City Jail, I had no tools with which to influence the nameless, faceless prison administrators who would soon decide to send me to another institution to await trial. Before I turned twenty-four, marshals transferred me into the madness of a large county jail, exposing me to new and different experiences of confinement.

Hard-liners may disapprove of jailers or corrections officers providing an opportunity of any kind to people who have been charged with wrongdoing. The idea of allowing inmates to earn their way into taxpayer-funded cells with televisions may be a bit hard for them to swallow. Such people cling to concepts of vengeance, and thirst for a more punitive criminal justice system, expecting those in confinement to suffer through every stage of the process. America has the world's highest incarceration rate, accompanied by the world's highest recidivism rate, suggesting that such hard-line stances may make for bad public policy, and an ill-advised drain on the public purse.

2

While I was being held in Kent, I didn't know how good I had it. How could I? I was in jail. Since I had never been locked up before, the thoughts passing through my mind were about my longings for home and questions of how much time would pass before my release would come. I did not yet have any concerns for my safety during my impatient wait for the ordeal to end.

That complacency changed quickly the morning guards ordered me to roll up my bedding and prepare for transfer. It was an abrupt command, and as a new prisoner I did not expect that others could uproot my life so easily. I wasn't told where I was going, but after marshals wrapped me in chains and packed me into the backseat of their Ford LTD, they drove south. I surmised that they were transferring me to the Pierce County Jail. The sudden change ended my ruminations about the future. It gave me more immediate concerns to consider. I knew I would need to adjust and fight it out through each day.

As in most large jails, administrators jam Pierce County with well over double its intended capacity of inmates. Locking several hundred inmates into separate wings of five floors, that jail stuffs fifteen hundred prisoners into a building designed to hold fewer than eight hundred. When a prisoner enters, guards record his fingerprints and snap those snazzy mug shots. They eventually lead him from the bullpen to the assigned cellblock. As I took those steps I had been a prisoner for several months already, but I was not prepared for what was to come in this new environment.

After a new prisoner passes through those gates of hell, an immediate assault to the senses slams him. So many bodies crammed into the concrete block create an overwhelming noise and stench. Always on, the television blasts out sounds of rap music. The pungent odor of dried urine and tobacco mixes in the air. New prisoners carry a vinyl mat on which they sleep; each prisoner finds his own floor space. Bodies sprawl all over the floors and tiers of the block in no discernible pattern. Walking into a large jail is like being sent to the rough part of town to set up house on the sidewalk of a crowded street.

When I entered the county jail, my days of being locked in a small, well-designed, and efficiently managed suburban jail were behind me. I was not helping prosecutors, so they had no reason to coddle me. It was time to live with the consequences of the choices I had made. And the newest consequence was the foreboding environment of a large, overcrowded county jail.

With thousands of prisoners to manage, guards in large penal facilities consider prisoners the way fishermen consider the thousands of fish they haul in with a good netting. The job description requires the guards to treat each prisoner the same, so they make no effort to consider the individual. No classifications separate rapacious predators from obvious prey. Everyone survives—or not—in the same pool.

The large county jails differ from the small, well-run Kent city jail in many ways. The most glaring, to me, is the lack of any constructive outlet for nervous energy. Prisoners overflow with it. In my experience most penal administrators place a fairly low value on enlightened concepts such as the use of merit systems to shape behavior. That seems the primary focus for administrators who manage the daily lives of the prisoners in Kent.

There may be good reasons for such a stance. Swelling population levels in large jails may so overwhelm administrators that implementing and monitoring merit systems or other quality-of-life and rehabilitation programs is simply impossible. Whatever the reason, in large city or county jails, where we measure population levels in the multiple thousands, and where many offenders begin serving their terms, administrators herd prisoners together and essentially ignore the adjustment inside the cages. It is interesting to note that because this kind of environment is the first stop for so many prisoners, it is perhaps extraordinarily important to the way that men new to the prison system set their expectations, and methods of behavior, for their entire terms.

Ronald MacLean describes his first encounter with the criminal justice system, which he experienced when he was twenty and admitted into the Baltimore City Jail, in Maryland. His descriptions remind me of those months I served in the Pierce County Jail. I met Ronald while we were serving time behind the fences of the federal prison at Fort Dix, New Jersey. Both of us had more than a decade of imprisonment behind us when we spoke. He and I were assigned to the same housing unit, and we sat at an outside picnic table while he told me about the early days of his first period of confinement. When locked up, he said, each prisoner must fend for himself.

Like many prisoners who serve time in large city or county jails, Ronald said the environment he remembers resembles that of a gladiator school. "That place is a tough jail, man, I mean *wild*. It don't make no difference if a guy wants to mind his business and do his time. Unless he knows someone that is known up in the jail, or cats know him for having some power out in the streets, a muthafucka better be ready to get down, to fight for real. And I ain't talkin' 'bout with these here," Ronald explains while holding up clenched fists. "A cat gotta make his self known. Better he gets hisself a shank, or if he ain't got time to find no blade, then a nigga better be lookin' for a mop ringer, a chair, or a pool stick. Word! 'Cause as soon as a muthafucka come through the do', and the po-lease lock that gate behind his sorry ass, it's on. Every nigga in the block gonna be scheming on his shoes, his watch, his cig'rette, and the ways he carry hisself. If a muthafucka be soft, or pretty, cats gonna notice and word gonna spread. He gonna be tried. Oh believe dat! Niggas gonna try him. Dey want dat ass."

Ronald is describing how events unfold for the new prisoner who walks into the bullpen, a large cage where jailers hold prisoners during the receiving and admittance procedures. The tank, with three solid concrete walls and one wall of steel bars, is about half the size of a typical high school classroom, perhaps twenty feet by fifteen feet. In a large city jail like Baltimore, where police constantly arrest felons and lock them into custody, the jail's bullpen always resembles a can of packed meat. Ronald estimates the bullpen holds forty people, and during peak times the population inside the cage can double, to more than eighty.

After Ronald's own arrest at one in the afternoon, guards processed and then placed him in the cage at four. He remained there until guards assigned him to a housing unit after two the following morning. Some prisoners, he says, are crowded in that cage for more than twenty-four hours before a cell opens for them.

It is when guards lock the prisoner inside the bullpen, Ronald explains, that all the other prisoners' eyes bore into him. I certainly know what that is like. Experienced prisoners constantly observe the goings-on of everyone and everything in the cage. They watch how a man reacts when another prisoner asks him for a cigarette. Someone else might demand the sandwich from his lunch sack. Prisoners take kindness for weakness in jail. It is more acceptable to throw food in the garbage than to allow another prisoner even to insinuate that he is applying pressure to take it.

Other prisoners listen to a man's tone of voice, observe his posture and the personal space he commands within the jail tank. A mean face helps. Most important, those looking to extort, otherwise known as "putting their press game down," will try to ascertain whether new prisoners know anyone in the jail or the prison system. Predators will mark for exploitation the poor souls who lack contacts or acquaintances in the jail, the ones who appear lost, vulnerable, or frightened. As Ronald explains, "Niggas gonna try anyone who be soft."

Ronald grew up in the Westport Projects, a tough neighborhood in South Baltimore. Rather than blemishing or disgracing one's character, in his community being arrested and confined brings a badge of honor. "I don't give a damn 'bout doing time. I always expected it. And when my time comes I intend to stand up and bring it like a man. I know I can do mines anywhere."

He is close with three of his uncles, each of whom is serving a multiple life sentence in the Maryland prison system for murder. "My uncles is the type a muthafuckas they ain't never gonna let outta prison. But they tough and they get mad respect up in the joint. Ain't nobody gonna fuck with me in the jail 'cause every swingin' dick up in there knows I'm playing for keeps. Anyone who comes at me gonna have to see my peoples too."

Within a few hours of the time that guards locked Ronald in the holding tank, prisoner orderlies managed to smuggle him some cigarettes. That simple gesture let others in the tank know that Ronald had friends in the jail, that he was not alone. There were scores of prisoners already settled in who resided in the same housing projects where Ronald and his brothers lived. Through telephone calls home, those prisoners already knew that Ronald had been arrested; they rightfully surmised that he would soon be in the holding tank awaiting transfer to the living units.

News in confinement spreads like a gasoline fire. It did not matter to which housing unit guards assigned Ronald. With each unit holding more than one hundred men, Ronald expected that he would have relationships through his criminal network wherever guards sent him.

Whereas administrators ordinarily assign new arrivals at the Kent City Jail to a barren receiving unit and encourage the prisoners to behave in a manner that allows them to advance to better housing, at the Baltimore jail, and in most large detention centers, prisoners await the first available bed. Each housing unit is identical in its furnishings. Once guards assign a prisoner to a particular unit, only a disciplinary infraction results in a change to a different housing unit. Behavior in violation of the rules can result in a transfer to more onerous conditions, but good behavior will not result in any appreciable difference for the prisoner. My experience of living as a prisoner for nearly two decades, and the information I have gathered from interviewing hundreds of other prisoners, convince me that this is a consistent management formula among correctional administrators.

Ronald says that he did not proceed into the jail with any notion of changing his behavior for the better. Nor did the corrections officers express any interest in whether Ronald corrected his behavior or changed his values. He was arrested for participating in the drug rackets, and he expected to return to the drug rackets upon his release from his four-year term. Ronald knew that his initial prison term would enhance his status, that it would show he could take the punishment and survive a stint in even the toughest of conditions. He would emerge from prison with more power and street credibility than he had when he went in, enabling him to expand his criminal enterprises.

Influenced by twenty years of living in an urban ghetto, with family members, acquaintances, and role models all having served time, Ronald was committed to a life of crime and what he considered easy money. For Ronald, a stretch in confinement was an obligation incidental to the choices he made. As a young black thug who quit school in the ninth grade, being locked up was something he knew he would face more than once in his life. He lived the prophecy.

After Ronald passed ten hours in the holding tank, guards finally escorted him to Unit N. Unit N, like all the living units in the Baltimore jail, has an open floor space on the lower floors known as the flats, with a parallel row of approximately twenty-five two-man cells stretching along the walls. An identical row of cells sits directly above the first-floor cells on a second tier.

The cells are of concrete construction and so small that a man can touch the opposing walls by extending his arms; only one person can stand on the floor at a given time. Two metal racks for sleeping mats hinge to one wall, one directly above the other. If the jail is crowded, guards assign another prisoner to lie on a floor mat beside or under the lower rack. A commode-and-sink unit stands between the bed's end and the far wall of the cell. Approximately two feet of narrow walking space separate the rack's edge from the opposite wall. An incandescent bulb lights each cell, illuminating graffiti-covered walls full of gang member's names and signs. From a guard's station at the end of the unit, jailers control the sliding steel bars that lock the occupants in their respective cages.

Each unit contains a common area where the men can watch television, mostly rap videos, or play table games. Young thugs control the televisions in large jails. If they don't broadcast music videos, they tune in to talk shows. Tables are used for games, not writing or reading. The flats also contain a community shower room where up to eight prisoners shower side by side, locker-room style.

The community showers, Ronald says, sometimes serve as a center for horseplay. He remembers one incident where the horseplay turned nearly fatal. "There be this bully in the unit who goes by the name Money," Ronald tells the story. "Money be the kind a muthafucka who like to start shit up. A new cat, Young Buck, come on the block. As he be walkin' out the shower, Money, always playin' a nigga for a fool, taps Young Buck on his ass. Young Buck don't go for that.

"Later that afternoon, Young Buck calls Money out the cell. The cell is at the end of the tier. When Money steps out the cell and onto the tier, Young Buck has him trapped in the corner with nowhere to turn, completely out of sight from anyone who isn't on the ramp. Now Young Buck be a big cockstrong muthafucka, a real live muthafucka from the hood, know what I'm sayin'? When he has Money trapped, Youngster just starts driving that steel up in da bitch. My cell is right next doe. As I hear the work, I step out my cell to see what da fuck up. Know what I'm sayin'? Money is tryin' to fight him off, but he just losin' too much blood. Muthafucka just keeps stickin' da bitchass muthafucka with that shank over and over again. And hard. The piece is hittin' him in the eye, in the neck, in the face, in the chest. Eve'y muthafuckin' where. Blood is shootin' out, splatterin' the walls and coverin' Money's face. I just step back in my cell and let Young Buck handle his bi'ness. Know what I'm sayin'?"

Ronald describes several other incidents of violence that he claims to have seen while locked in the Baltimore jail. Stabbings occur regularly, he says, as tension constantly fills the cellblock. "It's hot up in dat bitch! I'm talkin' a hun'red degrees with no air circulatin'. Niggas go mad crazy."

Many of the guards working in the jail hail from the same Westport housing projects where Ronald lives, and he doubts the ones he knows receive much training. Indeed, Ronald claims that while on the street he sold drugs to several of the people who were then working in the jail. Some of the female guards, he claims, supplement their income by working as prostitutes in the jail. "I popped a few a dem hos my damn self. Sheee-it."

According to Ronald, while he was there, many employees made his time easier by smuggling contraband to him. It is not unusual, he says, for guards to work while intoxicated or high, and many are susceptible to bribes or corruption. "Niggas come work in there for a paycheck, but it be straight ghetto. What dey really after be a bribe for bringin' in some dope or booze or whatever. Guards is quittin' or gettin' fired on the reg'lar, some be gettin' busted; some worked for only a few weeks before movin' on. I'm tellin' you, man, the jail is just like the projects."

Ronald's description of the Baltimore jail reminds me of Pierce County. Those jails differ from the small Kent City Jail. Yet they are like what I hear from scores of other prisoners locked in other large detention centers—places like Rikers Island in New York, the Cook County Jail in Chicago, or the Los Angeles County Jail in California.

Architects design large jails and detention centers to hold thousands of prisoners as they wait through court proceedings, or prisoners who are serving sentences of less than a year. They focus their resources on confining rather than even making the pretense of "correcting" anything.

The operations at the Kent City Jail, I conclude after my many years of experience living in confinement, are the exception rather than the rule when it comes to jail design and management. In Kent's jail, community showers do not exist. And guards do not tolerate horseplay of any kind without sanction. There are few areas out of staff members' direct line of sight, and electronic surveillance equipment keeps sentry whenever the human eye is blocked.

The merit-based housing system gives the prisoners a sense of control over their own lives. It is a management technique that, in my opinion, results in better working conditions for staff, less volatility, and more control over the jail or prison population.

During the many months I served in the Kent City Jail, there was not a single incident of violence, with or without a weapon. Prisoners focused their energies on incentives and the attempt to improve their lives in confinement. I did not notice any problem with staff turnover; they managed with what seemed to me a high degree of professionalism. Administrators in the larger facilities that others

describe to me and that I have experienced may simply lack the resources to manage their jails in such a manner. Or they may lack the
vision to appreciate the advantages that come with management
through the promise of incentives rather than through the threat of
punishment. Some administrators are certainly indifferent to a prisoner's adjustment, as long as he is locked up. The security of the institution is paramount, and the prisoner's preparation for release is
of secondary, and in some cases zero, importance.

3

A few weeks after Judge Tanner imposed my sentence, my status in the criminal justice system changed further. With conviction, the class switches from "pretrial" to "convicted felon." Numbers replace names. A move follows into the correctional system, which considers the men more like packages than people. The system determines the appropriate institution as the classification process begins.

Prisoners never meet or speak with the corrections professionals who decide where they pass their first years. As convicted felons, they do not interact with the people in charge of structuring their lives. Only objective data from the written record matter. From their formulas and systems, administrators make their decision. In my case, they ordered a transfer from the Pierce County Jail to a United States penitentiary in the East.

That order would separate me from my family and support group in Seattle. Despite my having no history of violence, weapons use, escape attempts, or previous confinement, I had just learned that an institution *The New York Times* describes as the most violent federal prison in America was about to swallow me.

The system would cage me within the forty-foot walls that surround that penitentiary alongside nearly three thousand men, many of whom never expect to leave prison. Those felons live without hope of anything better. Every prisoner in the penitentiary breathes only whispers away from extortion attempts, from savage gang rapes, from bludgeonings and stabbings.

"It's muthafuckin' ruthless up inside dis bitch. Vicious! And I likes it," a fellow inmate called Crip Tank told me while waiting for guards to process us inside. Crip comes from Compton, the California city that gangster rap music glorifies. He proudly asserts his allegiance to thug life, and especially to his particular set of the Cali Crips. Crip's speech pattern flows with the loud, violent, rapid-fire sound of a submachine gun blasting bullets. "It's all about da block up in dis bitch muthafucka. Tic tic tock it's da block. Know what I'm sayin'? Give it up or get fucked up."

Within each large prison system, like the Federal Bureau of Prisons (BOP) or any state-level department of corrections, administrators operate multitudes of individual institutions. Those systems operate supermax facilities to hold offenders who pose the most dangerous threat to society. A step below supermax is the penitentiary, a high-security institution filled with men convicted of violent crimes. Administrators call medium- and low-security prisons "correctional institutions." Those with minimum-security classifications serve their time in camps. All prisons differ from jails and detention centers, which are intended for short-term stays.

In prisons, especially penitentiaries, a new inmate must situate himself among thousands of men who have decades of confinement either behind them, in front of them, or both. A distinct culture exists inside, and a wild anarchy dictates acceptable behavior. Some men, such as Crip Tank, instinctively like this environment, but the penitentiary was a new world to me. I was still in my early twenties when I began my immersion in the rules, policies, and customs of high security.

Walking into that penitentiary, I know that only my mind and my will can carry me through; I haven't yet developed the temperament "to be 'bout my work," as Crip Tank advises me. I recognize that I make it through with a guardian angel watching over me, because in spite of the constant madness, some good force keeps me from crashing. Walking into that penitentiary corridor is like driving the ramp to the freeway in the opposite direction of traffic; it is like speeding headfirst into an onslaught of danger.

The penitentiary corridor is twenty yards wide and as long as a football field. It connects all of the housing blocks, each of which holds more than five hundred men. Except during the brief windows of time when guards authorize prisoners to walk from one area of the pen to another, the main corridor is like a long, narrow cavern. The floors shine brilliantly from countless coats of institutional wax. It is quiet except for the light buzz from the ballasts of fluorescent lights that never rest and the jingling keys of a few guards who patrol the corridor.

That calm changes with the quickness of a lightning storm when guards announce movement. The corridor becomes electric as thousands of men bust through the newly unlocked doors and rush in every direction. The air is charged with explosive energy.

Crip Tank thrives in such an atmosphere of chaos. "You gots to take shit up off muthafuckas up in here. Be 'bout yo business. Dis da penitent'ry. A cat gotta be strong in dis muthafucka. A nigga gotta live, gots to move quick, be on top yo toes. Can't never slip. 'Cause if you slip you might get got. Dis da block, muthafucka, where a nigga gots to make a bitch hurt in da dirt, in da glass in da ass." He speaks so fast that his words tumble into each other. "I'm gangsta, an original gangsta. O.G. muthafucka and don't get it twisted. Dis my house, where a real thorough muthafucka knows how to get down."

It's as if Crip Tank is psyching himself up when he is about to walk into the corridor and enter "the mainline," the penitentiary's general population. Some guards, I see, make more allowances for the high-energy tension of penitentiary prisoners. That becomes obvious as one of the officers gives an order for Crip Tank to step away from the locked gate leading into the corridor.

"Fuck you, bitch. Who da fuck you think you talkin' to? Suck my dick! I'll fuck you up right here right now." The guard just looks on as Crip stands there spitting venom. It is as if the guard hears it all every day. Another prisoner walks by wearing a dark blue sweatshirt with a blue rag hanging from the back left pocket of his sagging khaki pants. It is the traditional attire of Crip gang members.

"Wussup, homey?" Crip yells as the prisoner steps past us, on the same side of the locked gate as the guard.

"Where you from, cuz?" The prisoner stops by the guard to respond.

"Compton. Santana block, cuz."

The guard looks at the newcomer as if he might bring a calming presence. "Is this your homey?"

"What dis bitch muthafucka want?" Crip Tank is back into the conversation. "He be talkin' that punkass shit to a muthafucka." Crip Tank grabs the steel bars of the gate and shakes it on its hinges. "Let me out dis muthafucka!" he yells.

"Yo, homey. Chill. I got dis." The new prisoner, Woo Woo, is a Crip member of a different set. He speaks with the guard and agrees to escort Crip Tank to D house.

"Keep your boy right," the guard says to Woo Woo as he begins to unlock the gate. "Boy!" Crip yells. "Who da fuck you callin' boy? I got ten inches a black dick I'll stick deep in yo ass, muthafucka, you talk to me like that."

"Chill, cuz." Woo Woo tries to calm the fire in Crip Tank. "It's live up in here but you gots to fall back a minute." The guard ignores the commotion and unlocks the gate. The movement is on.

During that ten-minute span, the corridor is like a hurricane of activity. It brings an opportunity for the thousands of men locked in different blocks to meet, to mix it up. A thriving illicit economy makes for all kinds of action. Those movement times give prisoners opportunities to settle accounts, penitentiary style. The corridor is packed with people, some running, some walking. It is like the exits of a stadium following a football game. Some think it a good time to draw blood.

Tank passes through the corridor while Woo Woo stops other Crip members to introduce him. They clench fists and bump knuckles in greeting. Tank does not know the others, but their Crip affiliation makes them family.

"You a Crip till you die. Any time you see a Crip in distress, anywhere, ev'ywhere, you get down. We be the untouchables," as Crip Tank tells it. "And I'm in da game deep. I think 'bout Crippin' when I sleep. I think 'bout Crippin' when I wake. I won't stop. Can't stop till the last drop. Won't stop till I hit da dirt."

As Crip Tank and Woo Woo weave their way through the madness in the corridor, Crip Tank spots two cats talking with their back against the wall. Just then a raging Mexican, wearing a hairnet, his arms sleeved out with tattoos of señoritas and daggers, rushes one of the men. "Wuzz up now, *vato*," Tank hears the man say as he slams a sharpened piece of steel down into the startled man's shoulder. Blood springs out in spurts as the man tries to run away. The attacker chases after him in hot pursuit.

"Shit be jumpin' up in dis bitch," Crip Tank says to Woo Woo. "Looky dat nigga there. He leakin'. Das what I'm talkin' 'bout. Dis wild. I likes dis action here. Muthafucka betta be 'bout his business. I need to get me some heat up dis muthafucka here. I gots to stay strapped twenty-four-seven."

"You got that, homey. I'll get you right," says Woo Woo, assuring Crip Tank that he will supply him with a weapon.

"That's what I'm talkin' 'bout. A muthafucka gots to stay ready so a nigga ain't got to get ready."

"I feel ya, cuz."

Just then Gangsta Pimp catches a glimpse of Crip Tank as he and

Woo Woo turn into the D Unit cell house. "Wuzz up, you lil' young muthafucka? I knowed you wasn't goin' to make it out there in Lompoc. Git me my money."

Gangsta Pimp, who leads another clique of thugs, is happy to see Crip Tank. They are on good terms from the time they spent locked up together previously. Gangsta Pimp, who has more than twenty years in on a life sentence, had bet Crip Tank that his red-hot temper would result in administrators transferring him far away from the penitentiary in Lompoc, which is close to Crip Tank's family in California. "What you need up in here?"

"I'm a need ev'y muthafuckin' thing, you black muthafucka. I'm jus' now comin' up off lockup."

"My nigga," Gangsta Pimp says as he knocks knuckles with Crip Tank. "Woo Woo, I got him. Come up wit me. I'm a bless you up in here."

Gangsta Pimp leads Crip Tank to his cell. As a consequence of the influence he wields over so many other prisoners, Gangsta Pimp enjoys the privileges of a single cell. Inside, he keeps a commissary worth thousands. "Ooh, my nigga. You got cake up in here." Crip Tank admires the rich belongings of his homey. Gangsta Pimp grabs two large knit laundry bags and starts loading them with food, toiletries, and clothing to set Crip Tank up. Then he hands Crip Tank two balloons. "Dat's you there, muthafucka."

"What da fuck is this?" Crip Tank asks.

"Just take it, muthafucka. It's eleven-five. Give it to your homeboys. They'll tell you what's up in here. I gots to scatter. Meet me out by the chapel on the next move."

"I ain't going to no chapel, nigga. The only god I pray to is da Crip god."

"Man, cut all that bullshit with me, nigga. Meet me by the chapel. I'm a bless you with some heat."

Crip Tank lugs his two bags of belongings to his tier. He walks into his cell and starts stacking the commissary in the locker. Junebug, his homey from the Ace-Trey Crips, comes by to welcome Crip Tank to the Penitentiary. "Nigga, what you doin' up in my house? I thought you was headin' out to Lompoc."

"Man, fuck Lompoc. Some nigga dropped a dime on a mutha-fucka out there. Had me locked down in the box for six months. I'm here now. Wussup? Wuss poppin' in dis joint?"

"Nigga, this muthafucka's the livest. And we deep wit homeys up in here." Junebug runs down all the action. The gambling. The drugs. The excitement.

"Well I need a drink up in here. What you gonna do for a nigga?"

"I got two gallons up my cell. I'm a bring 'em out. You got dat." Junebug promises to share some of his prison-made wine with Crip Tank. Then, after he has all of his belongings put away, Crip Tank pulls out his two balloons that Gangsta Pimp had given him and sets them on the cell's metal table. Junebug holds the balloons in his hand. "Nigga, you gettin' blessed already."

"Dat's rizzite muthafucka. It's eleven-five. What dat shit go for up in dis bitch?" Crip Tank wants Junebug to move the heroin Gangsta Pimp had passed to him in the balloons; pen slang for heroin is "eleven-five." Other names include "chiva," "negra," "horse," "man," and simply the letter H.

They cut open the balloons with a razor blade Junebug keeps hidden inside the lining of his jacket. Despite the heat, prisoners always wear jackets in the penitentiary if they live in the action. "Dis shit here eight hun'red in each balloon."

"Cool," Crip Tank says. "Cut dis one up into fo' pieces. You take one piece. Dat's two hun'red for you. Get me fo' hun'red in commissary and two hun'red in cig'rettes on this pack. And get me eight hun'red on the wire for the other."

"You got that, nigga. Let me go get to workin'," Junebug says as he runs out to meet with others to sell the heroin. He returns in less than a half hour. "Yo, cuz. Give me a name for that wire. You can call in an hour and it'll be there. And I'm a have that commissary for you tonight too."

Crip Tank gives Junebug a code name for one of his girlfriends in Compton. He calls her his Crip-lette. Then he calls and instructs her to use the code name so she can retrieve the money from a Western Union station. The eight hundred dollars arrives as promised. So does the commissary that Crip Tank ordered. Within hours of walking onto the prison compound, Crip Tank is gangstered up—"G'd up"—and making moves. Thug life. He later makes the hookup with Gangsta Pimp and collects a bone-crusher shank. Crip Tank lives ready for whatever might come his way.

My own adjustment to penitentiary living lacked the color of Crip Tank's. I did not know what to expect from imprisonment. I only knew my intention to survive, to find some way to conquer the fear I was masking and grow through it.

Those initial months and years, for me, brought many thoughts and anxieties about what I would face when imprisonment ended. I set my focus on the first ten years ahead. The scheme under which Judge Tanner sentenced me dictates that—with no change—I serve twenty-six years inside. I knew that upon that distant release I would have no vehicle, no clothes, no place to live, no work unless I made something happen. The punishment for my crimes does not end with confinement. I knew that the bad decisions of my early twenties were going to afflict and shape the rest of my life, and I could also sense that the decisions I would make in the coming months and years would have an equal effect on my future.

Crip Tank made his choice to run with the penitentiary. Realizing the challenges ahead, I knew that I had to serve my time differently. Although I had earned respect from those with whom I interacted prior to my confinement, in the penitentiary I was nobody. I could not pretend that I was a gangster, a wiseguy, or a killer. I would never convince the real killers around me. The structure of the pen influenced the behavior of others; anticipation of the future influenced mine.

Whereas Crip Tank saw nothing but penitentiary life, I decided in those early months in the pen to define and refine a clear strategy to help me overcome the obstacles I would face upon release. That strategy gives me a reason to stay out of trouble. I structure time in a way that minimizes my exposure to problems. With the skills I develop, I help others around me. Through that assistance I form alliances with other prisoners. I help prisoners like Crip Tank, Gangsta Pimp, Woo Woo, and others when they need to file grievances or appeal disciplinary infractions. Those alliances keep me away from problems that tear apart so many other lives in the penitentiary.

Other prisoners with whom I live consider it a waste of time to focus on release. "I ain't tryin' to go to no school. What the fuck good that gonna do me? I got forty motherfuckin' years, holmes. Teach me how to use a knife or how to score some dope up in this bitch. That's what the fuck I need to know."

I never judge people who live by such codes. In fact, it is crucial for me to live as a neutral force. I am not affiliated with any gangs, but I am on good terms with several gang leaders of every race and geographical location, those men who "call shots" or "call dogz." Communicating with those prisoners in a nonthreatening way is essential to my achieving the goals I set for myself.

The consequences that follow disciplinary sanctions do not faze other long-term prisoners in the pen. They consider problems, either with other prisoners or with staff members, as being incidental to living in prison. For some, like Crip Tank and Gangsta Pimp, living on the edge breaks up the monotony. "I likeded the drama," Crip Tank says.

I cannot afford it.

I feel as if each day brings me an opportunity to build another step on the ladder that will lead me out of the pit my convictions have dropped me in. I avoid activities that threaten my progress. Whereas I successfully avoid altercations, I live in the midst of thousands of men who consciously or unwittingly invite violence and conflict into their lives daily. My sharing bathrooms, dinner tables, and small spaces with them keeps me in the eye of the hurricane. Over the decades I have served, I have seen blood spilled, weapons manufactured, and schemes orchestrated. Classes I teach in prison open relationships for me with prisoners who embrace a ruthless code of life, and with the weaker prisoners whom predators prey upon. My companions in prison are the men who spill blood, manufacture weapons, and orchestrate schemes, and the men who are manipulated, dominated, and exploited by the prison's ruling classes.

My experiences with these men, dangerous and heartbreaking though they have been at times, make it possible for me to provide a glimpse through this window I am opening into the world of penitentiary living.

4

A massive riot sent parts of the U.S. Penitentiary up in flames a few months before I arrived. Prisoners upset with a recent legal decision laid siege, taking nearly a hundred hostages and destroying several buildings. Those prisoners kept control of the penitentiary for over a week. After authorities squashed the disturbance, they erected several new buildings inside the walls. Among them is a large detention center that includes the prison's visiting room.

One sunny Saturday morning, a few years into my sentence, I walked down the long corridor leading to the visiting room on the third floor of that new detention center. Dr. R. Bruce McPherson, a professor from Chicago who had become a mentor to me, flew in for a visit.

While waiting outside the visiting room, another prisoner whom I did not recognize stood beside me. At that time, rules allowed prisoners to wear sneakers purchased from the commissary into visits. Since those earlier years of my sentence, administrators have figured out that prisoners smuggle drugs into prison through surreptitious sneaker exchanges during visits. They changed the rules. Now men in high security wear only prison-issue transparent plastic slippers and institutional jumpsuits for visits.

"Nice shoes," I said. The man wore a pair of white leather Reeboks. "Did you transfer in with them?" I knew that the prison's commissary did not sell such shoes.

"Yeah. I just got here last week," he told me. "They wouldn't let us wear tennis shoes to visits where I was before. My son's gonna get a kick out of seeing me in these."

"Where did you come from," I asked.

"Just got in from Marion."

The United States Penitentiary, Marion, in southern Illinois, is one of the most secure prisons in the United States. When I stood there speaking about it with the other prisoner, it was the nation's only supermaximum-security prison.

Guards lock only certain prisoners in USP Marion—the men they consider too dangerous or threatening to mix with general prison populations. Its reputation suggests a difficult existence for men condemned to serve time there. Some prisoners who pass several years without incident at Marion can transfer to other high-security penitentiaries. Administrators call such moves a part of the step-down program. USP Marion feeds many of those prisoners who once had been considered the worst of the worst into the general population at my current prison.

"Were you in the control-unit program up there?" I asked. As a consequence of my studying prisons, I have read a lot about life in supermax. Besides my readings, I listen to stories from other prisoners who have struggled through experiences at USP Marion. Many of those men are confined in USP Atlanta.

"That's right," the prisoner said. "Lockdown in the cell, all day, every day."

"How long were you there?"

"I've been down for twelve years. The past six I spent in Marion's cages."

"How do you spend six years locked in a box like that without flipping out?"

"I'm a writer," he said. "I spend my time writing."

"Really," I said, even more interested. "I'm learning to write myself. What kind of writing do you do?"

"I write screenplays, scripts for television. My son's in the entertainment business. He helps place my work."

Before we could finish our conversation, the guard gave me an order to report for my visit. As I left, the other prisoner told me his
name was Chuck. We agreed to hook up later. I sat down with my
friend Bruce and told him about the interesting character I had just
met from Marion. Everyone from the supermax has a story to tell,
and I wanted to learn about Chuck's.

I did not know why Chuck had been in Marion, but I know the
types of prisoners administrators confine there. Tall and lean, fifty-
ish, with sandy hair and a clean cut, he reminded me of Clint Eastwood. At first glance Chuck does not look like a man who would
inspire terror. He walked into the visiting room soon after me. His
visitor surprised everyone in the room. Chuck's son, it turns out, is
Woody Harrelson, the famous movie star of such big-screen attrac-
tions as *Natural Born Killers*. I wondered whether Chuck had done
any writing for that film.

Chuck and I met to speak after our visits were over. Guards, I
learned, locked Chuck in supermax as a consequence of his conviction. He is serving a life sentence for charges related to his alleged
job as a hired assassin. Some Texas drug lords wanted to kill a federal
judge; authorities contend that the dealers hired Chuck for the wet
work.

Contract killing is the kind of crime that leads to confinement in
supermax. A few years after Chuck earned his way into the general
population through the step-down program at Marion, he made an
attempt to scale the forty-foot concrete wall that encloses my current
prison. Guards caught him. They sent Chuck to Administrative-
Maximum Penitentiary Florence, the federal prison system's newest
supermax, also known as the Alcatraz of the Rockies.

Many Americans have a vague understanding of the old penitentiary on Alcatraz Island, in San Francisco Bay. It now serves as a

popular tourist attraction. At one time it was our nation's most secure penitentiary, home to such notorious felons as Al Capone. Hollywood made the prison famous with films like *The Birdman of Alcatraz,* starring Burt Lancaster, *Escape from Alcatraz,* starring Clint Eastwood, and *The Rock,* starring Sean Connery.

The Bureau of Prisons opened Alcatraz in 1934 for "habitual" and "intractable" federal prisoners. Until its closure in 1963, Alcatraz housed the federal government's most highly publicized offenders, its most sophisticated prison escape artists and riot leaders, and its most assault-prone inmates. Even so, Alcatraz had nowhere near the security measures that exist today at its successors, the nation's supermax prisons. At Alcatraz, most prisoners ate together in a regular mess hall and congregated in a large recreation yard; with few exceptions, most any prisoner on the island could mix with other prisoners.

After prisoners made a few escape attempts, and the popular media generated considerable amounts of bad publicity, the Bureau of Prisons closed Alcatraz. The United States penitentiary at Marion, Illinois, replaced Alcatraz as the nation's only maximum-security prison, holding America's most troublesome prisoners; later it became known as a supermaximum.

Still, up until the middle 1980s, being confined inside USP Marion was not too much different from being confined in any of the other high-security prisons in America. As was the case at Alcatraz, most prisoners in Marion were allowed to congregate. But a measure of further security was introduced, as the guards confined Marion's most troublesome prisoners to the "Control Unit," also known as "H-Unit."

Marion's Control Unit has four ranges, known as A-range, B-range, C-range, and D-range. Each range has nine single-man cells that are side-by-side concrete blocks with sliding, steel-cage gates that lock each man in his cell. Guards lock those in the small cells of the Control Unit for at least twenty-two and a half hours each day.

The corridors on the range outside the cells are about ten feet wide and about one hundred feet long; a shower room is available at the end of the range. Within a range, prisoners can talk to each other between cells.

Although policies have since changed, prisoners used to be given an opportunity, individually, to leave their cells and walk along the range for an hour of recreation each day. They could stop in front of other caged cells to talk during their recreation period. Inmates confined on different ranges were not allowed to mingle, but they could shout to each other through the bars. Those confined to the Control Unit eat in their cells rather than in the mess hall with the prisoners in Marion's general population. After the Bureau of Prisons closed Alcatraz in 1963, the Control Unit at Marion became known as the most secure section within the most secure prison in the Federal Bureau of Prisons. Generally, it holds the most notorious prisoners, those who threaten the security and order of the more general prison population.

Despite the tightened security of Marion's H-Unit, prisoners were occasionally able to stage a series of violent episodes. Those explosions of violence eventually led to the building of even more secure supermax prisons, like ADX Florence. Murders on the Marion block began it all.

In late 1979, Clayton Fountain, a prisoner in Marion's Control Unit, asked to take his recreation time together with Hugh Thomas Columb and Charles Stewart, who were confined in different cells on the same tier as Fountain. Although Fountain and Columb had passed their out-of-cell time together in the past, they had never done so with Stewart.

In order for Control Unit prisoners to take recreation together, each man had to submit a form in writing indicating that he was willing to spend his allotted time with the other prisoners. After receiving such a request from Fountain, Stewart, and Columb, a guard approached each man individually to confirm that he had agreed to the joint recreation time. After each man confirmed that he had agreed, the guard unlocked each man's cell gate from a remote post off the range. The men were then supposed to walk to the end of the range, where they would put their wrists through a gate that separates the guards from the prisoners so an officer could fasten each prisoner's wrists into handcuffs. Once the three prisoners were cuffed, a guard would lead them to the isolated outdoor recreation yard.

Fountain and Columb were celled side by side at the far end of the range, and they left their cells first. They walked down the range toward the guard's gate as if they were going for handcuffing. But when they came to Stewart's cell, which had been unlocked, guards saw Columb abruptly jump into Stewart's cell. His arm was raised high above his head and ready to slam down like an ax splitting wood. Fountain stood post outside of the cell.

The guards, separated from the range by a locked gate, heard a scream as soon as Columb jumped into Stewart's cell. Stewart and Columb rumbled out of the cell. As they did, Fountain and Columb began to beat Stewart. Stewart tried to escape the beating by running away, but he eventually fell to his knees. Guards saw that blood was pouring out of Stewart. They realized that he was being stabbed. A stabbing is not an unusual event in the penitentiary. Although Stewart tried to defend himself, both Fountain and Columb overpowered him. Stewart collapsed in a pool of his own blood. The guards saw that Fountain and Columb each held a sharpened rod with both hands. While Stewart lay dying on the concrete range, Fountain and Columb kept stabbing him. They used an overhead motion as if they were driving a pick into a block of ice. They stabbed Stewart in the back and head while one was heard to yell, "Die, you son of a bitch!"

After the two had stabbed Stewart numerous times, Fountain walked toward the locked gates where several guards were standing

and ordered them not to come onto the range unless they wanted to
endure the same savage wrath. The guards stayed put. Fountain then
rejoined Columb and the two stabbed Stewart several more times.
When they finished, both Fountain and Columb walked to the front
of the caged area and handed their knives through the handcuff window to the guards. Stewart died of fifty stab wounds. Besides enhancing their prison reputations, both Fountain and Columb were
convicted of voluntary manslaughter and sentenced to fifteen more
years.

The shocking violence of Stewart's murder provides a glimpse of
the type of prisoner behavior that led to the creation of the modern
supermax penitentiaries. They represent society's response to prisoners who kill repeatedly, as Fountain did. Indeed, a couple of years
later, in the fall of 1981, Fountain participated in another murder in
Marion's Control Unit.

On that occasion, Fountain joined his pal and fellow member of
the Aryan Brotherhood Tommy Silverstein for a joint hour of recreation on the range. They were released from their cells after dinner
and walked back and forth in front of the other cells. Soon after they
finished their recreation and returned to their cells, a black prisoner
named Chapelle was found dead on the floor inside of his locked
cell.

Chapelle had run afoul of the Aryan Brotherhood for several reasons. I have served time with many people who knew Chapelle and
they described him as a sexual predator who was aligned with the
DC Boyz prison gang. It was also known that he had disrespected a
prisoner named Vargas, who was a rising star in the Mexican Mafia,
another prison gang with close ties to the Aryan Brotherhood. All of
the gangs are lethal, and gang members commit themselves to
avenge any form of "disrespect" with violent death.

Medical evidence showed that Chapelle had been strangled with
a cord about an hour after eating. Fountain and Silverstein were

convicted of choking Chapelle while he lay on his bed with his head leaning against the bars. In a legal proceeding, Silverstein bragged that he and Fountain had "yoked the nigger." Fountain told another prisoner, "I'm glad we killed him." And Silverstein added, "I'm just sorry I had to kill him through the bars and couldn't get next to him."

After all the lethal violence on Marion's Control Unit, prison authorities decided to take additional security measures. They required three guards to handcuff and escort either Silverstein or Fountain anytime one of them left his cell to walk to or from the recreation room, the law library, or the shower. That was not enough. On a fall morning in 1983, while three guards escorted him from the shower to his cell, Silverstein stopped next to the cell of Randy Gometz, another prisoner on the tier, and inserted his cuffed hands through the bars of Gometz's cell.

Two of the escorting officers stood at a distance from Silverstein, but a third was close enough to hear the click of Silverstein's handcuffs unlocking; the guard also saw Gometz raise his shirt to reveal a steel shank sticking out of his waistband. Some prisoners make weapons out of anything they can; someone made the shank that Gometz gave Silverstein from the steel leg of a bed. With his unlocked hands, Silverstein drew the knife from Gometz and attacked one of the guards, Clutts, stabbing him at least twenty-nine times and killing him. Silverstein said that he felt Clutts had disrespected him, and in order to restore his pride he was duty-bound to seek such revenge.

Later that same day, while three guards escorted Fountain back to his cell from the recreation room, Fountain stepped alongside the cell of another Control Unit prisoner. Fountain slid his handcuffed hands through the bars, and when he brought them out he was out of the handcuffs and holding a shank. Fountain attacked all three guards, killing one named Hoffman with multiple stab wounds, some inflicted after the guard had already fallen. Fountain also injured the other two guards, permanently disabling one. After other guards dragged the two who were not killed to safety, Fountain threw up his arms in the boxer's gesture of victory and, laughing, walked back to his cell.

The above cases illustrate the difficulty prison administrators have in confining the most recalcitrant prisoners of a large prison system. In one landmark case, the United States Supreme Court held that the paramount responsibility of prison administrators is to maintain the safety and security of both staff and inmates. But the actions of Clayton Fountain, Tommy Silverstein, and others confined in Marion's Control Unit show that such an undertaking is not easy. The state of California, which confines nearly as many people in its prisons as the Federal Bureau of Prisons, responded to this challenge by opening the Pelican Bay State Prison in December of 1987.

As the ranking leader and shot caller of the Crips from Compton, Crip Tank frequently brought his gangbanger friends to see me. They were constantly in trouble and regularly needed someone to help them express in writing their grievances with the prison system or the courts. Lunatic was one of the people I met through Crip Tank. As a hard-core gangbanger, Lunatic came to the federal penitentiary where I was housed soon after his release from Pelican Bay State Prison's supermax unit. His descriptions gave me an idea of how difficult it is to serve time in such an environment.

The Pelican Bay penitentiary is located in the remote northwest corner of California, nearly four hundred miles north of San Francisco. It is a modern prison complex with three completely separate facilities. It has a maximum-security prison with approximately two thousand prisoners in its general population, and a minimum-security prison that holds about two hundred prisoners. Besides those two facilities, Pelican Bay also operates a security housing unit, commonly referred to as the SHU, which is located in a separate complex inside the security perimeter. That is where Lunatic spent his time at Pelican Bay.

By design, the SHU at Pelican Bay imposes conditions far harsher than those found anywhere else in the California prison system. It confines between one thousand and fifteen hundred prisoners to small windowless cells for twenty-two and a half hours each day. Those assigned to the SHU are denied access to prison work programs and group exercise yards. The SHU cells are reserved for those prisoners in the California Department of Corrections system who become affiliated with a prison gang or commit serious infractions once in prison, prisoners too violent or disruptive for other settings.

The chief judge from the federal court in the Northern District of California presided over a lengthy trial through which prisoners challenged the constitutionality of their confinement at Pelican Bay. The judge authored an extensive legal opinion, exceeding one hundred pages, from which I draw much of this information about Pelican Bay's conditions. I include it to provide readers with documented information that describes the culture spawned in supermax penitentiaries.

The judge wrote that the SHU of Pelican Bay is far removed from the usual sights and sounds of everyday life. From the outside, the SHU resembles a massive concrete bunker. From the inside, the SHU is a windowless labyrinth of cells and halls sealed off from the outside world by walls, gates, and guards. "The physical environment," said the judge, "reinforces a sense of isolation and detachment from the outside world, and it helps create a palpable distance from ordinary compunction, inhibitions and community norms."

"A muthafucka feels caged up inside them walls," Lunatic said. "I got homeys locked down in SHU, death row, waitin' to die. They're so fucked up they don't know the floor from the ceiling."

The design of Pelican Bay's SHU renders it impossible for prisoners to commit crimes like those for which Fountain and Silverstein were convicted while confined in Marion's Control Unit. The cells of the SHU are concrete blocks with solid steel doors. Designers have outfitted the doors with a narrow trapdoor (that is usually locked) at knee level, and a small window through which guards can observe the cell's occupant. The cell contains no bed frames from which steel shanks can be made, no sliding steel gates through which prisoners can pass hands for assistance in removing handcuffs. Further, SHU prisoners are not allowed out of their cells to roam corridors without restraints. What has been conceived and implemented is a system of total control.

With buildings of modern design, equipped with cutting-edge technology and security devices, administrators consider Pelican Bay a prison of the future. Its intent is to incapacitate completely the prisoners it keeps locked in concrete. Its configuration gives an incredible power to the prison officials, who have the "unenviable task of keeping dangerous men in safe custody under humane conditions," as one judge described the job of prison officials.

Over two centuries ago, William Pitt observed that unlimited power is apt to corrupt the minds of those who possess it. In the supermax-security prison, of which Pelican Bay's SHU is a prototype, a federal court found a tremendous potential for abuse of powers by the custody staff, which at Pelican Bay has led to a conspicuous pattern of excessive force. Indeed, the court found that "the use of unnecessary and excessive force at Pelican Bay appears to be open, acknowledged, tolerated, and sometimes expressly approved."

Coercive environments tend to create us-versus-them atmospheres, and there are few environments more coercive than prison. Many prisoners feel as though their life is like a stone that is being struck not by a sledgehammer, but by a constantly swinging wrecking ball. Bang . . . bang . . . bang. Every hour there is some new blow to one's sense of self.

At Pelican Bay, as in most prisons, administrators make minimal use of incentives or positive reinforcement. Every policy or rule comes with the threat of immediate, severe, and often painful punishment for those prisoners who fail to comply. Charles A. Graner Jr. describes well the experience of working in a prison. He had been a prison guard before he was called to active duty in Iraq. In a court proceeding inquiring into the abuses at Abu Ghraib prison, a whistleblower quotes Corporal Graner: "The Christian in me knows it was wrong," Graner is reported to have said about his abusive use of force. "But the correctional officer in me cannot help but love to make a grown man piss himself."

The custody staff at Pelican Bay, indeed, the entire institution, is led by a management culture with zero tolerance for prisoners who violate the rules in any way. Those prisoners who do violate a rule, the federal court found, are met by a use of force that "is so strikingly disproportionate to the circumstances that it was imposed, more likely than not, for the very purpose of causing harm, rather than a good faith effort to restore or maintain order."

Perhaps not all staff members at Pelican Bay condone the policies and procedures at the prison, but like in any prison setting, expressing any misgivings would serve only to slow or halt their career advancement. No one wants to be labeled a "weak sister." As I have been told by many correctional officers over the course of my imprisonment, the only thing lower than an inmate is an "inmate lover," a "hug-a-thug." Those are the pejorative terms guards use to describe staff members who take the side of prisoners or fail to abide by the ethos of the prison administration.

A powerful code of silence exists in the prison culture, meaning that staff members are expected to support one another, violations of truth or morality notwithstanding. Those who violate the code of silence risk open hostility from other staff. In such a culture, where prisoners are marginalized to a subhuman status, abuse runs rampant. And if staff members are questioned by investigators, with notable frequency they report "that they had just looked the other way, been distracted by something else, or had their visibility impaired at the moment the alleged misuse of force was said to have occurred."

Another case of prison abuse that received widespread attention occurred in the federal penitentiary at Florence. I have known several prisoners who served time inside the walls of the Florence penitentiary, and they describe how a group of correctional officers formed their own prison gang. The officers called their gang the Cowboys, and the prisoners with whom I serve time told me how the Cowboys would inflict pain on prisoners whom they deemed a problem.

I accept the veracity of such accounts of prison brutality, but I am conscious of how others distrust anything a prisoner may say about those who confine him. That is why I turn to legal documents to confirm that the brutality commonly reported by inmates I have known is real. Indeed, federal correctional officers who are admitted members in the Cowboys, or who plead guilty to civil rights violations, have on several occasions cooperated with the government in order to reduce their own exposure to prison time on criminal charges. The officers testified to participating in the beatings the "gang" of correctional officers inflicted on prisoners. Other members of the Cowboys gang were said to threaten those nonparticipating officers who complained about ongoing abuses to ensure their silence and protect the offending officers.

One of the cases that was heard in federal court describes how several officers invaded an inmate's cell while he was in full restraints. Cooperating witnesses said that Cowboys acted as vigilantes and kicked, hit, beat, slapped, and punched the inmate. Other officers then allegedly joined the frenzy, hitting the inmate in the genitals a number of times, punching him, and choking him. These are not descriptions of abuses in Iraqi prisons, but abuses right here in the United States prison system, for which officers have been indicted, and in some cases convicted; federal courts confirm the existence of such violations of law in our correctional system.

During the first few years of Pelican Bay's SHU operation, the use of force by custody staff was both overwhelming and regular. There are too many documented episodes to describe. A representative example is one that occurred when a prisoner named Castillo protested against an officer who he said had disparaged him and other prisoners with derogatory names. In the SHU, prisoners eat meals that officers deliver to their cells on trays. The rules require that after mealtime prisoners must pass the trays through the knee-high trap in the cell's door when staff direct them to do so. In protest against the name calling, Castillo left the food tray near the front of his cell but refused to pass it through the trapdoor. The supervising lieutenant then authorized his sergeants to remove Castillo forcibly from the cell.

Although Castillo was small in stature, and neither possessed nor threatened to possess any kind of weapon, guards fired two rounds from a thirty-eight-millimeter gas gun into the cell. The gun looks like a shotgun rifle and shoots rubber blocks at high velocity that ricochet off the cell's concrete walls. Guards also fired a Taser gun at him, which struck Castillo in the chest and stomach. The Taser is an electrical gun that shoots darts which connect to the gun by wires and deliver up to fifty thousand volts of electricity, incapacitating the victim.

Castillo testified in the judicial proceeding that after he had been shot with the Taser, a number of officers entered his cell and marched toward him. An officer struck Castillo on top of his head with the butt of the gas gun, knocking Castillo unconscious. When he regained consciousness, Castillo's face was on the floor and an officer was stepping on his hands while beating his calves with a baton.

Castillo passed out a second time. After he regained consciousness, officers dragged him out of his cell facedown. His head was bleeding and a piece of his scalp had been peeled back. Eventually, Castillo was taken by ambulance to a hospital, where a medical report described the wound on Castillo's head as "a seven-centimeter by eight-centimeter avulsion with a deep groove underflap that appeared one-half centimeter deep, running from the frontal to the parietal area of the skull."

The Castillo incident is only one of many examples of excessive force that the court found at Pelican Bay. Ostensibly it occurred because Castillo, an unarmed prisoner confined to a small prison cell, refused to pass his food tray through the port in his door. My experience suggests that the guards retaliated because Castillo challenged their absolute authority. In the environment cultivated at Pelican Bay, such challenges cannot occur without swift and certain response.

After evaluating testimony of both staff and prisoners, the judge found numerous other incidents of violence against prisoners who were not resisting. Several officers forcibly removed one prisoner, Martinez, from his cell and put him in restraints. After they restrained him, the officers threw Martinez against a concrete wall, rendering him unconscious. While Martinez was knocked out and not moving, the guards kicked him in the head, face, neck, and shoulders. The violence resulted in Martinez losing teeth, receiving a one-and-a-half-inch laceration to the back of his head, and abrasions to the head, face, back, neck, chest, and both legs.

In another incident, the judge found that a guard ordered a prisoner to back up to his locked cell door and bend down so he could pass his arms through the food slot for handcuffing. As the prisoner inserted his arms through the slot, a guard yanked them through the steel door's opening, then bent them up, causing the prisoner excruciating pain. Another guard then rammed his body weight against the prisoner's arm until the bone audibly snapped and broke. Other reports describe officers striking with a closed fist the head of a prisoner in handcuffs and leg irons who was offering no resistance.

Another prisoner, Dortch, a mentally ill African American man, smeared his cell and himself with his own fecal matter. Guards forcibly removed Dortch from his cell and escorted him to a bathtub in the SHU infirmary. According to a nurse who witnessed the episode, five or six correctional officers who were present managed Dortch's bath. They cuffed Dortch's hands behind his back. A guard held him down in the bathtub by the shoulders while another guard ran scalding hot water.

The nurse testified that she heard one of the officers say, "It looks like we're going to have a white boy before this is through, that his skin is so dirty and so rotten, it's all fallen off." The nurse testified that from just below Dortch's buttocks and down, his skin had peeled off and was hanging in clumps around his legs. The officers wanted to escort Dortch back to his cell in such condition, and disparaged the nurse when she insisted on taking Dortch to an emergency room. He was ultimately taken to a hospital for treatment of the third-degree burns the correctional officers had inflicted.

In the "total control" atmosphere of Pelican Bay, administrators use many methods to assert their force, their absolute power over the lives of prisoners. One method is using the fetal restraint, or in prison parlance, "hog-tying." It involves handcuffing the prisoner's hands at the front or rear of his body, placing him in leg irons, and then drawing a chain between the handcuffs and leg irons until only a few inches separate the bound wrists and ankles. Guards repeatedly put prisoners whom they consider troublesome in fetal restraints for up to twenty-four hours. At least one correctional officer asked why fetal restraints are used, and a program administrator responded, "Because we can do it." The officer then asked an associate warden, who replied, "This is Pelican Bay State Prison, and if you don't like it, get out. . . . We're going to do it our way."

"Shee-it," Lunatic told me. "Hog-tyin' ain't the worst thing they do to a muthafucka. Them crackas strapped me down in a four post. I told one them bitches to suck my dick. Next thing I know they spreadin' a nigga out like Jesus, lockin' my arms and legs to one them posts on each co'ner of the concrete rack. I'm lyin' facedown, naked, pissin' and shittin' myself from the mo'nin' to the night shift. It's fucked up."

Administrators also encourage other methods to humiliate and dehumanize prisoners. At Pelican Bay, they positioned several cages at various locations around the outdoor prison compound. Each cage was about the size of a telephone booth and constructed of woven steel mesh. Guards would strip the prisoners of their clothing and lock them naked inside the small cages. Those who suffer the cage are forced to withstand the elements in plain view of anyone who passes by. The cages are visible from the main administrative offices of the prison, and the judge found that "such naked cagings would be known to, and thus implicitly, if not explicitly, condoned by supervisory staff."

One educational program supervisor testified that on a cold morning in January or February, when it was pouring rain and she was wearing gloves and a heavy jacket, she observed two African American men being held naked on the yard in two cages. Another prisoner testified that he had been held naked in an outdoor cage despite his having been bleeding from the nose and mouth after a physical altercation with several correctional officers.

A few years after Pelican Bay opened, the Federal Bureau of Prisons began transferring the most troublesome federal prisoners to its brand-new administrative maximum-security prison, known as ADX Florence. ADX Florence is part of the large prison complex in Colorado where I have served some time in the adjacent minimum-security camp. Administrators built the ADX as a direct response to the murderous behavior of Tommy Silverstein and Clayton Fountain in the USP Marion Control Unit.

Both Fountain and Silverstein had already been serving multiple life sentences, and neither had any hope or expectation of ever leaving prison; having seen and taken the worst the prison system had to offer, both had shown that they had no compunction about killing again. Then–BOP director Norm Carlson decided to do something about holding such prisoners. The ADX would become the supermaximum prison to hold those prisoners who have so conditioned themselves to prison living that they are able to fashion lethal weapons out of nearly anything, snap themselves out of handcuffs with amazing efficiency, and kill at will without remorse or consequence.

ADX Florence has room for more than four hundred prisoners. According to published reports, Blake Davis, a high-ranking Bureau of Prisons official, said that more than half of the prisoners confined at ADX Florence have been convicted of murders, and at least a third of the men are members of prison gangs like the Aryan Brotherhood, the Black Guerrilla Family, the Mexican Mafia, and the Dirty White Boys.

The prisoners pass at least twenty-three hours of every day isolated in their own concrete bunker. The bed, the desk, and the stool are made of poured concrete. Toilets are specially designed in a way that does not allow prisoners to flood their cells in protest. In order to prevent the prisoners from unscrewing the taps in sinks to convert plumbing parts into shanks, architects designed sinks and showers built directly into the cell with push buttons to regulate the flow of water. Prisoners never have to leave their cell, and except for guards and other prisoners with whom they mix occasionally, those in the ADX Unit have no human contact. Yet, in the spring of 2005, prisoners in the ADX who did have a rare occasion to mix used the opportunity to stomp one of their fellow prisoners to death.

Many men at ADX Florence will pass decades, some the rest of their lives, in such conditions. They will never see plant life, animals, or natural scenery again. They will never smell perfume. They will never touch a woman or a child. The supermaximum-security prison is how administrators respond to the threat posed by violent, predatory prisoners.

Supermaximum-security prisons present difficult living conditions for the men confined inside of them. The endless time of idleness, tedium, and tension can drive one to madness, but the cells are so secure that suicide is not a viable option. The supermax prison is designed to isolate, punish, and remove the most volatile, intractable prisoners from the general prison population. Only those who have proven themselves disruptive in other settings or have extremely high profiles—fewer than 1 percent of the nation's prisoners—are held in such facilities.

Some examples of high-profile prisoners held in the federal supermax include prisoners like Timothy McVeigh, before his execution. McVeigh was convicted of blowing up the federal building in Oklahoma. Ted Kaczynski is another. He is the man known as the Unabomber. The vast majority of prisoners never see supermax. They serve their time in either high-security prisons, medium-security prisons, low-security prisons, or minimum-security prison camps.

As would be expected, the higher the level of prison security, the more expensive the prison is for administrators to operate. High-security prisons require heavily fortified walls, ceilings, and floors, and sophisticated electronic systems to monitor every aspect of every prisoner's life. Administrators spent over sixty million dollars to build ADX Florence, which comes to well over one hundred thousand dollars per cell. It was built in the early 1990s. The high construction costs, however, are dwarfed by the costs of staffing such prisons over a period of years.

In supermaximum-security prisons, prisoners, for the most part, do not work. Correctional staff members who earn union wages, together with minimum-security prisoners held in adjacent camps, provide virtually all services, maintenance, and sanitation work.

Although supermaximum-security prisons hold men whom administrators deem the most disruptive in the system, each individual is confined to a completely isolated cell. Such a design provides staff members with total control and essentially eliminates the possibility of riots, inmate disturbances, or murders like the ones committed in USP Marion's Control Unit. On the other hand, such facilities present a heightened risk that correctional officers will use abusive levels of force, as a federal judge found at the Pelican Bay State Prison, and as has been accused at the United States penitentiary in Florence.

Lord Acton wrote over one hundred years ago that power tends to corrupt and absolute power corrupts absolutely; unfortunately, that maxim has seemingly been proven true in the nation's prison system.

5

I am serving the last years of my sentence in a minimum-security camp, and as I write these words I am a few steps away from the adjacent supermax in Florence, Colorado. For a while, I held a job inside that labyrinthine structure. Many people with whom I began serving my sentence are now locked inside the ADX. I am glad that I only walked through the empty corridors while working and have never had to suffocate in the concrete cages of supermax.

By design, supermax facilities separate prisoners from others for years or decades at a time. Most of the men inside those bunkers never expect to leave a life of confinement. Although not all are eligible, some hope to join regular prison populations, which will bring them into contact with other felons. The best they can hope for is a transfer out of supermax to a high-security penitentiary.

Prisons of every security level have their own ways about them. Living in high security differs from living in maximum security, where prisoners spend all of their hours locked down. Like Crip Tank, those in the pen freely mix with more than a thousand other convicts. It's a walled city of madness where men, many with histories of and proclivities for violence, strive for nothing more than making it through one day and on to the next. For them, the penitentiary is the last stop. Everyone feels the tension, the constant possibility of lethal violence.

Little Mick lived in the next cell over from mine. Serving life for a hate crime, he understands the penitentiary. It is the expectations and values of the world outside of prison that he has trouble comprehending. Instead of focusing on strategies that might send him to lower security, or preparing for a contributing life, Little Mick does not concern himself with anything other than the tough time he leads inside.

As we leaned over the beige steel tubes of the mezzanine railing outside our cells, waiting for our unit's release, Little Mick slapped his hands against his pockets.

"Ah, fuck," he said. "I forgot my goddamn piece. Hold up, holmes. I gotta strap down."

Like many men in the penitentiary, Little Mick doesn't like to go anywhere without a weapon. For our journey to lunch he carries his minidagger. It's a heavy needle he stole from the prison factory; the needle is designed for sewing tufts in mattresses. Little Mick conceals the needle inside the casing of a Bic Clic Stic pen. "Slam a motherfucker in the eyes with this," he said while clicking the pen to reveal the point, "and he'll sure 'nough fall the fuck back."

For Little Mick, another advantage of the hidden needle is that guards are less likely to suspect it as a weapon. Steel pipes and heavy "bone crusher" shanks are a bit more obvious, difficult to conceal for a casual stroll to the chow hall.

Seasoned administrators expect convicts in the pen to gather weapons to arm themselves for lethal hand-to-hand combat. That is one of the reasons wardens frequently order institution lockdowns. They want to provide staff members with an opportunity to disarm the volatile men, to confiscate the prisoners' weapons.

During general operations in the penitentiary, guards unlock the heavy steel cell doors each morning at six. Prisoners are then free to leave their cells. They walk to the chow hall for breakfast, to the job details that counselors assign, to the recreation areas, or to watch television. When the loudspeakers blare "Institution lockdown!" all activities for the convicts stop. There are no work details. No recreation. No education programs. No movements to the chow hall.

The only way a man leaves his cell during a lockdown period, for any reason, is if guards first bind and lock his wrists in handcuffs. Those lockdowns give guards an opportunity to search every nook and cranny of the penitentiary for contraband.

To those uninitiated regarding prisoner ingenuity, staff members often appear callous and overzealous in their treatment of the men in prison. And as staff members work through months, seasons, and years, the culture of prison does indeed harden them, perhaps understandably. Witness to so much violence and unhappiness, officers often become an extension of the steel and concrete that smothers the humanity from so many lives. Staff members see too much. Before long, they suspect that all convicts are as alike as the uniforms they wear. All of the men who wear prison uniforms contribute to the sentencing practices that lead to long-term imprisonment; they also contribute to the policies, perceptions, and practices of penal administrators. All of these factors are interlocked in the vicious circle of the prison system.

When administrators order a total lockdown for a weapons search, teams of guards approach each locked cell, one at a time. They unlock the trap within the steel door of each cell. Through the small opening, they direct one man to move to the cell's back wall. They order the other prisoner to place his back against the door. "Cuff up," the guard orders, directing the prisoner to slide his wrists through the door's opening so the guard can bind them in steel. Once he is secure, the guards order the prisoners to change places. After they switch, the guard secures the second man locked in the cell.

With both men in irons, the team members use their skeleton keys to turn the heavy steel bolt and unlock the cell's door. The guards then direct the cuffed occupants out of the cell. If the men refuse to "cuff up," the guards summon the larger and more intimidating Special Operations Response Team (SORT) to initiate a "forced cell extraction."

Prisoners know that forced cell extractions bring violence and a lot of pain. Indeed, when called upon, eight to ten SORT members approach the cell in full-battle uniform with military precision. SORT members generally are the most physically imposing of all staff members. For a cell extraction, SORT members outfit themselves with helmets, padded clothing, and heavy plastic shields to eliminate the possibility of team members being hurt. The SORT members are less than sensitive to inmate pain as they rush into the cell to subdue and extract the recalcitrant convicts. In order to avoid cell extractions, I always cuff up if directed.

After the men vacate the cell, either voluntarily or by force, one team of guards moves inside for the search. To facilitate shakedowns, policies restrict the amount of personal property each inmate can accumulate. Everything a prisoner possesses must fit inside a waist-high locker that is less than three feet wide and two feet deep. Shakedown teams rip through all the personal belongings of each inmate, including papers, photographs, and books. They tear open the seams of clothing, mattresses, and pillows. They take apart lights and plumbing fixtures. They open vents and the speakers used for institutional announcements. The guards explore every opening where inmates might conceal contraband or weapons. When the search team finishes, the small cell looks as if a tornado has blown through. Only the concrete walls and fixed steel apparatus remain in place.

After a particularly brutal gang killing, where Buzzard, Beast, and Rock, members of one gang, plunged their shanks into the flesh of No Good, an enemy who had wandered away from his own pack of thugs, the warden put the pen on lockdown for a month. He ordered a thorough weapons search. Lockdowns are part of his attempt to quell the rising tensions and escalating violence.

During the lockdown, while one team of guards searches the unoccupied cells for weapons, another team escorts prisoners to a series of more invasive searches. At the first stop, each prisoner has to
sit for an X-ray examination. This procedure allows guards to scan
the prisoner's body and head for any type of weapons he may be
concealing inside his body's orifices. The electronic examination requires the prisoner to position himself in such a way that the machine can make a recording of the man's ears, nose, throat, and body.
It is a thorough search for any type of foreign object that the prisoner fashions to inflict harm or death on another.

The next stop brings the digital examination. For that humiliating
experience, the prisoner stands in a designated area in front of several guards. They unshackle him and order the man to strip naked
and discard his clothing into a laundry bin. Guards know that some
prisoners conceal razor blades or other weapons by sewing them
into the seams of their clothing. They will issue each prisoner new
clothing to wear upon the examination's completion. The guards order the naked prisoner to proceed through a series of movements so
they can inspect all areas of the man's flesh, including under the testicles and between the buttocks. On a complete weapons search, like
lockdowns I know from the USP, the guards instruct the naked man
to bend forward, exposing the guards to a clear view of the anus. A
guard may then insert a gloved index finger into the anal canal to
complete the inspection for contraband.

Some may think such examinations would yield nothing but a
disgruntled prisoner population and staff members upset with their
scatological duty. Not so—experienced administrators expect to
find weapons, and the prisoners in the pen never disappoint. Besides
collecting a plethora of knives, pipes, spears, and swords throughout
the penitentiary, guards always find a few prisoners who conceal
weapons in the most private parts of their body. During one spring
season, guards found a steel knife that Pig Pen had inserted into an

empty tube of toothpaste. He concealed the tube by coating it with Vaseline and stuffing it into his rectal cavity.

The guards' discovery of weapons that prisoners hide does not stop the men from procuring more. The penitentiary holds hardened convicts, men unperturbed by prison discipline. They have no concern for pain or for the length of time they serve.

T-Rex serves a thirty-year sentence for armed robbery. He sharpened a steel rod and applied some tape around its base for a better grip in the event that he would have to skewer an enemy. T-Rex hid the spear inside a metal flap on the inside ledge of his locker. Guards found it during a weapons shakedown. Administrators submitted the case to the U.S. attorney, who prosecuted T-Rex. After T-Rex's conviction, his judge imposed an additional five-year sentence.

"You think I give a fuck 'bout five years?" T-Rex asked. "You cocksucker motherfuckers gave me thirty motherfuckin' years already. What the fuck is five more pussy-ass years? Fuck you. I live up in this bitch. You pussy-ass motherfuckers just work here." A month after T-Rex's return to the pen, guards found a homemade steel knife buried, but within easy reach, inside his pouch of tobacco.

Like T-Rex, most prisoners in the pen keep a stash of weapons. They bury knives and pipes in the yard, and they hide them in other common areas where they can access them at will. Guards spend a considerable amount of time using metal detectors looking for weapons on their contraband hunts.

During the years T-Rex and I shared living space in the housing block, he was caught three times with knives. Administrators referred him for new criminal charges only once. The last time they caught him on a routine pat-down as T-Rex was leaving the chow hall. The guard found a knife that T-Rex kept inside a pouch he had sewn inside the sleeve of his jacket.

After locking T-Rex away, another guard went to search his cell.

T-Rex's cellmate, Dice Man, was in the cell. "Get out. Shakedown."
The guards gave Dice Man the order to leave.

"Fuck you. I ain't leaving. Why you fuckin' with me, dog?"

Dice Man insisted on staying put. He knew that if the guards
came in to tear up the space in a shakedown, they would find a steel
knife he kept hidden inside his pillow. That could lead to new criminal charges. Dice Man's defiance, he knew, would buy him a little
time. With his refusal to leave the cell, the guard locked Dice Man in
his cell so he could summon the SORT team for a cell extraction. It
takes fifteen to twenty minutes for the SORT group to gather and
suit up in their gladiator uniforms.

While the guard left to call for the SORT team, Dice Man put the
knife inside a plastic toothbrush holding tube. Then he slid the tube
up his rectum. Although Dice Man knew the SORT team would extract him and lock him in segregation, he did not anticipate the
X-ray machine. He hoped to bring the knife with him into segregation, then find a way to dispose of it while he was under less intense
scrutiny.

The SORT team marched in lockstep onto the tier. They stood
outside Dice Man's cell and ordered him to cuff up.

"Fuck you," came the challenge from inside the locked cell. "It's
gonna take more than you pussy motherfuckers to take me down.
I'm ready for you punkass bitches."

SORT members unlocked the door. "Last chance to cuff up," the
leader said.

"Suck my dick, motherfuckin' punk. Come get me if you can."

The team drove its way inside the cell, eight huge men in battle
uniform. Sounds of the thundering rumble flooded the block. The
team succeeded in binding Dice Man's legs and fists. They carried
him out horizontally by the limbs. His mouth was bleeding, but the
blood did not stop the invective from spewing out. "You ain't nothin'
but a bunch of punkass bitches. Take these cuffs off and I'll beat your

motherfuckin' asses. You motherfuckers ain't did nothin' to me. You ain't shit."

Dice Man served six months in the hole before he returned to the prison's mainline. "I knew I could've cuffed up after I keistered the joint," he said. "But fuck it. I like the contact. I like the violence. I like the blood. Anytime I can hurt one of these motherfuckers I'm gonna take it to 'em. The hate keeps me going. Besides, by fighting I figured those bitches would lock me up right away. They didn't. Cocksuckers got my knife." Dice Man served time in the hole, but he did not return to court to face new criminal charges.

That same summer, guards called in the SORT members to extract Bug from his cell. They chained him up, then escorted Bug to the X-ray machine. The guards were looking for weapons that Bug may have concealed internally, as he had done before. They performed a digital rectal examination. One of the guards felt a hard foreign object lodged deep inside Bug's anus; the guards were unsuccessful in extracting it. They therefore locked Bug inside a "dry cell," one with no running water or other means to dispose of contraband. Ultimately, Bug defecated into a bedpan. The search through Bug's excrement yielded yet another weapon in the form of a sharpened plastic knife. He had wrapped it inside plastic and a washcloth.

When charged with offenses related to possessing weapons in federal prison, prisoners argue that the racially charged atmosphere of the penitentiary requires them to violate the law by arming themselves. Bureau of Prisons administrators refuse to segregate housing units, and the convicts express a need to keep weapons in order to protect themselves from incidents that racial hatred motivates. Trial judges have not accepted this defense. They agree with government prosecutors and hold that such a scenario is insufficient to warrant the men's continued accumulation of weapons.

Several questions may come to those without prison experience.

How, for example, does a man procure a knife in prison? Obviously, the prisoner cannot search through *Soldier of Fortune* magazines or other catalogs to find advertisements for distributors of daggers and switchblades. Of course, the answer is that prisoners make their own weapons. Those who engage in such practices are often only too eager to describe their ingenuity.

Crip Tank considers himself an expert at making bone-crusher shanks. "I likeded it when that bitchass counselor put me in landscaping," he said when describing a new job assignment that came as a result of a disciplinary infraction. Crip Tank had been working as an orderly in the housing unit. When guards discovered his winemaking operation, the counselor assigned him to the landscaping detail. "That nigga done fucked up. From landscaping I done got me a whole new hustle making knives."

The landscaping department is located in the same cluster of buildings as all the industrial shops of the prison. Crip Tank had access to plates of steel, cutting torches, and grinders. "I put the template over the muthafucka and cut damn near twenty them bitches a week. I makes sure all the homeys stay strapped."

After he cut the flat metal sheets into the shape of a knife, Crip Tank sharpened the edges and point on the grinder. He wrapped the handle end of the weapon with a towel and tape, looping a cord of rope through a hole he cut in the handle. "I wrap the rope round my wrist. That way when a nigga slam a muthafucka the shit don't slip out the hand. Whizzam." Crip Tank made a stabbing motion by slamming through the air the pen he was holding in his clenched fist. "Dat's how you stick a muthafucka. The rope keep the shit in a nigga's hand in case it pop a bone."

Working in landscaping made it easy for Crip Tank to smuggle the bone crushers from the industrial shops back into the prison's yard and housing units. "I just passed them through the fence to my homey. He taped them to the bottom of the wheelbarrow and rode 'em right through the metal detector. Muthafuckas beepin' but he slides through as if he's goin' work. They can't stop no real live G from gettin' it on."

Little Man, a long-term prisoner who lives as an independent thug, neutral with the prison gangs, began serving time when he was twelve. At eighteen he transferred into the USP, and at five four, weighing 115 pounds, he came in looking for the edge that weapons provide. "Since only a fool expects a fair fight in prison," he said, "every edge is crucial. There is a time and place for all kinds of weapons. The experienced con can find weapons anywhere. The important thing is never to be caught without."

Soon after Crip Tank walked onto the penitentiary's mainline, members from his street gang embraced him as if it were a family reunion. They "blessed him with heat." Being new in the penitentiary system, Little Man did not have such connections. He made his own weapon from a simple soda can. "Man, I had a piece before lights-out on the first night. I cut open an empty can of Pepsi with my mustache scissors. Then I stomped on the metal to flatten it out. With that flat piece of metal, I folded it into flaps, then pressed the edges together. Rubbing it across the concrete surface, I made a glistening blade. It ain't pretty, but it's sharp enough to slice through a motherfucker's neck."

Another popular weapon in the penitentiary is the zip gun, which men manufacture from a standard number two pencil, some matches, a little dental floss, and some oil. They use ball bearings for ammunition. To make the weapon, the prisoners first grind the sulfur from a few packs of matches. They pull the eraser from the pencil, leaving the cavity in the metal tip open. By burying the ammunition into the cavity and packing it tight with the finely ground sulfur, they can use the oil-dipped dental floss as a slow-burning wick. In igniting it, the prisoner uses the zip gun to fire the ball bearing into another man's face.

When hard weapons won't do, others in the pen use "napalm." They fill a cup with a mixture of baby oil and Vaseline. They heat the oil in the microwave until it becomes bubbling hot. "If a mother-fucker brings me problems," Little Man said, "I solve them with the quickness. Throw that napalm on a bitch's face and I get the edge in a hurry. Then I get to working, stompin' the shit out the mother-fucker with my boots. I don't give a fuck how big he thinks he is, that napalm is bringin' him down."

One of the reasons administrators transferred me from the penitentiary system into lower-security-level facilities is that I have no history of violence. Instead of looking for weapons to solve my problems, I make decisions and structure my time in a way to avoid them. In nearly two decades of continuous confinement, I have never felt the need to make or use a weapon. The strategy for me is in keeping good relations. In addition to pursuing my own goals, I take caution never to threaten or judge the values that guide the lives around me; while I certainly wish that every other prisoner adhered to the same standards and lifestyle that I have chosen, I have no illusions that the prison system will ever be free of homemade, viciously deadly weapons.

6

My forty-five-year sentence meant that I would serve most of my twenties, all of my thirties, and nearly all of my forties in prison. It is a long time to fathom. The advice I started hearing from other long-term prisoners was to breeze through the years one day at a time. They refuse to focus on the future. "I can't live in two worlds at one time, so I'm a live in dis one," as Crip Tank tells it. Rather than anticipating the troubles that follow confinement, such prisoners live in the moment. I decided early on to serve my time differently.

In the beginning I mentally carved my sentence into blocks of time. The first block was ten years. The rest have been blocks of five years. I envision clearly defined goals that I commit to accomplish during each block. This strategy of focusing on the end of each block and placing myself in it helps me make it through. I still use that strategy today.

I hope that through continuous work and service, I can achieve measurable accomplishments that will help me transcend the stigma I expect to follow more than a quarter century of continuous confinement. When I began the term in USP, the strategy came to life. It is tripartite, requiring me to educate myself, to contribute to societies inside and outside of prison boundaries, and to demonstrate discipline. Living this strategy represents a part of my commitment to atone and reconcile with society. Keeping it at the forefront of my mind helps me navigate my way through prison life.

The decisions and activities I pursue, I hope, will validate me as a contributing human being upon my release. In prison, they have no meaning. Outside, redemption, commitment, and sustained discipline stand for something. Those virtues lead to integrity, temperance, and good character. Inside, where rules and policies discourage individual growth, where no vehicle exists for men to distinguish themselves formally in a positive way, each man lives by his reputation alone, not by meritorious accomplishments.

Prison is a class-based society. Whereas educated people reach positions of high social standing outside of prison, an entirely different set of values dominates the culture inside. Those convicted of leading large drug organizations together with those who have ties to organized crime represent the top of the heap. They are the Brahmin class of prisoners.

Because such prisoners are leaders of men, able to thrive in a world where they make their own rules, staff and other prisoners alike bestow a backward "convict dignity" upon them. If a man accepts a long sentence without whining, if he proceeds through trials without ever admitting guilt or expressing remorse, without ever contemplating the thought of cooperating with law enforcement in order to catch a break, he will live as a hero inside. By remaining resistant to authority, projecting a fearless demeanor, and embodying repugnance for anything contrary to the criminal code, such a man can ensure his place at the highest level of prison society. Inside, such men live only to preserve the integrity of their reputations, consequences be damned.

Big Paulie is a leading crime syndicate figure from the Northeast. "I been arrested more than tree hun'red times," he told me. "I didn't even know it was that much, fuhgedaboutit. Cops been harassin' me since I was ten, eleven years old. But I didn't know nothin' 'bout no tree hun'red times. My lawyers were tryin' to free me on bail. That's when I heard the numba. Cocksucka prosecuta jumps up and starts yappin'

'bout my record like I'm some kinda common criminal. Muthafucka.
I'm ready to post the bond. It don't matta. A mill. Two mill. Whateva.
Cocksucka judge won't go for it. Like I'm gonna run away or somethin'. Where the fuck I'm gonna go?" Paulie holds his hands up and
shrugs as if in bewilderment. "This is the life I chose. It'll be the end of
the fuckin' world before I run away from somethin'."

Paulie is serving a forty-year sentence for racketeering convictions. He was in his midfifties when the judge imposed the term.
"This is the last stop for me, kid," he said, accepting the likelihood
that he will serve the remainder of his life in prison. Rather than
whine about the time, Paulie embraces it. "What the fuck I'm gonna
do? Go cry like a little girl to some prosecuta or judge cocksucka
'bout how I'm sorry and how I'll say whateva the fuck they want so's
I can get out? Fuck that. Muthafuckas can suck my prick. I ain't sorry
'bout nothin'."

Big Paulie is known as a "made man." It means that the leadership
of New York's five criminal families accept him as a bona fide
wiseguy. He is "straightened out," entitling him to a fawning rever-
ence from others who embrace the criminal way of life. In the penitentiary, it means that Paulie does not wait in commissary, chow, or
laundry lines. He has scores of minions eager to perform such services on his behalf. Paulie lives as if he is an ambassador in the penitentiary, a celebrity whose influence extends not only to the streets of
Brooklyn, but from cellblock to cellblock across the country.

The reputations of top-tier prisoners precede them into the penitentiary. They live as prison royalty among their peers, legends in a
world forgotten by normal society. Less brilliant stars of the criminal
world must enhance their reputations by putting in work. They may
become shot callers, men of respect by virtue of their toughness,
their commitment to fight to the death for their beliefs.

One need not struggle through academia, achieve success in a
career, or communicate with eloquence in order to earn a solid

reputation, as one must in the broader society. Indeed, in higher-security prisons, such aspirations do more to diminish a man's reputation than enhance it. They would let the population know that he is abandoning the vicious circle, leaving the cycle of crime, thus marking him as soft, a potential target of ridicule or exploitation.

On the other hand, even the simpleminded car thief can become a powerful gang leader, a real man, feared and respected inside these abnormal communities. He simply must demonstrate his commitment to the specific values for which society builds these prisons. As one convict said, all it takes to survive in prison is a steel ball of hate and a knife.

Big Country, for example, who leads his gang of thugs from Alabama, talks proudly about the criminal actions that led to his confinement. "I started out as a young G. Know what I'm sayin'? I be crawlin' out the window while my moms was sleep. I just went out. Know what I'm sayin'? I be robbin', stealin', just takin' shit up off a muthafucka. I got mad squabbles, good hands. I can fuck a nigga up. I be fuckin' hos and jackin' niggas for they rides and shit. I be like goin' to the Church's Chicken? Know what I'm sayin'? I orders some food and when the muthafucka axes me for some money I whip out the burna. Know what I'm sayin'? I just point the pistol in a nigga's face and say let me git dat out da register, bitch, befo' I pop a cap in yo muthafuckin' skull. Word! Dat's wuzz up."

Big Country serves a life sentence for killing a man during the course of a robbery that brought him less than twenty-eight dollars. But his relatively unsuccessful criminal background does not interfere with his status as a shot caller in the pen. "They does what I tells 'em 'cause they knows I got they back. Know what I'm sayin'? Man gonna respect man. And I'm a look out for my dogz any fuckin' way. Ain't no muthafucka fittin' to get over on no Bama boys. Fuck dat. I'm a serve up any muthafucka who even thinks 'bout creepin'."

The explosive use of violence will lift a man's credibility in prison. Much like the use of a platinum card can help people in society find better seating in a restaurant, a man who is known to give no quarter may receive a single-man cell and a job assignment of his choosing. Despite Big Country's failure in society, he is a big man in prison, with a single cell and a cushy job that allows him as much free time as he wants.

Some offenders, however, regardless of how they behave in prison, will have no possibility of enhancing their reputations in the eyes of their fellow convicts. They are the lowest of the prisoner class, the pariahs.

In higher-security prisons, if a man becomes known as a snitch, a rat, "a no-good hot motherfucker," he can never redeem himself in the eyes of the unforgiving convict population. Others will ostracize him. They will not allow him access to seating in the dining room, to use the recreation yard, to watch television. Such a man will not find peace anywhere. Others will mock him continually, force him to live each day of his sentence in the midst of hundreds who constantly express their vitriolic hatred of informants. Many want these men dead, and it's usually only a matter of time before someone pays a few packs of cigarettes to force the suspected informant off the compound, or bring him the heat.

This is not to imply that there is a shortage of informants in any prison setting, even the high-security penitentiaries. Gaspipe, for example, had been a leader of New York's infamous Lucchese crime family. During his years at the highest echelons of the Mafia, Gaspipe built a fearless reputation as a ruthless killer. "Gaspipe is the meanest person I've ever seen. There is a simple evil about him. He'd whack you for bein' late to dinner," Scotty Black said. Scotty Black is an associate of the Lucchese family. In prison we became friends and he told me about his experiences working under Gaspipe. Despite his savage reputation, Gaspipe became a cooperating witness upon his arrest and now serves his time in protective custody with other high-profile informants. No one doubts his ferocity, but his reputation as a rat makes it impossible to survive on any penitentiary's mainline.

Many men lose their spine and break upon arrest. They cooperate with law enforcement prior to confinement not as an act of contrition or remorse, but in a diabolical exchange for leniency at sentencing. Such prisoners rarely experience conflict in minimum-security camps, as camp prisoners focus more on the proximity of their release dates than anything else. If these men serve time on the mainline of higher-security prisons, however, and the population of felons becomes aware of their duplicity, they will assuredly attract serious problems.

Louie is another wiseguy, from Jersey, who likes to gangster it up on the compound. He serves a thirty-five-year sentence for his conviction following a drug bust. America's fascination with the Mafia extends inside the prison system, and some wiseguys play into the folklore. They cultivate the image, pursuing a following and the status that comes with being connected.

Louie talked the gangster talk. "No-good rat cocksucka muthafuckas. There's no more honor in this life. Everyone's tryin' to save they own ass. A man pays his dues to make his bones, but even then he's gotta watch his back for some stool pigeon cocksucka whose tryin' to put the squeeze on." Louie enjoyed the prestige of his Mafia connections for several months. Then other gangsters from New Jersey's DeCavalcante family showed up on the mainline. "They pulled his ho card," as Crip Tank says, revealing that Louie had cooperated with officials in New Jersey on an earlier charge in state court to save himself from a mob-related murder conviction. When word spread, Louie ran to the lieutenant's office for protection before other wiseguys had an opportunity to serve him street justice.

Besides those who cooperate with law enforcement prior to confinement, every prison has a percentage of inmates who provide information to staff members in exchange for privileges. Indeed, many people in prison are of weak character despite the bravado they project. They are accustomed to lives of immediate gratification; they regularly follow bad decisions with efforts to erase the consequences for themselves.

In institutions of total control, where administrators manipulate virtually every aspect of each prisoner's life—including the food he eats, the clothing he wears, the quarters in which he sleeps, the medical attention he receives, and the contact he has with others—some men find it to their advantage to whisper into a staff member's ear or pass a note. In exchange, the informant may receive exoneration from a disciplinary infraction, a transfer to a preferred prison, a cigarette, or an extra scoop of cereal. Staff members will do what they can to protect and coddle their informants because inside, like anywhere else, information is power.

If word ever spreads about their betrayal in higher-security prisons, however, consequences will follow. If the gangs, shot callers, or wiseguys detect a traitor, lethal violence will often ensue. Pariahs must navigate their way through prison compounds, enduring the constant threat of reprisal from thousands of violent men committed to exterminating rats.

It is not only the snitch who lives as a pariah in prison. Those convicted of crimes against children and women, too, live in an underclass of untouchables in the prison community. Once others in the pen learn that a man is a snitch or a sexual offender, that man becomes a complete outcast. Although he may try, there is nothing he can do to reverse the reputation.

Battle is a prisoner convicted as a rapist and murderer. He and I both began our lives as federal prisoners in 1987. He first went to USP Lewisburg, where he ran into some problems as a consequence of his pariah status. Those problems brought a transfer to USP Leavenworth. The problems followed him again, and guards transferred

Battle to the USP where I was housed in 1993. At each stop, Battle did what he could to keep the details of his conviction a secret, but to no avail.

Like many people in the penitentiary, Battle has a hard time reading. He relies upon others to help him. While at USP Lewisburg, Battle hoped that he could win some relief from his case. Not knowing how to begin a search for judicial relief, Battle turned to Jerry the Jew, a jailhouse lawyer and stand-up convict. "There may have been mistakes in the case. Bring me your legal papers and let me see if I can help," Jerry offered.

Upon reading the legal documents, Jerry says, he discovered that Battle was serving time for a rape-murder conviction. He promptly returned the paperwork to Battle. "Here's your motherfucking paperwork. I can't do nothin' for you. I don't work with cases like this or with guys like you. Stay the fuck away from me." Like other stand-up convicts, Jerry the Jew cannot stand the presence of rapists. He spread the word about Battle's treachery. Soon thereafter, other convicts pressured Battle into protective custody.

Battle wanted respect in the penitentiary. He is a killer, a man serving a life sentence. Those attributes generally bring a man status in the perverted communities locked inside walls. Not so for Battle. The fact that his victim was a woman complicated his standing among the other dangerous felons, who feel that the only acceptable reason to kill a woman is for retribution in response to a betrayal. With a conviction for a sexual assault, Battle would never receive the respect he sought. Others in the pen looked down on him, dismissed Battle as a pariah, cementing his status as an outcast in the society of felons.

"You can't get no props for no rape-murder, muthafucka," Crip Tank scolded Battle. "Ain't no real G gonna respect dat. Dat's somebody's mama, somebody's sista, muthafucka. Don't come round me or I'll serve yo ass." Crip Tank was warning Battle to stay away. "You gonna get yours someday, muthafucka. Niggas don't stand for dat. You gonna pay da pipa. Believe dat, muthafucka, you gonna pay da pipa."

Battle had been run off two penitentiary compounds already. Word was spreading in the USP, and Battle was thinking about steps he could take to redeem his reputation. He did not want to live as a pariah and thought about killing again. This time he would kill a man, another convict. In prison, the more explosive, violent, and public he made the killing, the better would be his chances of enhancing his reputation. For a man like Battle, there are no other opportunities in his power to redeem himself in the unforgiving world of the pen. His actions had dumped him into a sewer of a world, and he had to slither through it.

If Battle thought about killing another prisoner, there were countless ways he could achieve such an end. While another prisoner used the phone, for example, Battle could sneak from behind and plunge a knife into the man's neck. He had killed with a knife before, so the action would presumably not daunt him. Such a brutal murder would likely result in massive bloodshed, splattering the walls and ceiling, causing people to talk for days. The murder would have to be public and very visible, thus bringing Battle the criminal credit which he may have craved. People would fear him, and to many of the perverted minds of the penitentiary, the ability to instill fear is a quality beyond all others.

Stabbing another prisoner, however, was evidently not enough for Battle. Hardly a week would pass during those years that I served in the federal penitentiary, it seemed, when I did not hear teams of guards running to help a man being stabbed or beaten. There was a lot of gambling. The penitentiary was infested with drugs. As men ran into trouble with the rackets, perhaps unable to pay a debt, some type of violence would inevitably follow. Evil lives inside those walls, and in order for Battle to overcome his pariah status, he would have to shock the already world-weary collective conscience, to ratchet up the violence quotient. Stabbing another prisoner would not necessarily achieve this goal. But killing a guard, that was another matter.

After a public run-in with Officer Tucker, Battle evidently found his target.

Tucker was a hip guard, straight out of the housing projects that surround the USP. He spoke the same ghetto English as convicts in the pen, and he likely grew up with or knew countless men who were imprisoned in the pen he was charged with guarding. Tucker was working on a deal to smuggle some dope into the pen for a con named Lucky when he locked horns with Battle. That move marked Tucker for murder.

"Wuzz up wi' chu, muthafucka," Tucker said to Lucky as he caught him walking out into the corridor during the busy early-morning move.

"What da fuck you think is up, blackman? Wha'chu gonna do for a muthafucka?"

"Tell a nigga wha'chu need," Tucker said. "You know I'm straight out da hood. Ain't nothin' changed. Dis just a nine to five for a muthafucka."

Lucky knew Tucker was hoping to supplement his income. Hints had been exchanged before, as Tucker knew that Lucky was a G. It was time to cinch the deal. "Check dis out den. Looky here. I'm a bless you wit twinky-five hun'red. Know what I'm sayin'? I needs you to meet my girl and pick up dis package. Bring it to a muthafucka."

"Okay. Okay. You got dat. Dat ain't no problem. She gonna have my paypa?" Officer Tucker wanted to make sure he would receive twenty-five hundred dollars cash as payment for his end of the deal.

"Dat ain't nothin', nigga. You gonna get dat. Just bring me my shit. Here's my girl's number. Give her a call and get dis shit right."

Just then, Tucker spotted Battle making his way to C Cellhouse through the crowded main corridor. "Look at dat muthafucka right der," Tucker said to Lucky as he spotted Battle's approach.

"Who you talkin' 'bout," Lucky asked. Hundreds of convicts were crowding their way through the corridor. Tucker didn't respond to Lucky because Battle started walking through the door. The officer spoke directly to him.

"Hey, muthafucka," Tucker called out to Battle while Lucky stood by watching the exchange. "I heard you is in here for rape-murder."

"You don't know what da fuck you talkin' 'bout. You don't know nothin' 'bout me, bitch." Battle stepped right up in the officer's face, as if to challenge him.

"Oh, now you tough all of a sudden," Tucker baited Battle. "I know more 'bout you than you thinks I know." Lucky watched, not liking what was going down. He didn't want anything to happen that could threaten Tucker's agreement to mule his package of heroin into the penitentiary.

"Fuck that, you muthafuckin' cop. Don't make me kill again, you bitchass muthafucka," Battle said. "I'll put yo ass in da dirt."

Lucky stepped between the two, addressing Battle. "Yo yo yo, calm down, baby boy. Calm down. Don't get trapped off in here behind no stupid shit. Go head on. Be 'bout yo business. Dis ain't da time."

Battle allowed Lucky to lead him away. "Man, you betta let dat muthafucka know who I is. I ain't da one."

"Okay, okay. Dat's cool," Lucky said. "Let me holla at da poe-poe. I'll holla back at you lata."

After sending Battle on his way, Lucky returned to his conversation with Officer Tucker. "A yo, my man, looky here. Hustler to hustler, pimp to pimp, you gots to fuck all dat dumb shit, man. You gots to stay focused, to be 'bout yo work up in dis bitch if you wants dees chips. Know what I'm sayin'?"

"You right, you right," Tucker acknowledged. "I'm a call yo girl tonight." But the officer never got the chance.

Battle had returned to his cell on the upper tiers of C Cellhouse. He was furious at the guard for belittling him. Battle was determined that others would not run him off another penitentiary mainline. He was ready to serve Tucker, to let others know "they better find someone else to play with." Soon he would kill a staff member. Such a murder would demonstrate his potency, Battle reasoned. It would teach others to respect him as a man rather than to scorn him as a pariah.

After his altercation with Officer Tucker, Battle went to see his friend Bill Hester. He gave Hester two phone numbers. "Dis da numba a my daddy an my sista. If sumpin' happens today, I wants youse to call 'em and let 'em knows dat I'm in trouble, dat I won't be callin' no time soon." Battle knew he was going down. He had made his choice and he was committed to it.

Battle saw Richard Boone, a con serving fifteen years. Richard worked as a plumber, so he regularly came into C Cellhouse with his tool pouch. Rather than work on plumbing, Boone strapped his tools over a chair while he caught the grooves on the rap video station.

"Yo, Rich. Let me get dat hammer up off you. I gots some bi'ness to handle."

"Wha'chu need da hammer fo', you country-ass muthafucka? I'm only gonna be here a minute."

"Man, jus' let me use da bitch. I gots me sumpin' I gotta do."

"Take da muthafucka den."

Battle held the heavy ball-peen hammer in his hand. He gripped the long wooden handle, then banged the head into the palm of his other hand. He grimaced as he gauged the weight of his weapon. Then he lurched beneath the stairs and hid near the vending machines. He looked at Officer Tucker and seethed with anger. Tucker's back was turned, and like the vicious predator that he was, Battle took his opportunity. He stepped behind Tucker. Then he slammed the steel of the hammer into Tucker's head. Tucker went down, and

Battle continued to pound the hammer into the officer's skull as if he were slamming to bust through concrete. "Dat's wha'chu get fuckin' wit me, you bitchass muthafucka! You done picked the wrong one!" Battle screamed.

With the guard's body dead on the red tile floor of C Cellhouse, Battle tossed the hammer beneath the vending machines. Other guards heard the commotion and rushed to Tucker's aid. Blood was splattered on the wall. It was too late. Tucker was by then a corpse lying in a pool of his own blood. Battle stood by observing, blood on his clothes, blood dripping from his hands. The guards took him down.

Officer Willis, one of the first guards on the scene, asked Battle why he had killed Officer Tucker.

"Fuck dat nigga. I had a dance wit him. You wanna dance, muthafucka?" Battle yelled. "He fucked wit me. He harassed me. He slammed my doe and called me a black muthafucka." Battle continued, "It don't botha me dat he's dead. He fucked wit people. I ain't no punkass bitch."

Battle was led away, taken out of the penitentiary to a solitary cell in another prison. When interviewed by FBI Agent Fred Pickens, Battle revealed that he felt attacking a guard would bring him more respect. And in the world of the penitentiary, where people are anything but corrected, it may have. Yet the attack also made Battle a candidate for the death penalty. He now waits in an ADX cell while judicial proceedings continue to play out.

Whether Battle is executed or not, it is certain that he will never walk on a prison compound again. The best he can hope for is to die in a solitary cell, still a prison pariah.

7

Every prison has boundaries that separate convicted felons from the broader society. Within each prison lies a special housing unit, also known as a SHU, pronounced "shoe." In prison argot it is also called "the hole." The special housing unit represents both a jail and a prison within a prison. Administrators send those whom they want to remove from the mainline, for a variety of reasons, to serve a portion of their time in the SHU. Prisoners spend time in the hole because staff members place them under investigation. Others "check in," seeking protective custody because they fear for their safety in the general population. Most prisoners in the hole serve time as a consequence of guards charging them with a disciplinary infraction of some kind. Time on lockdown represents one of the sanctions administrators can impose on those who guards suspect violate prison rules.

As a general rule, guards search all prisoners before admitting them into the SHU. Sometimes they pat frisk the men. More frequently the guards order the men to strip naked for the search. Other prisoners must proceed through X-ray and digital examinations before guards will lock them in a SHU cell. Prisoners in the hole wear a different class and color of clothing to distinguish them from those in the general population. In the federal system, prisoners in the hole wear oversized orange jumpsuits, while those in the general population wear khaki trousers and shirts.

Prisoners that guards lock in the special housing unit do not have access to the same privileges as those men in the general population. They do not report to job assignments. They cannot access open recreation areas. They do not have easy access to the telephone or visiting privileges. They cannot watch television, and rules restrict access to personal property. Guards lock those in the hole for twenty-three hours cell time each day. Guards deliver boxed food to the men, who eat in their cell. Guards handcuff and escort prisoners scheduled for the caged shower, for the locked recreation cage, or for any other movement within the self-contained unit. Living in the SHU is like living in supermax.

SHU cells are barren. Two steel plates mounted against a wall serve as the bed frame. A thin mat lies atop them as a mattress. The cell has a metal commode and sink, no mirror, no locker to store belongings. Prison systems across America operate well in excess of capacity, and the special housing units frequently represent the most overcrowded parts of each prison. The cells, designed for one man in solitary confinement, frequently have two racks, yet guards may assign three or even four men to serve time inside a single cell. In such cases, one man sleeps on each rack. Another stretches his mat on the floor beneath the bottom rack. The other stretches his mat along the narrow walking area of the cell and sleeps with either his head or feet abutting the toilet.

Some prisoners languish in the most squalid of conditions, locked in the hole for months or years at a time. Others serve only days or weeks in lockup. There is a constant rotation of cellmates. Since no one has much in the way of personal belongings, living in the hole is a lot like living as a homeless person, squeezed in with other vagrants. In crowded cells, the men must sometimes restrict their movements to only the bed itself.

Although guards have locked me in the hole for a few hours over the years for administrative reasons, I have never been sanctioned to pass days, weeks, months, or years in the SHU for disciplinary reasons. I consciously avoid behavior and relationships that can lead to such further restrictions on my life. In order to reach the goals I have set for myself, I need access to the library, to typewriters, and to a desk. I know that a trip to the hole would interfere with the deadlines by which I live. It would likely result in the loss of my books and other belongings. It is a disruption I do not need and so choose to avoid.

The structure I impose upon myself accounts for every hour of every day. I constantly look ahead to what I commit to accomplish. By holding myself accountable to achieve specific goals in the weeks, months, and years ahead, I give myself a reason to guard against the loss of the minimal freedoms I have. Structuring my time helps me work toward specific goals; it also lessens the likelihood of confrontation with others. That strategy minimizes my exposure to disciplinary problems or investigations that can lead to hole time.

By completely committing myself to the course I have set, I am able to live my life as an open book. I do not make efforts to fool anyone; despite the forty-five-year sentence I serve, I do not pretend to be a gangster. Others in the pen cannot live so openly. Such people have histories that complicate their standing with the convicts whose presence they cannot escape. As New Jersey Louie experienced, when a man lies to enhance his reputation, it is only a matter of time before someone shows up on the compound and exposes him. Louie's efforts to masquerade as a wiseguy in good standing with the DeCavalcante family came to an abrupt halt with his sprint to the lieutenant's office in search of protective custody.

Puppet had a similar problem, but with deadly consequences. Puppet, in his midthirties, walked into the penitentiary carrying a lot of personal baggage. His judge had sentenced him to serve thirty years. On the surface, such a sentence recommends Puppet as a stand-up convict, a right guy, solid by penitentiary standards.

The trouble is, several years previously Puppet had faced charges from an earlier and separate drug conspiracy. In that case, Puppet cooperated with authorities and testified against his partners at trial. In exchange, the judge spared Puppet by sentencing him to probation. On his current case, the judge slammed Puppet with real time, and administrators ordered him to serve it inside the walls.

"Hey, *vato*," Speedy, a shot caller with the Mexican Mafia, said to Toker, his young associate. "*Ese pinchi bolillo* is a fucking *rata, un hijo de la chingada.*" Using the vulgar language common inside the walls, mixing Spanish and English at will, Speedy identified Puppet as a snitch. He did not know Puppet, but Speedy had received a message from one of his homeboys serving time in another prison. Word had spread by mail and telephone. From penitentiary to penitentiary, convicts were looking for Puppet. When he turned up, Speedy assigned the job of serving him to Toker. Toker was eager to stick Puppet in order to prove his allegiance to La Eme, pronounced "em-may," as the Mexican Mafia is known in the pen.

Toker had his shank ready. Another associate who worked on the maintenance crew had planted it in the gymnasium's bathroom, using duct tape to secure the steel blade above the fluorescent-light fixture. Shorty, Puppet's workout partner and an affiliate of a white-supremacist gang with close ties to La Eme, was to lure Puppet into the bathroom at six o'clock under the pretense that the two could get high. Toker stood lurking in one of the bathroom stalls, waiting for the smell of the reefer as his cue to put in his work.

"I was ready for that *pinchi gavacho* in the *baño, ese,*" Toker told his tale. "I went to the fucking *peluquería* and filled my *cachucha* with *pelos* from the *pinchi mayates*. I was going to slam that white-boy *rata* motherfucker in the *pecho* and in the stomach, leaving his guts spilling out of him like an open enchilada. *Ese pinchi guey* was going down, *vato. Simón.*"

Toker had collected hair from the floor of the barbershop that he suspected had come from black prisoners. By sprinkling the hairs inside his skullcap, he hoped to throw off investigators. He wanted them looking for a black inmate instead of a Mexican. Toker had cut eye holes in the skullcap, his *cachucha*. He intended to emerge from the bathroom stall with the cap pulled tightly over his head and plunge his shank into Puppet's chest, and then slice Puppet's stomach open to dig his guts out.

It was not to be. Toker was left waiting in the bathroom stall, all dressed up with no one to stab. He had hoped to make his bones, to prove himself worthy of the trust placed in him by a shot caller of the Mexican Mafia. But Puppet sensed that he had been marked as a snitch, a prison pariah. Rather than join Shorty for his scheduled workout, Puppet turned himself in to the guards, seeking protective custody.

Protective custody, though, means a trip to the hole. And with the crowded prison system, special housing units are even more packed than prison mainlines. There is no protection in the sense that people usually associate with that word. A check-in is locked in a cell with whoever else might be there. The guards assigned Puppet to a cell with KooKoo.

KooKoo had recently transferred into the penitentiary from a medium-security prison. Rather than behaving in ways that might result in more freedom with a transfer to lower security, KooKoo had filled a tube sock with combination locks to slam another prisoner in the head; there had been a disagreement over which television show to watch. After the incident, guards raised KooKoo's security level and sent him to the pen. Upon hitting the compound, he cliqued up with Red Dog and his pack of thugs from the Georgia hills.

KooKoo's transfer to the pen did not have a calming effect on him. He kept himself mixed up with trouble and frequently made rounds to segregation. KooKoo was serving a brief stint in the hole as a consequence of guards discovering a stash of wine that he had hidden inside the vents of his cell. Guards disrupted KooKoo's private hole time when they unlocked his door and ordered Puppet inside.

Not wanting his new cellmate to know that he was a check-in, a protective-custody case, Puppet told KooKoo that he was serving time in the hole because guards had found his stash of weed. That story lasted for less than a week. The day after Puppet made his check-in move by running to the lieutenant's office, Smoke was released from the hole. Knowing that Puppet had been tight with Shorty, Smoke stepped to him. "A yo, Shorty," Smoke called. "I saw your boy down on lockup. They got him in the cell with KooKoo."

"Fuck that bitch muthafucker," Shorty said. "He's fucking PC." Shorty was letting Smoke know that he wanted nothing to do with Puppet. Being a solid convict, Shorty then passed the word back to Speedy, the shot caller for the Mexican Mafia.

"*Simón, vato,*" Speedy said. "Good lookin' out, holmes. *Oralé carnal.* I got something for that *pinchi rata.*" Speedy could use that information about Puppet's whereabouts in the SHU. With it, he could pass word to KooKoo, a convict who made his hatred of rats known.

Speedy then wrote a letter for KooKoo. He buried inside the text enough information to let KooKoo know not only that his cellmate, Puppet, had checked in for protective custody, but that he was "a nogood rat motherfucker who testified against others in an earlier case. Some homeboy," he said, "caught an asshole load of time because of Puppet's testimony. *Simón.*"

Speedy used an old penitentiary trick to deliver his message to KooKoo. He used KooKoo's name and registration number for the return address. Then Speedy created a fictitious name and address for the intended recipient. He applied postage and dropped it in the prisoners' outgoing-mail box. When the postman recognized the undeliverable address, the Postal Service returned the letter to the prison, marked "Return to Sender, Address Unknown." The mailroom officer

performed his usual search for contraband, then delivered the envelope to KooKoo's cell. Message delivered, just as Speedy intended.
With it came the end of Puppet's protective custody.

After the four o'clock census count, guards deliver the mail to the
cells. Generally, guards demand that prisoners stand for the four
o'clock census count. In the hole of the penitentiary, however, guards
don't bother because the prisoners don't budge. The prisoners in the
pen respond to count announcements with a defiant "Fuck you" or
"Count these nuts, motherfucker." KooKoo had a look of surprise
when he saw the envelope slide beneath his door. He had no connections or support group outside of prison for correspondence. When
he saw the outer markings on the envelope, he knew it was a kite; the
prison grapevine was sending him a message. KooKoo opened the
envelope and read the letter while Puppet stood over the toilet taking
a whiz.

KooKoo had accepted Puppet at face value when the guard locked
him inside the cell. Puppet's story of being in the hole for some weed
was plausible enough. Although they had not spoken on the mainline, KooKoo knew that Puppet walked the yard with Shorty, a solid
con. The kite from Speedy changed those perceptions. With the
note, KooKoo knew that his cellmate was a check-in. He played it off
until evening, when he would make his move.

Without weapons available to him in the hole, KooKoo had to
plot his attack. "Yo, Puppet," KooKoo said. "I can't get no fuckin' air
down here on this rack. How 'bout switchin' up for a few days? I
can't breathe down here." The ploy worked. Puppet was happy to
give up the top rack. It hurt his back to climb down from the top
each time he had to use the toilet.

That evening, after mealtime, KooKoo climbed up onto his rack.
Both men lay reading. When KooKoo heard Puppet begin to snore,
he hopped to the floor as if to use the toilet. Instead, KooKoo straddled Puppet's body, pinning him down. KooKoo positioned his

hands over Puppet's neck and squeezed, strangling the life out of him as Puppet kicked helplessly from beneath. A silent and bloodless death came in place of protective custody.

Following the murder, KooKoo tore a pillowcase into strips of cloth. He stretched one between the wall to the lower bunk and tied it to the dead weight of Puppet's lifeless wrist. When the guards snooped into the cell door's window as they made their rounds, KooKoo would be reading on the top rack; he tugged on the pillowcase strip to make it appear as if Puppet's corpse was shifting beneath the sheets. Puppet lay dead in his rack for two days while KooKoo ate double meals.

On the third day after Puppet's murder, guards came to the cell and ordered KooKoo to cuff up. His hole time had expired. He was to return to the penitentiary's mainline. "What's up with your cellie?" one guard asked.

"That motherfucker sleeps all fucking day," KooKoo said. The guards chose not to disturb Puppet's sleep. They locked the door and escorted KooKoo back to the prison's compound.

KooKoo hit the yard by noon. "¿Qué pasó, vato?" Speedy asked him. "Didn't you get my kite?"

"Yeah, I got the motherfucker. That dude is dead as dead. He's out."

"What do you mean he's dead? Then how did you get out?"

"I left his punk ass under the covers in the cell. Cops think he's sleepin'."

"You're fucking crazy, ese. Ruthless. I like that in a gavacho. Simón," Speedy said.

KooKoo remained on the compound for more than twenty-four hours. The guards did not discover Puppet's corpse until four days after Puppet's murder. They were trying to lock another man inside to share a cell with Puppet when they found him dead and stinking. So much for protective custody. KooKoo's lawyer was successful in using the late discovery of Puppet's corpse as a defense strategy to negotiate a lighter sentence for KooKoo. He pleaded guilty to manslaughter and received an eight-year sentence for the killing. KooKoo boasts about it.

Some may think a killing in the hole would be an isolated incident. After all, unlike with the convicts assigned to the general population, guards thoroughly search each prisoner before admitting him into one of the special housing unit cells. Manufacturing a weapon in such close and barren confines is not likely. Further, with the guards having to deliver all meals and necessities, those in the hole endure much more scrutiny than those assigned to regular units. Still, violence in the hole is not unusual. In fact, action can thrive anywhere in prison. As some prisoners like to say, "A muthafucka can get served anywhere."

Despite the heightened security in the special housing units of every prison, they remain dangerous places. They are dangerous because of the men who occupy the SHU cells. When a man lives to break prison rules, administrators use time in the hole as a method of punishing him. For some men, placing them in the hole is like poking a caged animal. It enrages them, pushing them to further disruption. Many look for opportunities to interfere with or agitate the operations of the SHU.

Scores of caged men yelling obscenities all through the day and night fill the special housing units. "Hey yo, muthafucka, send me down some fuck books," one yells from down the tier.

"I'm a light dis bitch up," comes another holler.

Another prisoner calls out chess moves. "It's yo move, nigga, I said knight to B4."

The madness never ends. They bark, howl, and snarl, imitating the sounds of fighting animals. They stuff blankets and sheets into their toilets, then flush them repeatedly to flood the cell. The water eventually flows out from under the door and onto the tiers, flooding the unit. It creates more work for the officers working in the SHU.

Some men refuse to cuff up. Others ignite their mattress into flames with matches. Angry men use any method available to cause disruptions. Without access to the necessary materials for fabricating weapons, they will use what is available. They collect urine and excrement to throw at officers. Some have been known to bottle crushed hot peppers, jalapeños, and hot sauce in order to squirt the blinding mixture into the eyes of others. The hole is bedlam.

Saxon, a skinhead and hardened convict with tattoos of swastikas and symbols praising the righteousness of Adolf Hitler, tried to advise Dirt. Dirt had fallen into debt with some of the dopers and was trying to lie low for a while until the money he was expecting came in. He wanted to check in. "You can't PC up," Saxon told him. "You can't go to the man and lock up for protection. That's a bitch move. You'll never be safe. The only way to get off the yard and alleviate your problems with a little respect is to go to the hole for something that's honorable. Violence is honorable. Trying to escape is honorable."

Despite the solid convict advice, Dirt approached an officer and said that he needed to check into the hole for protective custody. The guards assigned Dirt to a cell that Brick and Stone, two cousins from the South Pacific, already occupied.

The cousins are tight, members in good standing with the islander cliques of the penitentiary. They are not tall men, neither reaching the height of five seven. Brick is stocky, big and round. His hair is wavy and hangs to his shoulders. Not quite as big, Stone is slimmer. He wears a goatee and has hair down to his waist. Both are tough men. Pumped up and prison tough.

Soon after Dirt checked in, Stitch, a leader of the Dirty White Boys prison gang, called Tiny, one of his soldiers. "I need you to get into the hole. Spread the word about that rat motherfucker Dirt. The cocksucker bitched up and PC'd. He's tryin' to stiff me for two bills."

Tiny didn't question the order from his shot caller. He purposely got into a scuffle with a comrade, and guards took them both down.

They escorted the men to segregation and locked them inside. Once there, Tiny passed the word that Dirt was a check-in. It may as well have been a death sentence.

Brick and Stone had been entertaining Dirt. The cousins were sharing some wine they had been brewing in the cell. All three men were close to drunk when the word came down from Tiny about Dirt. "What's this shit about you being a punkass check-in?" Brick demanded. He slapped Dirt with his open hand.

"I didn't check in," Dirt said. "That motherfucker don't know what he's talkin' about." Dirt stood nervously, shaking.

"You callin' Tiny a liar? That what you doin'?" Brick slapped Dirt again. "I think you're the fuckin' liar, bitch. How you gonna come in here and disrespect me, drinkin' my shit when you know you're nothin' but a rat motherfucker?"

Stone egged his cousin on. "Beat his punk ass, Brick. Fuck that motherfucker up. We can't let no pussy-ass check-in bitch hang with us."

Dirt ran to the door's window, banging on it to catch the guard's attention. He pleaded, screaming for the guards to move him to another cell. Dirt wanted the guards to separate him from the crazed cousins. They were like two rabid pit bulls.

A correctional officer came by to peep into the cell from the outside window. He snickered. "Who's winning?" he asked. Then the guard walked away with his keys jingling, leaving Dirt to fend for himself.

Dirt pleaded with the guard as he watched him walk away. "No, no. Come back." He pounded on the door. "Don't leave me in here. They'll kill me."

Brick fired on him, blasting him with a punch that knocked Dirt's head into the wall. "Stop your whining, bitch. It's time to meet your maker. Stand tall, motherfucker." Brick nailed him with his fists and hooked him with an elbow to the jaw.

Stone reached up and grabbed his razor. "Hold the mother-fucker." Brick reached beneath Dirt's arm and grabbed him in a full nelson. Stone used the razor to slice through Dirt's extended neck, cutting through veins and arteries as blood pumped out of his body.

"That's what you get, motherfucker!" the two cousins yelled as Dirt's corpse collapsed to the ground. They kicked him in the head, stomping him. Then Stone straddled Dirt's dead body and sliced him open. They used their hands to rip his liver and guts out. The two then started chewing on his insides.

Prosecutors charged both cousins with Dirt's murder and sought the death penalty for them. Dirt received his death penalty without the benefit of trials or appeals. It was a consequence many hardened convicts deem necessary for those who betray the convict code by seeking protective custody.

Prisoners who fall out of favor with staff members, for whatever reason, are especially vulnerable when faced with confinement in special housing units. Such prisoners may not be well liked by staff members because they are leaders, because they file papers seeking administrative remedies, because they do not show proper respect or deference to staff.

It is easy for guards to lock such a prisoner into a cell with con-victs like KooKoo, Brick, or Stone. The guards can then hint or in-sinuate that the man is in the hole for reasons not accepted by the convict code. Irrespective of the truth, convict justice will prevail.

8

For those who walk into the penitentiary without connections inside, or without hard, street-tough credibility, it is not the guards or possible trips to the hole that fill them with anxieties and apprehensions. It is the fear of prison rape. Weakness and fear smell as delicious to sexual predators as hot buttered popcorn does in a movie theater. Every week the bus serves up scores of new prisoners. For those without friends or penitentiary savvy, the tests begin at once. Some pass. Some do not.

Although I am not inclined to participate in organized religion, I feel a spiritual connection. It helped me through those early tests. From the beginning, I felt God's presence steering me clear of altercations and opening opportunities for me to grow. The blessing comes in networking skills and absolute faith that I will survive and emerge from the prison experience as a stronger man. The journey for others does not always pass as smoothly.

Not all prisoners who fall victim to sexual abuse stand out. A typical heterosexual who has not a trace of feminine tendencies can find himself confronted if he walks into the pen without the hardened demeanor forged through years of tough living. For such a man, death, his own or someone else's, is sometimes preferable to the never-ending battle of fighting off sexual predators. Todd is one such prisoner whose struggle begins hours after his admittance. His is a story that happens with alarming frequency in high-security penitentiaries.

Being of average height and build, with sandy blond hair, an easy smile, and no tattoos, Todd is vulnerable from day one. He walks into the pen with a sentence of twenty-five years. Prior to this day, Todd has not been incarcerated before. He was reared in suburbia, was active in high school athletics, and looked forward to following in his father's and grandfather's footsteps with a professional career.

While in undergraduate school, however, Todd detoured from academia. He began selling marijuana to supplement his income. By his junior year of college he was the go-to guy for those wanting to score weed on fraternity row. That led to larger and larger quantities. Then the Ecstasy rage hit on college campuses across America. Todd became the man, organizing groups of distributors who worked with him to move tens of thousands of Ecstasy tablets each month through university campuses across the western United States.

Being the big man on a university campus does not necessarily translate into being the big man on a prison compound. Especially not a federal penitentiary. In the pen, Todd is nothing more than a pretty face. He is released into the general population with a roll of sheets and a blanket, then is greeted by his new cellmate, Stump, with an attack.

Stump is a shot caller for a California clique. He serves a double life sentence and has over a decade of confinement at prisons like USP Leavenworth and USP Marion behind him when Todd comes into his life. While in the chow hall for the evening meal, one of the clique's hangers-on runs in to tell Stump that a new punk has just moved into his cell and that he is making up the top bunk.

An aggressive sexual predator, Stump returns to the cell. He sees Todd standing on a chair, tying his sheet in a knot to secure it around the thin mattress that stretches across the top steel rack. "Get the fuck up off my chair, bitch," is all Stump says as the cell's door closes behind him.

"Oh, I'm sorry. The guard assigned me to this cell. I'm just making up my bed."

"I don't give a rat's ass who put your punk ass in here. You're on my chair, bitch. Now get the fuck off."

Todd takes in the vibe. He had been scared to begin with upon his transfer to prison, as he had heard plenty about the pen. Prior to coming in he had vowed to make it through his sentence, whatever it took. Yet he did not expect a confrontation during his first hours of prison living. Indeed, Todd had gone through a year in county jails while he waited for trial. He passed more than a month moving through transit facilities on his way to the penitentiary. Not once did he have a problem. Now he is forced to consider Stump, an enormous white man who looks as if he has been transported from the days of tenth-century Vikings.

At six foot four, Stump towers over Todd. His arms bulge from years of lifting heavy weights in the prisons where he has been held before. His chest and back spread wide, pulling his shirt taut as if it were an expanse of tarp. Along with his long, ragged, and unkempt hair, he sports a goatee, the devil's beard that accentuates Stump's fierce look of hatred. Tattoos of skulls and swastikas and demons with daggers sleeve out his arms. The words "FUCK THE WORLD" are inked boldly in capital letters across the front of Stump's neck.

Todd takes a deep breath, sees the closed door, and knows he is trapped. He steps down from the chair. It seems that before his foot touches the floor, Stump is on him with a smashing fist to the side of his head. Todd crashes into the lower bunk with the blow, dazed and dizzy from the unexpected strike; the taste of blood begins to fill his mouth.

"Get the fuck up off my bed, bitch!" Stump yells.

Todd is weak. He grabs the bed frame and struggles to pull himself up. As Todd stands, Stump moves close. Less than an inch separates the two men. With one hand he grabs Todd by the lapels of his shirt, wrapping the material tight in his fist to the point of choking. Stump sticks out his tongue and licks Todd from the neck and up his smooth-shaven cheek. Todd squirms, hanging lifelessly as Stump slides his tongue across his face and jams it into his mouth. Then, as Stump pulls his face away, he says, "I knew you'd be hot."

Stump uses his free hand to reach down inside Todd's elastic-waist pants, beneath the boxer shorts. He grabs Todd's crotch. "You forget about this little dick and these balls here. You're mine now." Stump squeezes Todd's testicles with a vise grip, and Todd feels the fingernails digging into his scrotum. "What you've got is a pussy, bitch, a little cunt that belongs to me. I want you to keep it shaved, and you'd better not ever forget that Satan served you up to big Stump. You belong to me."

Todd stares bug-eyed as Stump kisses his lips hard, then shoves him back into the lower bunk. "Now what did I fuckin' tell you about being on my bed? Clean this fuckin' cell up, bitch. I'll give you a taste of that bed tonight." Then Stump storms out of the cell.

The entire episode lasts fewer than three minutes. But to Todd, it feels as if an eternity has passed. When Stump leaves the cell, Todd begins spitting blood into the sink. He tries to find some perspective on what has just happened. It all has come so quickly, and he is amazed at how impotent he was to counter the attack. Todd is speechless. His legs are shaking so hard that he can feel his knees colliding.

The threat of being locked in a cell with Stump then sets in. He does not know a soul in the penitentiary, has nowhere to turn for help.

Knowing that he is staring down the long end of a lengthy term, Todd refuses to seek assistance from guards. He is even more afraid of living through his sentence with a snitch label than he is afraid of Stump. Todd feels as if he has to handle the matter himself, and he reasons that violence is the only answer that will work in such a place. Todd knows that he needs a weapon of some sort, something to give him an edge. But only hours separate Todd from lockdown, when he will be trapped inside the locked cell with Stump.

Todd finishes making up his bed. He then walks by a "coun- selor's" office, where he fills out various forms that authorize him to make telephone calls and receive mail. The counselor is preoccupied with his computer screen, absorbed in a game of Tetris that he plays while supposedly considering inmate requests. A mug made of a smoked, heavy glass with an attached wooden handle sits on the cre- denza that Todd is using to fill out his forms. Todd sees an opportu- nity. While the counselor sits absorbedly clicking away at the computer keys, Todd slips out with the mug hidden beneath his shirt.

He returns to his cell. By wrapping his fingers around the wooden handle, Todd figures, he can use the mug as a weapon that will strike a devastating blow to Stump's head. But it is not enough. Stump is a big man, outweighing Todd by at least seventy-five pounds. A few punches in the head, even with a heavy mug, might not subdue him. Todd needs to cut.

It looks to Todd as if Stump has been street fighting all of his life. Todd decides to take a gamble. The mug is so constructed that if he holds the wooden handle, then smashes the mug against the cell's concrete floor, it might break in such a way as to leave the handle with chips of shattered glass attached to it. He makes the smash, and the mug breaks perfectly. Todd cleans up the broken glass, then leaves his cell to walk the track alone with the handle in his pocket.

The lockdown announcement comes and Todd returns to his cell. Stump is lying on the lower bunk flipping through the pages of a *Maxim* magazine. He does not say a word as Todd walks in. Todd stands by the sink near the door, washing his face. He then looks through the cell door's window, watching as the guards make their way around the unit, door by door, turning the huge steel bolts that lock men in their concrete bunkers. With his hand in his pocket, clutching the wooden handle of his weapon, Todd visualizes his exact movements upon lockdown.

The loud clank of the door comes as the guard turns his key. He pulls at the door twice upon locking it, to ensure it is secure. Bang. Bang. Steel banging against steel as the door hits the frame. The guard then walks on, oblivious of and indifferent to the danger brewing inside the cell. Once he passes, Todd feels dead quiet come over the housing unit. It is not yet nine o'clock in the penitentiary and all the convicts are locked in their cells.

Todd turns around and Stump sits up. "Come on over here and sit next to Daddy. Talk to me."

Todd stands motionless by the door as rage displaces his fear.

"Come on now. You're not still mad at me, are you?" Stump makes an effort to stand. As soon as he set his feet on the floor, Todd comes at him, smashing Stump's face with the shattered, jagged glass still attached to the wooden handle. It stuns Stump, knocking him back. Todd keeps swinging, pummeling away at Stump's face, cutting him in the eye, across the nose, the cheek. Blood begins pouring out of Stump's face, his head. He tries to cover it with his forearms, but Todd keeps swinging like a madman.

"You think you're going to fuck me? You piece of filthy shit. You picked the wrong man. I'm nobody's bitch, you faggot motherfucker. You'll never fucking touch me again, you get that, asshole!" Todd is screaming at Stump as he continues to pound him. The tables have turned. Todd has vindicated himself, penitentiary style. But the victory is short-lived.

When the guards come by to count the men in their cells, they see the blood. It has splattered on the walls, on the floor, on the white blankets that cover the beds. When the guards open the door, they see Stump, with his face and arms bleeding profusely. Todd stands, enraged, clutching the wooden handle firmly in his fist. Guards handcuff him, then escort him to segregation. They send Stump to the infirmary.

Todd is charged with several disciplinary infractions. Because he refuses to cooperate against Stump, the correctional officers sentence him to serve three months in detention and then order a disciplinary transfer to another penitentiary, where he will have to begin again.

Todd responded to Stump's aggression in the only manner that he saw available to him. Such a response was clearly not consistent with prison rules. Yet, as Todd saw things, it was prison rules and classification procedures that forced him to sleep in tight, locked quarters with a monster like Stump. Prison rules, he reasons, were not designed to save him. Todd expects that every day of his confinement will bring a threat to his safety, at least until he can persuade administrators to transfer him to a lower-security institution. Prisoners like Stump, however, will always prowl around the prisons where he is being held. Todd can control his own behavior, but he cannot control how others behave. Hence the danger of living in prison.

Todd certainly could have checked into protective custody, but as we have seen, such a choice would not necessarily bring him safety. Stump launched his assault on Todd within hours of his walking into the penitentiary. Todd did not do anything to provoke it. Stump considered him—a handsome young white man with all of his teeth and no whiskers—an easy piece of meat that he could snatch without resistance. Other predators lay the groundwork for sexual attacks more subtly.

Caspar and Bird rode into the pen together as codefendants. Like Todd, they are young and white, but they lack Todd's athletic build and confidence. Both are small-time hoods with long criminal histories. They have felony convictions for burglary and drug sales. For each of those offenses, the young men faced sanctions of probation, community service, and jail work-release programs. Their most recent offense is the sale of firearms. Because of their long criminal histories, the judge slammed them with lengthy sentences that brought them into the jaws of the penitentiary.

Immediately upon the newcomers stepping off the bus, the vultures from the pen begin their catcalls.

"Don't you worry 'bout a thing, bitch. Daddy gonna take care of you up in here."

"Look at those pretty muthafuckas there."

"My dick is hard for you bitches now, and you gonna taste it tonight."

"I need some new ass, and you is just what I'm lookin' for."

The calls come from every direction. Although Caspar and Bird are only two among many hobbling forth into the pen's receiving area while shackled in chains, they feel vulnerable. Rightfully so. Despite their pale skin's covering of chicken-scratch tattoos, their methamphetamine-devoured teeth, and the scraggly growth of facial hair, both are as slender as schoolboys. They look inviting to the beasts in the pen.

Although both Caspar and Bird try to hold their composure, the fear as they proceed through processing causes their bodies to tremble. Neither has suffered prison before. Each senses the evil lurking in high security. It is present in the air. They hear it with the slamming of steel gates. With the blaring institutional loudspeakers. They see it in the tough-looking cons who seem bigger, meaner, more frightening than any group of people either has seen before. The two feel like grade-schoolers in a rowdy biker bar.

"You two are lucky," the guard says as he escorts Bird and Caspar from receiving and discharge to A Cellhouse. "The pen has only one two-man cell that's empty. You guys got it."

"You mean we're going to be cellies?" Bird asks the guard.

"That's right. Believe it or not, today's your lucky day."

Each of them instantly breathes easier. They had been dreading the thought of guards locking them into a cell with one of the deranged men shouting threats as they made their way in on the chain. The two of them sharing a cell makes the idea of an escape from the madness possible, even if it comes only during lockdown periods. In the pen, everyone welcomes an interlude from the tension, no matter how brief the respite.

After settling into the cell, Bird and Caspar walk onto the tier. They see crowds of men. Some wear radio headphones from which music blares. At the steel tables men slam dominoes with a whack, as if striking to kill a resting hornet. "That's what I got, muthafucka. What you got?" Those sitting at other tables, or on any flat surface, slam cards with the same ferocity while they play games of spades or casino. Another group of men shoots dice against the wall. Despite the games in progress, both Bird and Caspar sense the predatory eyes weighing them, measuring them. They know where they are and they know what they are. They are insects in a tank full of hungry lizards.

They knock on the counselor's door. He allows a phone call for each, then issues a series of forms for visiting and regular phone privileges. By then it's getting late, nearly time for the nine o'clock lockdown. Although both are sweaty after a long day of traveling and intake processing, neither Bird nor Caspar can find the courage to shower. While walking loops around the housing unit, they make contact with Satyr.

"What's up, holmes?" He acknowledges them head-on, neither smiling nor threatening, in the penitentiary style of indifference. The greeting is the first sign resembling humanity either has received from those in the pit of felons into which they've been dropped. As one of the few other white faces in the block, Satyr eases their anxiety. He is in his early thirties, a decade older than either of them. Like both Caspar and Bird, his arms are covered with crude drawings in blue-green ink. His head is bald except for a goatee and a small tail he keeps knotted in the back. He wears sweatpants and a shredded tank top, flip-flops on his feet. Satyr is at home.

"What's up?" the two respond. "How you doin'?" Both are eager for some type of conversation, some news about their new world.

"Where'd you dudes roll in from?" Satyr asks.

It leads to a conversation. Satyr tells them about what to expect. He answers their questions and eases their concerns by telling them the prison isn't bad. "I'm just glad to see some white men hit the block," he tells them. "We need to stick together." The two have found a friend. Just before lockdown he leads them to his cell. "Let me fix you up with some toothpaste and soap and shit. I ain't got much, but fuck it, I can get you started."

"We'll pay you back," Caspar said. "I just talked with pops. He's gonna send me five hundred. I'll hook us up with some zoo zoos and wam wams. They got any dope round here?"

"Shit. We got every fuckin' thing. Weed. Meth. Drink. Horse. You fuckin' name it. I can get it," Satyr assured them. "I'm gonna come wake you for breakfast. But you better get back to your cell. Fuckin' hacks lockin' down."

At six the following morning the block guard starts turning the key, unlocking the steel door of each cell, click by click, to begin another morning of madness. Satyr is laced in his boots and standing by his door, ready for whatever. The instant the guard twists his key that reverses his door's bolt, Satyr is out. He walks up the stairs and peeps into the room of Caspar and Bird. They're sleeping. He walks in without knocking and pulls the cover down from Caspar's chest. Satyr shoves him gently.

"Let's hit it, bud. Breakfast is on. You comin'?" With Caspar waking, Satyr nudges Bird. "We gotta roll, holmes. It's time for chow." Satyr then waits on the tier smoking his Bugler rollie while Caspar and Bird dress.

"Man, I was out. What fuckin' time is it?" Caspar asks.

"It's a quarter after six now," Satyr says. "We gotta roll. They'll start breakin' down the line by six thirty and leave only scraps. You guys gotta get with the fuckin' program. When that cop cracks the door, you need to be up and ready. Shit can pop off around here at any time, and you don't wanna be sleepin'. We gotta look out for each other. That means no sleepin' in the day without a watch, and up with the first click of the door. I'm serious 'bout this shit. You with me?" Satyr advises the two on how to serve time in the pen.

By their third day, Satyr has shown them around everywhere. He tells them which TV room the whites use and walks them around the yard. He helps them land a job on the maintenance crew. The two are comfortable around him, as if they have an older brother lookin' out for them. Satyr really comes through when he surprises them with a tiny balloon of meth. It's a small package, but he shares it equally by drawing out three lines for one good snort each.

"Fuckin' A," Caspar says. "I needed that fuckin' jolt. I ain't had no good shit for fuckin' weeks, since I got locked up. That's just what I needed to get right."

"Oh yeah," Bird adds. "That's what I'm fuckin' talkin' about. I got the lightnin', the electricity fryin' my brain. This is the shit."

"We need a little snort around here to take the edge off," Satyr says. "A dude owed me. I wanted to hit you guys off with what I had."

"You're the fuckin' bomb, dude," Caspar says. "I just got my money on my books today. Can you get any more?"

"How much you lookin' to spend?" Satyr asks.

"I can get two hundred in commissary tonight."

"Bet. That'll get us off. You want some drink too?" Satyr asks.

"You got Budweiser?" Bird asks.

"The fuck you say," Satyr snickers. "We ain't got no fuckin' beer in here. This is the pen. We got pruno, bud, fruit wine. Five bucks a quart and it's gonna fuck you up for real. You need it with the crank."

"Check it out," Caspar says. "Get me a list for two hundred. I'll buy the hooch and anything else you want. Just make sure you bring back enough meth for the three of us. I wanna get fucked up."

"You got that, holmes." Satyr gives Caspar the list of food to bring back from the store. They agree to meet back in the cell at seven, when Caspar will have the commissary and Satyr will have the dope.

The time comes. Caspar and Bird are giddy with excitement at the prospect of getting high. "My pops is gonna send me five hundred a month," Caspar says. "We're gonna get it on once a week. This ain't shit."

Satyr walks in. "You get the shit?" he asks about the commissary. Caspar hands him two bags full of sweets, coffee, sugar, and juice. "That's what I'm fuckin' talkin' 'bout. A man of his word." He plops the balloons on the table. "Hold the shit here. I'm gonna go pay the man and I'll be back. Don't start the party without me."

Satyr returns carrying two quarts filled with pruno. "Let's get it on," he says. "Bird, you go watch out on the tier. We'll take turns here. Me and Caspar gonna have a snort, then I'll go out and watch for the cop while you come get yours. Take a swig of this first."

As Bird leaves the cell, Satyr draws out a few lines of the crystal powder on the desk. He bends over the table, presses his forefinger against the outside of his left nostril, and snorts the line up with his free nostril; he's a vacuum cleaner. "Yee haw," he says. "That's what the fuck I'm talkin' about. This is the shit here. Yowza! Go on and get you some," he says to Caspar as he fires a fist into the air.

While Caspar bends over to inhale the poison into his body, Satyr stands behind him, charged up with energy. He listens to Caspar snort, then grabs him from behind in a bear hug. "This shit makes me feel so fuckin' crazy," he says while pulling Caspar's body tight. He bites him on the neck.

"What the fuck?" Caspar yells. "Let me go, you crazy mother-fucker."

"Yowza!" Satyr screams as he throws Caspar aside. "I'm fuckin' wired, charged up. Damn this shit is good," he says before taking a swig of wine.

"You're fuckin' crazy, dude," Caspar says while laughing off Satyr's advance.

"Bird!" Satyr yells. "Get your ass in here and have a snort. I need some fuckin' air. I'll step out and watch the tier." While Satyr and Bird exchange spots, Satyr sees his buddy Wolf on the tier. They planned the meet earlier. "What's up, dude? I'm fuckin' ready," Wolf said.

"Hold up, big dog," Satyr says. "When you see me go back in, count to thirty, then come knockin'. It's live."

"Cool," Wolf says.

As planned, Satyr steps back into the room. "What you two little fuckers think? Does Satyr bring the shit or does Satyr bring the shit?" he asks while drawing out several more lines on the table.

"You're the fuckin' man up in here, dude. You fuckin' rock."

Just then comes the knock on the door. "Who the fuck is that?" Satyr yells, as if it's his room. Wolf walks in. The dynamics of the room change instantly. It crowds. Wolf towers over the others. He has a fierce look, and with his size, he is intimidating.

"What the fuck is goin' on?" Wolf demands. His voice is grave and loud. "You motherfuckers are makin' so much noise I can't hear my own farts. What's up?"

"Ah shit, Wolf," Satyr says. "Just a little party. A little crank, a little wine. Takin' the penitentiary edge off, you know."

"Yeah? I got a book," Wolf says. "Let me catch a ride." He offers a book of stamps as payment for a snort.

"Go on, Caspar," Satyr says. "Let my man Wolf buy a snort off you, make you a book of stamps for a line."

"Naw, fuck that," Caspar says. "We're partyin' here. You ain't got to pay me nothin'. Hit yourself up."

"Right on, little man," Wolf says. He bends over and snorts the two largest lines on the table. Then he lets out a wolf howl: "Ooo, ooo, ooo, ooo! This shit makes me want to fuck."

All the vibes change in the room. It's not so fun anymore as Caspar and Bird tremble at Wolf's naked aggression. Satyr isn't bothered at all. "Take a hit a this, brother," he says to Wolf while passing him the quart. Wolf turns the jug on its end and chug-a-lugs the wine while Satyr bends down for another snort.

Wolf slams the jug down on the table. Then he grabs Bird and pulls him toward him. "Oh, you sweet little young motherfucker. Gimme some of that pussy," he says while trying to kiss him.

"Leave me the fuck alone!" Bird yells while trying to struggle free. "Get him off me."

Wolf slaps Bird across his face, then picks him up by the shirt. "Don't you talk back to me, bitch!" he yells, then slaps him again.

"Make him stop," Caspar says to Satyr.

"Shit," Satyr says. "I can't do nothin' to make him stop. Wolf's his own man."

"Stop him," Caspar says again. Satyr slaps Caspar so hard he falls back onto the bed. "Shut the fuck up, bitch. You motherfuckers know what time it is." Satyr flips Caspar over onto his stomach, then crawls on top of him from behind and starts humping him through his pants. "This is what you want. You want this big fuckin' dick in your ass, and you're gonna get it."

"What are you doing?" Caspar cries. "I thought you were my friend. I thought you were someone I could trust."

Wolf sets Bird down, holding him by the shirt. "Motherfucker, you're gonna suck my dick. Now."

Bird is scared to death. He looks to the bed and sees his buddy Caspar, prone, with Satyr grinding into his rear. Wolf drops his pants to his ankles, then slaps Bird again. "Don't you fuckin' look over there. Now suck on this dick, bitch. And if you bite it, I'm gonna kill you. You got that. Get to suckin'."

Bird cries. He drops to his knees. He opens his mouth and places his head in Wolf's crotch. Bird takes him in. "That's right, bitch. Suck this big dick."

Satyr stands up from Caspar. Caspar gets up and stares unbelievingly as he sees his partner's head bobbing in Wolf's groin. Satyr smashes Caspar with a fist to his jaw. Caspar falls back into the bunk. "Get up, you little motherfucker," Satyr says as he pulls a shank out of his sock. He grabs Caspar and stands him up. Satyr moves behind him and presses the knife across Caspar's throat. "Now shut the fuck up, bitch, or I'll open your fuckin' neck. Take those fuckin' pants off." Caspar drops his pants to the floor. "Now step out the motherfuckers. I like my bitches bare assed all the way."

With Caspar naked from the waist down, Satyr walks him to the locker with the knife still pressed against his neck. "Grab that Vaseline out your locker, bitch, and lie down on the bed with your ass up just like you like it." Satyr dips his hand into the petroleum jelly, then smears a gob of the lubricant over Caspar's bare bottom. "Don't you scream, bitch, or I'll kill you." Satyr proceeds to rape the young prisoner while calling out to Wolf, "Now this is a fuckin' party here."

"You're damn right it is," Wolf calls over from the table. "Where's that fuckin' meth at?"

"It's right there on the floor in his pants, the right pocket," Satyr answers him.

Wolf pushes Bird off his crotch. "Stand up, bitch, and get naked, or do I have to slap you again?" Wolf digs out the crank and takes another snort. He sits down in the chair facing the bed while Satyr continues his assault on Caspar. "Come here, bitch," he calls out to Bird, his voice deep with bass. Bird is so terrified his legs can hardly support him. He's trembling. "Do you hear me, bitch? Bring your punk ass over here."

"I'm not like this. I'm not like this," Bird manages to say.

"You're my bitch," Wolf says. "Do you fuckin' understand me?

You're nothin' but a cocksucker and my fuck toy. Got that? I tell you what you're fuckin' like. You don't tell me shit. Now put this jelly on your ass and set it down on this big fuckin' pole. And grab that wine. I'm gonna fuck you while we watch Satyr stick it to your punkass friend."

And so it goes. The orgy continues until just before the nine o'clock count, as Satyr and Wolf hold Caspar and Bird hostage. They are sexual slaves in their own cells while the rapists have their way with the easy pickings of the pen. After the predators leave the cell for the count, Caspar and Bird lie on their bunks like two pieces of leftover meat, their humanity gone, taken. When the guards come by for the count, they plead to be taken off the compound. They provide statements about the rape and agree to participate in the prosecution of Satyr and Bird. All four men leave the pen.

Word comes back in time that both Satyr and Wolf received lengthy sentences for their attack. Administrators sent them to supermax. No one knows what became of Caspar or Bird, as administrators sent them elsewhere to serve their time. Although they likely transferred out of the pen into lower security, it is also likely that memories of the pen will haunt them forever.

The possibility of prison rape in high security is an unspoken fear for many inexperienced prisoners. I passed several more years behind penitentiary walls and watched scores of Birds and Caspars come through. Many take precautions against such attacks by joining gangs or cliques to gain protection. In so doing, they frequently become predators themselves.

9

Although I had never experienced incarceration before, as I came into the penitentiary system, I saw immediately that despite all the rules and regulations administrators impose, the prisoners create their own society. An underground economy drives it.

A typical penitentiary houses more than a thousand men. At USP Atlanta, we had nearly three thousand men during peak population levels. All of those men hold paying job assignments and many also have contacts outside of prison who support them financially. Transactions that total hundreds of thousands of dollars take place each month inside the walls. This illicit economy, and the quest for power within it, have spawned an epidemic of prison gangs seeking to control the economy.

Some of the gangs have a strict organizational structure, with clearly defined leadership. Prison gangs like the Mexican Mafia, the Aryan Brotherhood, the Latin Kings, the Black Guerrilla Family, the Vice Lords, and the Dirty White Boys have been around for nearly half a century. Members distinguish the generals from the shot callers, and the shot callers from the soldiers. All of those gangs have a presence in every high-security penitentiary. Their members recognize each other through hand signs, tattoos, and a criminal network that spreads across the country's prisons, from coast to coast, from border to border, like a vast spiderweb.

Others, like the Crips and the Bloods, have their origins in street gangs. They clique up as the members come inside. Inside, those gangs tend to have less formal structure. They are more like a group of cells with a common geographical interest outside that serves as an adhesive to hold its members together. For example, Crip Tank "calls dogz" for the Compton Crips. The Hoover Crips from Los An-geles, and the Ace-Trey Crips, from another part of the city, have their own leaders. Yet they all identify themselves as Crip gang mem-bers, and their relationships transcend prison boundaries. They de-rive their power as a consequence of the thousands of incarcerated Crip members who populate every high-security penitentiary.

Many prisoners in the pen aspire to gang leadership. That status does not come easily. Gang leaders enjoy fierce reputations for having "put in work," meaning that others know they will not tolerate any form of disrespect. Further, gang leaders must have the ability to think strategically. One gangbanger I know described the responsibilities of leadership. "They can't just do what a motherfucker wants to do, can't go to war over just any motherfuckin' thing. A real motherfucker knows how to look out, to make shit happen. And he can't just be 'bout himself. A motherfucker gots to know how to take a brother's back."

Gang life in prison is not about preparing for a law-abiding life in society, but about creating a thriving world for the brothers, the homeys, and the leaders themselves while in prison. "I can't live in here and out there," Lion says. "The motherfuckin' man tells me I gotta serve life. Fuck it then. I can do that. But I know that means I get out the rack every mornin' not knowin' whether I gotta move on a motherfucker, or whether some other motherfucker's gonna try and move on me. And if a bitch tries to move on one of my brothers, right or wrong, I got my brother's back. Doin' it all means I might serve time behind these walls today, or that some shit might jump off that sends me out to Leavenworth tomorrow. Or Florence the next day. Fuck it. I got my brothers everywhere. Wherever I'm at, that's fuckin' home for me."

Lion is the shot caller for a gang of white prisoners in the penitentiary. His gang is known throughout the prison system and has a reputation for explosive violence. It has a long list of members, associates, and followers. In the one pen alone, Lion says, he has sixty brothers and many more associates, making it a powerful force. It is deeply involved in every moneymaking racket possible. At thirty-nine, Lion is seventeen years into a life sentence. "I been through the shit, man. That's why motherfuckers respect me. I been in wars, you dig, and motherfuckers know when it's time to jump off, I'm gonna bring it all the way." He transferred to Atlanta after a six-year stint on lockdown at USP Marion.

Because he's a gang leader, his sixty brothers in Atlanta are willing to abide by his every command. In order to curry favor or lift their standing within the gang, the soldiers must abide by the customs and orders that Lion lays down. When Lion issues an order, the soldiers don't question. They act. They put in work. In exchange, they enjoy a piece of the power that comes with being part of an organization, albeit one that society and prison administrators frown upon. Legitimate society has rejected them and the values by which they live. Rather than attempt to reconcile with society, gang life provides its members with acceptance and even encouragement for their criminal histories and futures. The members pledge their allegiance to this lifestyle.

Being affiliated with Lion's gang, or any other, means that no member is alone. Wherever they go in the prison system, every gang member has brothers. Leaders like Lion orchestrate or oversee schemes to ensure that brothers never go without. Controlling the drug rackets provides Lion with the resources he needs to build unity, to impose his will, and to ensure that his every need is met. It also gives him the resources to branch out and control such penitentiary vices as gambling, alcohol, and extortion. With his mastery of turning correctional officers into mules that smuggle contraband into the pen, Lion controls the flow of money. And with that, he controls other men. "I got me all kinds a motherfuckin' cops," Lion says. "They don't make nothin' workin' in here. It ain't hard to get one. Shit. I'm with 'em all day. They know what I'm about, that I'm solid as that fuckin' wall out there. Ain't nothin' gonna shake me. I give my word to a motherfucker, that's it. It's done. A motherfucker knows he can count on Lion."

Every employee of the Bureau of Prisons has access to the central records file of every inmate. Whether secretary, chaplain, recreation specialist, or whatever, all employees are correctional officers first. By reading Lion's central file, employees whom he tries to turn can read his history. Those who do read his file see that Lion lives defiant of authority, as he has his entire life. They read that Lion has served seventeen straight years, all of which have been in penitentiaries. Lion's record and reputation makes clear that he is committed to convict life.

"I start out with the motherfucker just kickin' it 'bout sports, or broads, or some shit, you know. It don't matter what. We're both just men." Lion explains how he massages his relationship with O'Dell, one of the guards. "He's cool with me, so I start feelin' him out a little further, you know, like I ask for half his burger and a sip off his shake. It's still cool, you know, so I take it up a notch, and he brings me in some food once in a while."

Like Satyr soft-played Caspar and Bird, Lion slowly lures his target into his grasp. "Then I say somethin' like, 'Dude, check this out. I'm tryin' to get me a shortwave radio up in here.' I tell him I'm studyin' German and the only foreign music I can catch on the commissary radio is that beaner shit. He punks out and says, 'No, man, I can't do nothin' like that. It'd be my job.' I come right back at him, you know. 'Come on, brother,' I say. 'Look out for the white man. It's just a fuckin' radio. Check out my paperwork. You know I'm solid. I'm gonna give you five hundred to bring it in.' I look at his reaction.

'You'll give me five hundred just to bring in the radio?' he asks me. Then I know I got him. He's just like everybody else, you know, wants a few bills to flash at the titty bars and shit."

With the guard in agreement, Lion goes to Toro, one of his many contacts inside the walls. Toro also serves a life sentence for his convictions of being a high-level drug distributor, though he is not a member of Lion's prison gang. "Check this out, my man," Lion tells him. "I got a cop."

"What you mean you got a cop?" Toro asks him.

"I got a cop, man. I'm ready to move," Lion says.

"What you need?"

"I need you to have your people get a shortwave radio, a good-size one. Pack that motherfucker with an ounce of horse and have five hundred with it. Get it to my people outside. They'll give it to my guy to bring in. I'll use my people to move shit in here. Anything you need, I'll get that too. Tell me your costs. You'll get that off the top. I'll give you forty percent of everything we make, and you got my word that I'll always have your back."

Lion understands that he cannot come out and ask a correctional officer to smuggle drugs into the penitentiary. Not at first. A radio, though, sounds innocuous enough. And the five-hundred-dollar payment seduces O'Dell. The officer doesn't even have to hand the radio to Lion. They agree that the officer will set it on his desk. Lion has one of his soldiers snatch it and bring the contraband to his room. With the dope inside, Lion enhances his power. He disburses it, feeding his power base and securing his future.

"Toro's people pack the radio with the OZ and front the five hundred," Lion says, explaining how one of his deals actually goes down. "My people make the delivery to my guy, and he brings it in. It ain't nothin', a fuckin' radio. Once I got it through, it brings me thirty balloons. Each balloon has thirty hits. I give five balloons to my man, and he distributes them to the brothers. That's on me. I gotta feed 'em. The other twenty-five they move for me. In the walls a balloon goes for eight hundred. My brothers get me five hundred on the wire for each; they keep three for themselves. That's twelve five. After payin' the man, I split the ten thousand left over. I keep six for me and break Toro off four more. My guys can move the OZ in three, four days tops. But with it, I got a cop."

An exercise fanatic, Lion doesn't use drugs himself. He begins each day by stretching out on the floor of his cell and cranking out a thousand push-ups. He spends another two hours on the track and the weight pile. Lion uses all of the money he makes to support himself and his brothers in Atlanta and in other pens. With the allegiance of his sixty brothers, Lion has scores of people on both sides of the wall to handle the transfer of funds for him and other matters that support gang life inside.

"How'd that extra work out for you?" Lion asks O'Dell, the officer he's got hooked.

"Hey, Lion, my man," O'Dell says as if they're old buddies. They do the prison shake, bumping closed fists. "That came right on time. My fat-ass wife and smart-ass kids are drivin' me nuts. I just went out and parked it at Platinum's, pissin' away a load on drinks and lap dances with a tight little box who calls herself Lucy."

"Shit, Platinum's?" Lion asks. "You should've told me you was goin' to Platinum's. I got a few brothers whose ole ladies dance at that spot. I'm gonna hook you up."

"Man, I can't afford to spend too much time in a place like that," O'Dell says. "That place is for high rollers. It's eight bucks for a drink, twenty for a lap dance."

"Fuck that, brother. I said I'm gonna hook you up. Just be cool."

"That box helpin' you out with the German?" O'Dell asks.

"Check it out, bro," Lions says. "Fuck the German. I got four pounds a weed I got to bring in. It ain't shit. I can flip you two Gs if you pack it in for me. No one knows but us," Lion says while pounding his chest. "My word is my bond."

"Come on, man," O'Dell says. "A radio's one thing. Drugs is somethin' else. You're talkin' 'bout more than my job here. I can't do it."

"Just think about it. It's just you and me gonna know. And you walk away with a clean two thousand."

"How the fuck am I gonna walk in here with four pounds of weed?" O'Dell asks.

"Shit. That ain't nothin'. Just bring in a little at a time. Bring a pound a day. Just try it how it's right. You know you wouldn't be the only one to give it a go. Stick with me and I'll get you another five grand a month. Cash. And you know what I'm about, brother. Ain't nobody else in on this but us. I'll take it to the fuckin' grave."

O'Dell thinks about it. He agrees. Everything is a hustle in the penitentiary, and Lion uses his connections with O'Dell and others to make sure he and his brothers stay on top. Drugs are the big moneymaker, the steady flow of money that feeds the gangs. Like the heroin, there is a huge markup on the street price of marijuana, as well as an insatiable demand. Joints sell for ten dollars all day. His soldiers see to it that each of those pounds brings a thousand joints. Lion takes four thousand a pound, making himself two thousand profit on each pound he distributes. Besides that, he keeps his cop happy and feeds his entourage, building and solidifying his power base.

It's not only drugs. As a shrewd gang leader, Lion has several guards who move for him, male and female. Every convict with access to money wants something in the penitentiary. Wiseguys want food, wine, and scotch. Weightlifters want steroids and muscle-building supplements. Athletes want sneakers. And for those who can afford it, Lion charges between fifteen hundred and two thousand dollars for a few minutes of sexual bliss with one of the female guards with whom he has an agreement. Lion has the resources to bring in what he chooses. His power base and respect in the penitentiary give him the network to make use of his position.

Lion is a shot caller. As a gang leader, in the pen he is in his own element, standing head and shoulders above those who follow him. An aura comes with his power, and others aspire to it, want to be associated with it. Guards and other prisoners alike respect him. They know that his word alone can cause bloodshed, or stop it.

Many young guys who come into the pen feel the pressure. The gangs are filled with young soldiers and others who want the status that comes with the brotherhood. The only way in is through blood, and once in, the only way out is through death.

Aspiring gang members or those seeking to advance up the pecking order must demonstrate their fearlessness, their quickness to impose their will and command respect. Those who succeed come closer to leadership and higher status among their peers. At thirty-two, Poo is one of Lion's men moving up within the group. When his younger cousin, Woodpecker, comes in on the chain, Poo takes him under his wing.

"What the fuck you doin' in the pen, you little motherfucker!" Poo yells at Pecker as he sees him coming in through R&D, the release and discharge area of the pen. "Last I heard you was in some pussy-ass FCI." Poo thought Pecker was in a Federal Correctional Institution, a medium-security prison.

"That didn't work out," Woodpecker yells back while struggling to fight the resistance of the chain. "Had a run-in with one a them rat motherfuckers. Left him with his guts fallin' into his hands."

"You came to the right spot then," Poo says. "Check this out, Peck. I'm gonna go yell at the counselor, see 'bout gettin' you assigned to my block."

Woodpecker is only twenty-three, but serving a lengthy sentence, he is all about fitting into the penitentiary scene. He wants to prove himself, to build a name inside the system. Having an older cousin inside who runs with one of the most powerful gangs helps give the youngster a foothold. When Woodpecker comes into the cellhouse, Poo introduces him to his brothers, then walks him around the compound and instructs the youngster on penitentiary life.

"This ain't no fuckin' FCI, dude," Poo begins. "You got to stay right in here. I'm sponsorin' you, gonna look out for you, hook you up. But you gotta be your own man. There's three thousand motherfuckers runnin' wild in here. You got spic gangs, dago motherfuckers, Natives, and all kinds a niggers. You can't let nobody take nothin' from you. We run the shit on this pound, but that don't mean you can go disrespectin' other motherfuckers. You just can't do whatever the fuck you want to be doin' here."

"Man, fuck all that shit," Woodpecker says. "I ain't no punk, ain't new to this shit. I'm solid wood. This may be the pen, and I know you and your brothers been holdin' it down for a while. I respect that. But I was runnin' shit on the streets. I'm gonna be all right in here. I'm down for whatever. What I need to know is how much the shit is goin' for and who's got it."

Woodpecker isn't interested in educating himself, in doing anything to redeem his criminal ways. He is a convict. Like others in his community, Woodpecker is interested in making a life for himself inside. Gang life offers the possibility for instant respect. Poo is glad to have him come aboard, but sets him straight about the order of the gang.

"Look, you little motherfucker. I don't give a fuck what you think you were in the streets. You're in here now. You was still ridin' fuckin' bicycles when I started inside this motherfucker here, and I ain't never gettin' out. You're comin' into this on the strength of my word. You gotta respect that. Without it every fuckin' bull in here would be testin' you. That's for real, Peck. You're on my crew. If I say go, you fuckin' go. You'll have your day. But don't come talkin' this shit 'bout runnin' shit."

"Look, dude." Peck backs down a bit. "I know you're the man up in here. Ain't nobody tryin' to change that. I just need to come up a little. That's all I'm sayin'. I been locked down for six months and I'm ready to run. I like gettin' high, makin' a little dough for myself."

"That's cool, little brother. I'm gonna get you right. Now check this out. You need somethin', you let me know. If you want to take somethin' off a motherfucker, slap him down if he's a punk, then go to it. Just be sure he ain't runnin' with nobody. But don't go bustin' into no rooms or lockers. No one's gonna respect that. You'll get your props for takin' somethin' from a motherfucker face-to-face, from collectin', from whatever. We got weed and horse up in here now. When you're ready to move it, know that joints go for ten bucks. We get eight hundred for a gram of heroin. I'll take care of you outta that."

Soon after Woodpecker settles in on the compound, a test comes for him. It begins when Lion gets word from one of his brothers that Scooter, a new dude, gave up someone in another joint. "Hey, O'Dell," Lion says to his cop. "I need you to check the paperwork on this Scooter motherfucker. Here's his number." In order to confirm that Scooter is a rat, Lion tells the officer he's got to check his central file. When the correctional officer confirms that Scooter is hot, Lion wants him taken out. He gives the job to Poo.

"Check this out," Poo tells Woodpecker. "It's time to put in some work. I want that fucker Scooter leakin' by count time." He orders the hit on Scooter, giving Woodpecker a chance to prove himself with the gang. Woodpecker doesn't hesitate. He has Stick, one of his road dogs, hem Scooter up in a conversation as they climb the zigzag stairs leading to the upper tiers of the cellhouse. While they're talking on the stairs' landing, Woodpecker comes down and thrusts the knife into Scooter's kidney, leaving him collapsed on the stairway in a pool of blood. Woodpecker continues down the stairs, leaving his gloves and shirt in the trash can at the bottom; Stick walks up and returns to his cell. No one saw or knew they were there. Woodpecker is in.

Over the next several months, Woodpecker assembles his own little group of thugs inside the walls. They prey upon the weak, extorting them, beating them down for commissary. He starts moving drugs for his cousin Poo. Without a complete allegiance to the gang, Woodpecker gets the idea to smuggle his own dope inside. He can buy heroin through his contacts on the street for sixty dollars a gram. He convinces his girlfriend to pick it up, stuff it into balloons, then pass it to him through a kiss during their visits. Woodpecker wants to move his own dope instead of taking crumbs from Poo.

"A yo, Peck, hold up," Cadillac calls out to him. "I hear you're movin' the shit. Can a nigga get blessed?" he asks.

"What you tryin' to do?" Woodpecker asks.

"I'm sayin', muthafucka lookin' to put his own game down. I needs a hookup. What you give me a loon for?" Cadillac, who runs with the DC car, the gang of prisoners from the nation's capital, wants to buy a gram of heroin.

"You know the rate," Woodpecker says. "It's eight hundred a package."

"I'm sayin', my man, I ain't tryin' to pay no eight hun'red. Know what I'm sayin'? I'm talkin' 'bout settin' my own little thang thang down. You feel me? I'm tryin' to move some shit for you to the homeys. But you gots to do better than eight hun'red. A nigga can't eat off that. I gots to get me me."

"Check this out," Woodpecker says. "If you can be cool, just keep this between you an' me, I'll give it to you for five hundred. You got to have it on the wire for me today. Can you do that?"

Woodpecker is trying to build up his clientele by undercutting the market, and the gang that took him in. "Five hun'red," Cadillac says while scratching his chin. "Dat's what I'm talkin' 'bout, nigga. That's love dere. Bet. You got dat. Gimme a hookup. It's gonna be dere in a hour."

Woodpecker calls his girl and tells her to use the code name they have established to retrieve money from Western Union. When she confirms that she has the money in hand, Woodpecker delivers the balloon to Cadillac. Less than an hour later, Cadillac comes back to him.

"A yo, my nigga. I needs me three moe them things. Know what I'm sayin'? I jus' called my peoples. They done wired fi'teen hun'red to the same spot. I'm a come back when it's a wrap. You check what's up. Then gimme my three joints."

Woodpecker is ecstatic. Selling the other three balloons will lift his profits for the day to more than fifteen hundred after costs. That's more than he ever made selling drugs on the street, and he's making it in prison.

"Yo," Cadillac comes back to him. "Call yo peoples. That money is on the line now. Check it."

Woodpecker calls his girlfriend and tells her to call Western Union for confirmation that fifteen hundred dollars is available to her. When she learns that the money is there and waiting, she tells Woodpecker. He then tells Cadillac that he has the money and delivers the other three balloons that he has been holding. The deal is a seal, or so he thinks.

The following day, Woodpecker calls his girl after lunch. "Baby, it wasn't there," she tells him.

"What do you fuckin' mean it wasn't there?" he asks with fury. He had expected her to be flush with cash. "You fuckin' told me that you called and they said it was waitin' for you. What the fuck happened?"

"I did call," she says. "I don't know what happened. The lady told me over the phone that the money was waiting for me to pick up. Then when I went to get it, the lady said the money had been taken back by the person who sent it. You didn't call me back last night, so I couldn't tell you."

DC Cadillac has taken Woodpecker for a punk. By allowing him to collect the five hundred dollars for the first transaction, Cadillac earned Woodpecker's trust. But he used that information Woodpecker had given him about keeping it on the hush hush. To Cadillac, that meant Woodpecker was pulling a rogue move, running alone. He didn't have any support, so DC chose to take him down.

Pecker heads out to the yard looking for Cadillac. He doesn't find him, but walks into the barbershop where the DC Boyz hang out. Cadillac is lounging with his crew of thugs. "Cadillac," Pecker says. "I need to see you."

"Yeah," Cadillac says. "You seein' me. What's up? D'you get dat?" He snickers.

Woodpecker knows that he is sinking into quicksand. "Let me talk to you outside." Woodpecker doesn't feel comfortable in the barbershop, but he knows he is alone on this deal.

"Bitch, what you mean you needs to talk to me outside? I don't give a fuck what you need. Who the fuck you think you is, white boy? What da fuck you need to talk to me 'bout? You can talk to me right here." Cadillac stands up and confronts Woodpecker, looking down on him like a cobra that is ready to strike.

"I didn't get the money," Woodpecker stutters. "It wasn't on the line when my girl went to pick it up."

"You callin' Cadillac a liar? That what you doin', muthafucka? How the fuck you gonna come holla at me 'bout somethin' went down last night? You need to check yo bitch. Don't come tryin' to play no punkass game on me. I ain't dat muthafucka. You tol' me you had the money yesterday. Wuss up?"

Pecker does not strike back. He is strapped with a shank, but he has lost all of his courage as a consequence of Cadillac's aggression. He does not pull out the weapon. He is scared. "Let me check it out again," he says. "Maybe there's been a mistake." Woodpecker just wants out. He needs to get away and regroup.

"Look at dat muthafucka dere," Cadillac's friend says as Woodpecker walks out. "You done pulled his ho card."

Woodpecker is in trouble. And there is nowhere to hide in the pen. He knows he cannot contain what has just happened. He goes to find his cousin Poo and reveals all that transpired.

"What the fuck you mean you're makin' moves on your own?" Poo is furious. "I told you to fly straight in here, and your little dumb ass goes and does shit behind my back with a bunch of DC motherfuckers. Who the fuck you think you are? You're gonna answer for this, motherfucker. This shit ain't over. Come with me. We gotta see if we can handle this now, before the count."

While Poo and Woodpecker walk to the barbershop to talk with Cadillac, the word spreads. "Hey, *carnal.*" Choo Choo, a shot caller for La Eme, comes to see Lion.

"*Qué pasó* with the *pinchi mayates*? I hear one of your *hermanos* has a problem with DC."

"What?" Lion says. "Who? I don't know nothin' about it."

"*Simón, vato,*" Choo Choo says. "Just a while ago. The one they call Cadillac disrespected your youngster. I heard he didn't do shit. *Nada.* You better check him. The compound is watchin'."

"You're damn right I'm gonna check him," Lion says. "I'll let you know what's up by the count."

"Whatever happens, *vato,*" Choo Choo says, "we got your back."

The first that Lion hears someone from his crew has a problem with the DC Boyz comes from the leader of the Mexican Mafia. Then the leader of the Natives comes and tells him the same thing. The blacks are the most populous group in Atlanta. Although there are multiple gangs, they all join forces when racial problems are about to explode. Without knowing the nature of the dispute, shot callers from the Spanish and Native American gangs offer support to Lion in order to keep the balance of power inside the walls. By the time the count clears, Lion has brought in further reinforcements from the other white gangs. He doesn't know what will go down, but he prepares for a potential battle.

It's nearly recall when Poo and Woodpecker see Cadillac. Hundreds of convicts are returning to the housing units from the yard. There is not much time to talk, but everyone is watching.

"Say, muthafucka," Cadillac says to Woodpecker. Cadillac continues his act, as if he is in the right. "You check yo bitch? That ho stealin' from yo punk ass." Cadillac completely disregards Poo in a deliberate sign of disrespect.

"Hey, Cadillac," Poo says. "This is my cousin. Let me talk to you."

"Yo cousin," Cadillac says. "You ain't got nothin' to do with this cracka. Muthafucka comes to me tellin' me to keep it all quiet and shit. I ain't got nothin' to keep quiet 'bout. I paid the muthafucka. Now wuss up?"

Poo sees where it's going. He's got his shank ready, but he and Woodpecker are the only two white faces in a wave of black hostility. He needs to talk with Lion before this gets out of hand, before it explodes into a full-fledged race riot. Two guards see the commotion and the gathering. They break up the melee and push the crowd through the movement, ordering the men to return to their housing units for the count. "I'm a see you later, bitch," Cadillac says to Woodpecker.

During the count other black leaders step to Cadillac. "Yo, wuzz up nigga, wuzz up whi'chu?"

"It ain't nothin'," Cadillac says. "I done some bi'ness with that lil young muthafucka. Now the cracka muthafucka tryin' to say I didn't pay. Shee-it. You knows how it go up in here. A muthafucka ain't get no product till he pay. Muthafucka say he got the money yesterday and he gives me the three loons. Now he comes at me today talkin' some dumb shit 'bout how he ain't got it. Cadillac ain't da one. Cracka muthafucka tryin' to take a nigga for a sucka. I'm a check dat bitch after da count. Just grab my back if it goes any furtha." With that, the dispute becomes racial.

Shot callers from the Crips, the Bloods, the Black Guerrilla Family, the Vice Lords, and the Gangster Disciples join forces with Cadillac and the DC Boyz. Those who call dogz for the Philly mob, New York, and Florida are also riding with them. "Fuck it," Crip Tank says. "If them muthafuckas wanna bring it, we'll just run 'em off the yard."

Poo gets his chance to speak with Lion. When Lion hears what Woodpecker has done, he wants his head on a platter. "What is that little motherfucker doin', makin' moves like this? Is this you, Poo? Did you set this motherfuckin' mess up?"

"Ain't no way, dog," Poo assures him. "I would never cross lines like that."

"Well you brought him in, motherfucker. He's your problem. Cousin or no cousin. We'll handle this shit with DC. But you got to serve that little motherfucker. We can't have no shit like this goin' on."

After the count clears, the population empties from the housing units, block by block, as the men rush to the chow hall and to the yard. The tension is rapid and rising as the blacks come together, separating themselves from all other races. The Spanish and the Natives join forces with the whites. The gangs of thugs are ready to swarm and attack each other. It's quiet—everyone is waiting for action, though most of the men have no idea what brought about the tension. At this moment, it's just hatred, a hunger for action, for a break in the monotony. They see nothing else to live for.

The guards know something isn't right. Video cameras are placed throughout the penitentiary, broadcasting movements to the control center and other offices. Babcock, the captain of the security forces, keeps photographs of all gangs with mug shots of each known member and associate. He requires all guards to commit those faces to memory. All of those faces are clustered together on the yard. One side is all black; the other is white and brown. Even nongangbangers refuse to cross the racial divide. The captain is the coordinator of the guards. He watches the action from his monitor while staying in touch with lieutenants and guards in key positions at every post by radio. Something is going down. He knows it and orders security reinforcements in place to control it.

Poo and Woodpecker come down the walk toward the yard. Lion is talking with Stitch and Choo Choo, other shot callers with whom he has good relations. Lion explains to the two that he intends to quash the incident and use his own forces to discipline Woodpecker, but it happens too fast. Movement begins on the black side as Cadillac spots Poo and Woodpecker walking to the yard.

Cadillac steps up. "Yo," he says to Crip Tank and the other black leaders. "Fuck dis. I'm fittin' to go handle this shit now. Silk," he calls out, "come on wit me. Let's check dees cracka muthafuckas."

"We got yo back, cuz," Crip Tank says. "Go head on and handle yo bi'ness. Be 'bout yo work. Fire on dat muthafucka if he comes out da side his neck wrong. Any otha muthafuckas come in, we all go."

Cadillac and Silk walk toward Poo and Woodpecker. "What you got to say now, you cracka muthafucka," Cadillac says. Poo makes a move to stick him, but before the shank hits flesh, Cadillac fires on him. The four of them get to rumbling right there on the yard. Guards from the tower fire shots all around them. Announcements come simultaneously from all the loudspeakers. "Everyone on the ground. Now! Hands spread apart. Nobody move." Shots continue to pummel the yard, bullets piercing the dirt only inches away from the convicts' bodies. Guards are running into the yard. The captain has called it. He is rushing from his command post to the yard, radio in hand, barking orders to his lieutenants and staff.

"I want everyone back to their units! Total lockdown. Now. Separate them by housing unit."

Scores of white-shirted officers rush to subdue the prisoners. They come from every direction, from every department. They are yelling orders. "Alpha Unit in this line. On the ground. Nobody stand. Bravo Unit over here. I want Charlie house in this line. Delta house over here. Nobody fuckin' stand. Shots will be fired and my officers will shoot to kill. I repeat, they will shoot to kill."

The convicts scatter to their areas as designated, all on hands and knees. They try to bury their weapons in the dirt before officers come close. "Take those men there to the SHU." The captain singles out Cadillac and Silk, Poo and Woodpecker. "Get the rest of these men into their cellblocks. Single file, one unit at a time. Total lockdown. I want everyone locked in their cells now."

As the officers line the men up and march them away, Babcock goes to talk with his lieutenants. They shake hands and congratulate each other on a play well called. He then goes to see each of the men he locked in segregation. "What you got to say to me?" Babcock asks Cadillac.

"Man, I ain't got a muthafuckin' thing to say to you, bitch. You can suck my dick. Why ain't you go ax them cracka muthafuckas? I ain't did a muthafuckin' thing." The captain is used to such exchanges. Neither Silk nor Woodpecker has anything to say. He steps to Poo. "How 'bout you, Poo. You gonna tell me what's up?"

"What the fuck you mean am I gonna tell you what's up? Who the fuck you think you talkin' to? I'm about to handle my business. That's what the fuck is up. Now you handle yours and don't come 'round here askin' me nothin'. You know what time it is in here."

No information. Captain Babcock looks at his picture board. He knows the leaders of every gang. He orders the guards to bring Lion to talk to him in his office. "What's goin' on, Lion?" he asks. "You can tell me what's up or I'll order the buses in here right now and start changin' zip codes for everyone. We can stay on lockdown for a month. It's your call."

"Check this out, Cap," Lion says. "You know what I'm about, you know how I roll. I ain't gonna tell you a motherfuckin' thing. But I can squash this shit here. It's nothin' but a misunderstandin' that I can straighten out."

"You wanna squash it? Tell me how you're gonna do that."

"I need to talk to Crip Tank. Bring him down here and let me talk to him alone."

"And what am I gonna get if I make that happen?" Babcock asks.

"You'll see. Everything'll be cool. No problem."

Lion has an interest in keeping the status quo. He has power inside the penitentiary's walls. Although he knows that wars can ignite in an instant, as a gang leader he uses strategy to control the volatility around him. It is that influence he has over others that makes him a shot caller. In the free world, society looks upon him and other gang leaders as predators. But in the pit into which he has been cast, Lion is a king among his men.

"What's up?" Crip Tank asks him as the two sit face-to-face in a holding cell the captain locked them in. "I heard you wanna holla at me."

"Check this out," Lion says. "You know what I'm about. I know what you're about. We're both men. This ain't about us. My guy went outside the rules and regulations, pulled some foul shit. I'm gonna handle that; we impose our own discipline. Now I know Cadillac took him down. I'm gonna let that slide because I know Cadillac thought Pecker was on his own. Because he wasn't disrespectin' me or the brothers, I'm gonna squash this. Ain't no reason for no war over this here. It's a misunderstandin' that got way out of hand."

"I can respect dat," Crip Tank says. "You give me yo word you got yo people, and I give you my word that I can squash dis with da homeys."

The two gang leaders clash fists to seal the truce. With their word, the captain leaves the pen on lockdown for the night. At six the following morning, keys start clicking as guards start opening the doors in the cellhouses. It's back to normal operations, with French toast for breakfast.

Two weeks later, Lion orders the discipline on Woodpecker. Poo brings four of his men to Woodpecker's cell. Together they pummel him with their fists and boots, but no knives. "That's what you get, you little motherfucker, for violating," Poo says as his cousin lies broken on the floor of his cell. His skin, muscles, and bones ache from the beating. The brothers don't allow him to leave the cell until his bruises and black eyes heal. They bring him food, nurture him back to health.

While making his rounds a few days after the beating, Captain Babcock looks into Woodpecker's cell. He sees him recovering. "What happened to you?" the captain asks.

"Nothin' I didn't deserve, Cap. Just a little discipline. I needed it."

The captain looks at him for a moment, then walks on. It's another day in the pen.

10

The more time I spent in the penitentiary, the more I came to believe that it is truly a culture unto itself. It is a culture that perpetuates failure, at least as measured by free society's standards. The penitentiary discourages the men it contains from thinking that they can become anything more than prisoners. With Congress's abolishment in the mid-1980s of the possibility for federal prisoners to work toward advancing their release dates through parole, the pen has become a home devoid of hope for tens of thousands of desperate men. Those men make their lives inside of it, embracing values unrecognizable to most law-abiding citizens.

As a young man I had to come to terms with the fact that I would pass nearly three decades inside. Because the corrections system eliminates channels for men to distinguish themselves in a positive way, or to earn freedom through merit, few of those with whom I serve time have any reason to plan for more than the next few hours. For them, it's all about the pen.

The system encourages this life-inside mentality. Prisoners can see that the individual striving to prepare himself for the future is not the one who receives the single cell or the choice job assignment. Staff can walk over that prisoner without a second thought. Administrators concern themselves more with the potentially disruptive prisoner, the one presenting the threat of adding to the havoc in the penitentiary. In an effort to keep those volatile forces in check, corrections professionals appease such men with single-man rooms, easy work assignments, extra phone calls, and individual attention. Ironically, this system of corrections brings the unintended but inevitable consequence of giving power to those who further disrupt the system. Those who recommit to criminal values assuage the pains of confinement. On the other hand, those working to reconcile with society and prepare for release meet resistance; they live much more difficult lives inside.

With freedom gone, and the administrators' belief that separating men from their wives and girlfriends for decades at a time is somehow consistent with the stated goal of corrections to prepare felons for law-abiding lives, many of the men turn to erotic magazines to help them relieve their sexual urgings. "I been down so muthafuckin' long," Crip Tank says, "I don't need no women to satisfy me. Crip Tank know how to beat his own muthafuckin' dick. Believe dat. Crip Tank can take care a his damn self."

In the 1990s, Congress passed legislation that prohibits the introduction of pornographic magazines and the showing of films with R or X ratings for federal prisoners. But in older penitentiaries, where men have been locked inside for decades, thousands of "fuck books" remain in circulation. Some prisoners make a hustle of renting them out. Lion keeps stacks of such magazines as part of his full-service operation to satisfy cravings in the penitentiary.

It is not only prisoners who lust after the erotic photographs. When performing shakedowns, where officers rummage through the personal property of convicts in their never-ending search for contraband, some of the guards sit down in the cells and flip through the pages to enjoy the shots of naked women. Such an encounter led directly to an opportunity for Lion and his friends to find some relief.

A corrections officer named Nelson works as the officer in charge (OIC) of the cellhouse's third tier. As far as prisoners are concerned, Nelson is an easy guard. Some of his colleagues develop an obvious taste for the power that comes with their position. They get a charge out of degrading men by forcing them to perform mindless and meaningless tasks like raking rocks back and forth from one pile to another. Nelson is cool, laid-back as far as guards go. He does his job, performing shakedowns each night, but Nelson does not seem to make it his mission to aggravate prisoners further.

Like all guards, with regular shakedowns Nelson has developed a good idea of each prisoner's belongings and interests. Lion has a reputation as a shot caller in the pen, but Nelson knows that Lion also controls a considerable portion of the underground economy, including the distribution of pornographic magazines. When his shift eases up, or when Nelson feels like kicking back, he pops into Lion's room. "What's up?" the officer says to Lion. "Got any new fuck books?"

For security reasons, administrative policies discourage correctional officers from forming any types of bonds or friendships with prisoners. Yet after years of continuous contact in close quarters, some officers let their discretion slip and start to consider the prisoners as fellow human beings. The guards have access to considerable amounts of information about each prisoner. When they're comfortable, some guards will reveal a bit about their own personal lives.

"You know what the fuck I got, motherfucker," Lion answers while stretched out on his bunk. He has a Joseph Wambaugh paperback in his hands. "You're lookin' through my shit every day. Grab what you want and leave me the fuck alone."

Nelson sits at the table and starts fingering his way through the stacks of *Hustler, Penthouse,* and other hard-core porno rags. Lion preserves the pages of his merchandise by covering them with thick strips of a heavy, transparent tape. "I don't even know why you spend so much time lookin' at those skanks," Lion says. "You're fuckin' free. You oughta be gettin' all the snatch you need out there."

"I'm married," Nelson says while holding up his ring. "The same ol' shit every fuckin' day. Home's no different from here. I check these out to see what I'm missin', to get some ideas."

Nelson's wife works as a correctional officer in the penitentiary as well. They are both in their early thirties. He wears a crew cut in the military fashion. Nelson has his sedentary job, carb-rich diet, and lack of exercise to thank for his gut that has turned to dough. "If I wasn't so strapped for cash I'd be out there gettin' me some new shit. Even with overtime I'm strugglin'. I got child-support payments to two different women that are breakin' me." Nelson holds up a particularly lewd centerfold. "I'd like to get me some a that. Check out that box." Nelson tries to get Lion's attention away from his paperback.

"Man, fuck that skank," Lion says. "I'm fuckin' tired a lookin' at them pages. I've jacked my dick so many times to them broads that they all look the same. I need some real pussy."

"What you mean?" Nelson says. "There's plenty a pussy' round here. It just all smells like shit."

"I don't fuck with no punks. And you better watch what you're sayin' around me, Nelson. I'm a man. Remember that."

"Come on," Nelson laughs. "I'm just breakin' balls. After all the years you've been down, you probably wouldn't even know what to do with it."

"You're fuckin' crazy," Lion says. "I'd do anything for some pussy. I'd pay five hundred for a fuck. Just one come. No, fuck it. I'd pay a fuckin' thousand."

Nelson puts the magazine down and looks at Lion. "You'd pay a thousand dollars for one fuck? You're bullshittin'."

"The hell I am," Lion says. "I wouldn't need more than five minutes with that bitch, but I'd tear that pussy up. I'd damn sure get my thousand's worth."

"A thousand bucks for five minutes. That's fuckin' crazy."

"Shit. You try jackin' your dick for twenty motherfuckin' years," Lion says. "Then tell me about crazy."

"A thousand bucks, huh? I'm gonna keep that in mind. I might be able to help you out with this."

Officer Nelson leaves the pen that night. He cannot purge the thought of Lion's offer to pay a thousand dollars for five minutes of sexual intercourse. He thinks of all the bills the couple could pay with that tax-free money. Nelson talks it over with his wife, who initially rejects the idea. "Come on, honey," he pleads with her. "Just think of all we could do with a thousand dollars. You know I love you. I need you to help with this. The guy's been locked up for almost twenty years. You could make him come in five minutes. Maybe less."

"Well if he's anything like you I could," she says. "I would lose my job for this. I can't believe you want to take this risk."

"Nobody's gonna know. I'm the OIC. I'll sneak you in during a count. When the unit's locked down, you come in. You'd be in and out." Nelson cajoles his wife to have sex with the lifer.

"What if he hurts me?"

"He ain't gonna hurt you," her husband says while caressing her breast. "I'm gonna be right outside the door." Nelson convinces her with kisses to her body. In so doing, he excites them both into the wildest sex they have enjoyed in years. His wife fantasizes about the forbidden act with the gang leader. While the couple lies spent on the bed, his wife tells him that she wants to have the money in hand before she goes anywhere near Lion. "We're gonna have it, honey," Nelson says. "I'll take care of everything." He kisses her before drifting off to sleep.

"So you're serious about that thousand," Nelson says to Lion the following morning during the shift.

"Don't fuckin' jerk me around, man," Lion says. "I'm fuckin' serious as a motherfucker. Lion don't play."

"But you're in here. How you gonna get me a thousand dollars if I can pull this off?"

"Don't fuckin' worry about that," Lion says. "You know who I am. You know I got people on the street who will put a thousand down for me whenever I say, wherever I say. Now what's on your mind?"

"My wife," Nelson says. "She'll have sex with you if you get us the thousand."

"Your wife," Lion laughs. "How the fuck you gonna get your wife in here?"

"She works here. She's the corridor officer."

"You mean hot little Miss Nelson is your wife?" Lion asks. "Shit. I never put the two of you together. What the fuck does that tight little blonde see in you?"

"Fuck you," Nelson says. "Are you up for this or not?"

"Fuckin'-A rights I'm up for it," Lion says. "Just tell me how you wanna do this. You wanna meet my people outside, or your want me to put the money on the wire? I can have the money for you by chow time."

"No, no. I don't want no records of this," Nelson says. "Give me a number to call. You just tell him that I'm gonna call when I get off work."

"Done," Lion says. "Here's the fuckin' number. Just call after an hour or so. Ask for Striker. He'll be ready for you. But check this out," Lion adds with a hard glare. "Striker will have the cash in an envelope. You take that thousand, it's on. You don't want to fuck me on this. My brothers can reach out and touch anywhere."

Nelson smiles. "You think I'm bullshittin'? Just get that money right tonight. This shit is goin' down tomorrow mornin' before chow."

Nelson calls the number after work. Before going home, he meets with Striker as they had agreed. Striker passes the cash-stuffed envelope with hardly a word. Nelson counts it in his car, his eyes darting to the rearview mirror to make sure no one is following him. He drives home and shows the money to his wife. Neither of them has ever before held ten crisp one-hundred-dollar bills. It is tax-free money to them, a bonus. His wife begins to look forward to earning it.

At nine o'clock the following morning, Nelson calls a lockdown unit census on the third tier of the cellhouse. Most of the convicts are at their assigned work details or on the yard. Those few who are in the unit yell obscenities and return to their cells. They are angry at having to miss their morning dose of MTV. Nelson turns the bolt in each cell's door. He inserts his key into Lion's door, but doesn't lock it. When he reaches the rear of the unit, he unlocks the emergency exit.

As an important shot caller, Lion commands a single cell. It's at the end of the block, right next to the emergency exit. Nelson's wife creeps in. She slides into Lion's room, her heart racing as if she has just finished a sprint. Lion is ready. He is lying naked on his rack, a sheet covering him. He has a sex magazine in one hand, and he strokes himself with the other. He can't believe it's happening, and when she eases into the room, she shocks him. "Damn, honey," Lion says. "You surprised me."

"What are you lookin' at," she says with a bit of apprehension.

"I ain't lookin' at nothin' but you," he answers, throwing the magazine down and lowering the sheet. "Come on over, sweetness."

"We've got five minutes to do whatever you want to do," she says. "Put this on." She passes him a condom.

"What the fuck is this?" Lion says. "I paid a thousand dollars. I wanna feel what you got in there. I wanna taste you from the inside."

"I don't care what you paid, Lion. I don't know what you got, and I need protection. Let me put it on you. We need to get this over with."

As she fumbles to unwrap the condom, she's looking at how muscular Lion has built his body. It excites her. The extensive workouts have clearly defined his pecs, his shoulders, his arms. Lion's stomach is a slate of stone, and his cock stands rigid hard, straight up like a flagpole. She sets the condom down on his dick and unwinds it down the powerful shaft. "Don't hurt me," she says. "You're so much bigger, and stronger, and harder than my husband."

"Come on, baby," Lion says. "Take those off. I need you now."

"Just one second," she says while standing to walk toward the door. "I need to peek out the window to see my husband, to make sure everything's all right." As she looks out the window, she makes eye contact with her husband. He holds his hand in the okay sign and gives her a wink. He then holds up five fingers, letting her know that she has five minutes.

While she watches her husband, she quickly unbuttons her pants and slides them down to her knees. She lifts one leg out of her pants; she wears no panties. "Goddamn," Lion says while watching her. "You've got the prettiest, tightest ass I've ever seen. Come on over here. I need you. Show me what you got."

She walks over, excited, with all of her blood flowing.

"Sit here on my lap."

She sits down on Lion, with her back to his chest. He enters her. She moans, then starts wiggling back and forth, up and down. Lion is so hard, so charged up, that he can't remain seated. His large hands squeeze her waist, her breasts. Then, in one sudden movement, while licking the back of her neck, he stands up, leaning her over the cell's locker while he rams her like a locomotive, in and out, thrusting into her, fucking her with twenty years of fury. He covers her mouth to muffle the sound of passion. She is into the speed, the power, the rough sex. And less than two minutes after it began, Lion fills his condom with come.

"Ah shit," Lion says. "I need more of you than that."

Her heart is still pounding. She is delirious, then snaps out of it and remembers where she is, what she has just done. "That's all you get," she says. "Give me a towel to wipe myself." She pulls her pants back on, peeks out of the door's window. With the all-clear sign from her husband, she walks out of the cell. She scoots right and exits the unit through the back stairway, leading down toward her post as the officer on the main corridor.

The tryst comes off without a hitch. Officer Nelson doesn't think a thing about his wife's intercourse with Lion. The thought of bringing a thousand dollars into his household so quickly, so effortlessly, thrills him. Upon seeing his wife exit the unit, Nelson clears the census count and lets the men out of their cells. He purposely stays away from Lion until he can talk with his wife.

At home, the two Officer Nelsons talk about the day. Rather than traumatizing her, as Nelson thought might happen, his wife brags about how easily she brought Lion to climax. "It took me less than five minutes," she tells him. "I can't believe he paid us a thousand dollars for that." They celebrate with dinner and a night of passion. The danger brings Nelson the additional benefit of a spark to the couple's sex life. Nelson starts calculating how much they can earn.

"Did you get your money's worth?" Nelson asks Lion the following day.

"The dessert was good, just not enough of it," Lion says. "I only had five minutes with her. She could've stayed a little longer."

"Hold on, big dog," Nelson said. "You're the one who set the price. You even called it right, saying you'd come in less than five minutes. You got what you paid for."

"I ain't complainin', dude," Lion says. "I'd like a little more of it, that's all. I just don't want to go for no thousand every time."

"Well," Nelson says, "I can't back down now. Don't want to insult my wife. The price is a thousand."

"Fuck," Lion says. "How 'bout a blow job? What are you gonna charge for her to suck me off?"

"This ain't no smorgasbord, pal. You think they'd go easier on my wife if they catch her suckin' your dick than if they caught you pluggin' her? It's a thousand bucks. I don't care what you do in here, but she's not comin' in this room unless I've got a grand from you up front."

"All right, all right," Lion says. "Fuck it then. I'm gonna get you two thousand. That's good for two more hits at her. Call my man Striker. He'll take care of it."

Over the weeks to come, the Nelson team earns over ten thousand dollars from Lion. It's more money than they've ever had, and Nelson's wife is developing a real liking for her new job. Then Lion receives a visit from one of his brothers who lives in the same block. "Hey, bro," Stitch says. "What the fuck is goin' on?"

"Nothin's goin' on."

"Come on, Lion," Stitch says. "This is me you're talkin' to. I fuckin' live right across the hall. I see this broad creepin' in and out your cell. What's up?"

"Check this out," Lion says. "That broad is Nelson's wife. I'm fuckin' her."

"Get the fuck outta here," Stitch says. "You're shittin' me."

"I shit you not, bro. I been hittin' that shit for a month now."

"What about me, bro?" Stitch asks. "Let me get some of that."

"I can make it happen," Lion says, "but you gotta pay two thousand up front. It's fuckin' worth it though," he adds while holding his arm out to clang fists.

"I don't give a fuck," Stitch says. "Sign me the fuck up, bro."

The brothers are flush with cash from their drug-dealing, gambling, and other rackets in the pen. They don't have much opportunity to spend money, so Stitch is eager to pay the rate that Lion sets. The news takes Officer Nelson aback when Lion first tells him. "What do you mean you've got a date set up for Stitch?" Nelson asks. "My wife can't fuck everybody. She ain't no whore. No one is supposed to know about this."

"Yeah. She ain't no whore and I ain't no drug dealer," Lion says. "Stitch is my brother. What's the big fuckin' deal? He'll use a rubber. It ain't like we're droppin' a load in her. He lives right across the block and keeps seein' her creep in my room. He knows what's up. You don't gotta meet nobody new. Striker's gonna give you two thousand, one for me and one for Stitch. You set it up with you ol' lady."

With nearly three thousand deprived men confined inside the penitentiary's walls, and several hundred government employees mixing with them, Lion and the Nelsons are not the first to forge physical alliances inside. Others take advantage of the supply-demand imbalance as well. It's usually gang leaders like Lion who create and control opportunities for the prostitution of female staff members. Those staff members inclined to participate in such flagrant violations of institutional policy and law need to protect themselves against informants. Further, they cannot easily solicit clients without serious risk of getting caught. Working together with a highly respected and well-connected gang leader like Lion reduces the risk of detection. Such men wire themselves into the happenings of the pen; they know who can pay how much, and they have finely tuned instincts for the rackets they control.

The Nelsons work as a husband-and-wife team, which makes escaping detection easier. The complicity between the two ensures that the husband remains on point to watch for anyone who can spoil the operation. He has the power to lock other prisoners down in their cells while at the same time running interference against fellow correctional officers or lieutenants who might stumble onto the action. Others in the game do not enjoy the same assurance.

Choo Choo put his own moves on Ms. Luna, an attractive young lady who holds a teaching position in the penitentiary. Although gang leaders usually don't work, Choo Choo began volunteering in the education department soon after Ms. Luna came inside the walls. They both grew up in the Echo Park section of East Los Angeles. Despite Choo Choo's early commitment to gangbanging, the fifteen years of imprisonment he has behind him, and the life sentence that he serves, Choo Choo convinces Ms. Luna that they share a lot in common. About the same age, they have mutual acquaintances back in Los Angeles. When alone, he calls her Maribel, which is her first name.

"*Mira, linda,*" Choo Choo calls out to her. "Those boxes *están muy pesadas.* Let me lift those for you," he tells her one afternoon when he has stayed late to help Maribel organize the classroom. She keeps him there with her during the count, when the rest of the prisoners are locked in the cellblock. The time alone allows Maribel to talk about her private life. "I don't like it here," she tells him. "I miss my *familia,* my friends, the Chicano life of home. I haven't found any good Mexican food in this whole city."

"I know," Choo Choo said. "This place is full of *pinchi mayates.* Inside we've got *la raza unida.* But I miss Los too. I know why I'm here. *Lo que yo no sé* is why you're livin' in this *pinchi* city."

Maribel tells him her story. She followed a man to the East, bringing her two children with her. After they lived together for a year, he started to treat her badly, hitting her and cheating on her. They split up. She accepted a job with the Bureau of Prisons because it was growing so quickly and offered stability. "But I hate this work," she says. "I see all you homeys locked up, serving life and shit. I feel so bad for you. I'm just tryin' to save enough money to get me home, back to Echo Park with my family."

"*Oralé. Simón,*" Choo Choo says. "*Viva la raza.*" He continues to help her, smiling.

"*La raza,*" she says.

"So *qué vas hacer,* when you get back to Califas?" Choo Choo asks

what type of work she will pursue in California. "Are you still goin'
to *trabajar para los pinchis federales*?" He asks whether she plans to
continue her career with the federal government.

She laughs. "I'm thinkin' about it," she says. "It's fucked up, but at
least it's steady money. I'm tired of depending on an ol' man. I want
to be independent. Don't tell anyone here, but I used to dance when
I was younger. It's the only other thing I know how to do, but I'm too
old for that kind of shit now. This job gives me security. I never
wanna depend on a man again."

"Come on," Choo Choo says. "You know you're a beautiful *ruca,
una jaina preciosa.*"

She giggles. "Stop that."

"You could do whatever you wanna do," Choo Choo continues. "*Simón.* You don't have to work here if you don't like it. There are ways a
beautiful woman like you could support yourself. You could even earn
more here now, put together enough to make your move home."

"Yeah, I'll bet," she says. "I've heard about that in training. There's
no way I'm bringing any weed or dope in here. The only way I'm
comin' to jail is if they're payin' me for it."

"Ahh, you don't have to bring in no drugs," Choo Choo says. "You
could do plenty well just bringin' your *bella* self in. *Simón. Tú eres
una jaina hermosa, deliciosa.* You said you used to dance. It would be
just like dancin'. But you'd make a lot more."

"You mean having sex with strangers?" she asks. "There's no way
I'd do that. I'm no *puta, ese.*"

"Hey, come on," Choo Choo says. "Nobody's sayin' you're
nothin' different than one fine-lookin' woman. *Si yo no estuviera* in
this fucked-up situation I'd want you to be my lady. But this is
what I am. I'm just sayin' I could look out for you, help you put together the security you need. And we'd both be helpin' out the
homeboys."

They continue to talk while working side by side, stacking

curriculum folders in files. "How much does a girl make for something like that?" Maribel asks, curious at the prospect.

"I could get the homeboys to pay you a thousand dollars for about five minutes, *chica*. And I'd protect you, make sure it's okay. You could make twenty thousand in a couple weeks. *Simón.*"

"Twenty thousand," she says. "I'd have to fuck twenty guys." She laughs at the absurdity of it. Maribel has never allowed herself to think of so much money.

"Don't think of it like that, *mi linda,*" Choo Choo soothes her. "It's just like dancing. If I could I would give you the money myself. It's not like you'll be thinking about it. All the homeboys are clean, and you bring them all condoms. We could set it up during a movie night, where we'd all be lookin' out for you. You'd have all the money up front, before you even come in."

"I don't know," Maribel says. "It's scaring me to even talk about it."

"*¿Por qué tienes miedo?*" Choo Choo asks. "You don't have to be scared. You don't have to do *nada*. But if you want to, I can make it happen for you. I'm not going to let nothin' bad happen to my homegirl. This is just business for you, you understand, nothin' personal," he says while touching her cheek softly. "And nobody will ever know."

"But don't you want me?" she asks lightly, in a little-girl voice.

"Oh, *mamacita*. I want you so bad I'm walkin' around beatin' myself three times a day. *Simón.* But I care about you. I want to help you do what you want. It makes me feel a little bit human to do something for you."

She kisses him, takes his hand and lifts it to her breast. They enjoy the moment, but it's too dangerous for more. The count clears, and other inmates are about to roam freely. They continue their work. By the end of the evening, she tells him it's okay, that she wants him to do it. "I want you to start setting it up. But before I do anything with them, I need some time with you. I'm goin' to have you on the out count to be with me again tomorrow."

Choo Choo sets it up. More than three hundred men in the penitentiary roll with the Mexican Mafia. They come from California, New Mexico, Arizona, Colorado, and other western states. The BOP transfers gang members far from home as they stir problems in other pens. All of the members have their Mexican heritage and their commitment to convict life in common. Their money comes in the same way as all gang members'. They get it the old-fashioned way. They take it. They traffic in contraband. They perform contract hits. They run gambling operations. They sell weapons. They manufacture wine. They run the pen; it is their home.

Besides that, all have criminal connections on the street, some of whom support the members with financial resources in times of need. Since it isn't every day that an opportunity arises for sex, when it does come, prisoners are willing to pay. Choo Choo has no problem putting together seven players whom he trusts. All are willing to go for five thousand apiece. That gives each of them five trips to the nectar well, and thirty-five thousand in cash to little Ms. Luna.

He meets her the next day. When they're alone, Choo Choo gives her the news. "*Mija,* I got you thirty-five thousand dollars. *Dáme una* hookup for the money. They'll send it on the wire," Choo Choo tells her. "One thousand *cada vez.* They're ready to send *los primeros siete* today."

"Thirty-five thousand," she says. "That too fuckin' many. I can't fuck thirty-five guys."

"No, *mija,*" he tells her. "Only seven. They're each gonna *pagar* for *cinco veces. Yo tengo todo listo.*" Choo Choo tells her that he's set it all up. "Five guys a night. They're gonna draw straws to get the order right. We got it set up for Mondays, Wednesdays, and Fridays during the movie. The homeboys gonna work together to cover us."

The education department reserves Ms. Luna's classrooms on those nights for Spanish-language films. While the prisoners fill the

classroom, and with the lights off inside, the customers Choo Choo
secures have intercourse with Ms. Luna, one at a time, as the other
prisoners form a visual barrier around the windows, as if they all are
watching the film. Others are in the corridor outside the classroom,
standing sentry to send a signal in the event that another staff member patrols the area. Two weeks later, she has the thirty-five grand in
her bank account and the freedom to do what she chooses with her
life. Yet with the growth of her financial resources comes a growth in
her attachment to Choo Choo. She doesn't leave until the administration forces her out.

"*Venga, mi vida.*" Choo Choo calls her closer. "We can do it *aquí.*
My homeboys got our back." Choo Choo is in the hole, on the third
tier, the backside of the cellhouse. When Ms. Luna makes her rounds,
delivering educational materials through the wall of bars to the men
locked in cages, Choo Choo pleads with her to have sex with him.

"Baby, I can't do it here," she says. "The cops are walking all over
the place."

"Come on, *mi princesa.* I love you. I need you now. Do it for me,
baby. Just back up to the bars. I gotta have you now."

Ms. Luna doesn't resist Choo Choo's advance. While she stands
outside the bars as if she is talking to him, his arm slides through,
under her skirt to fondle his Mirabel. She doesn't stop him. She likes
it. It excites the woman. The danger of getting caught thrills her. She
turns around and hikes her skirt up while bending over.

Choo Choo has intercourse with her through the bars, ramming
himself through, ignoring the pain of his pelvis slamming into the
steel gates as he enters her. It is in that moment of action that Lieutenant Greer walks onto the tier, his keys jingling by his side as he approaches, catching the two in flagrante delicto. Choo Choo is
indifferent to the guard. He continues to pump, to pound himself
into her, refusing to quit until he climaxes inside. Only upon Choo
Choo's completion, when Ms. Luna straightens up and drops her

skirt to cover her bare bottom, does the lieutenant say anything. "Let's go," he says, then escorts her off the penitentiary grounds. Choo Choo is transferred to another penitentiary, but his name lives on as a legend inside the walls.

Life goes on for the convicts as they make the penitentiary their home.

11

By taking away an individual's hope to return to society, the penitentiary breeds chaos. Whereas the social structure outside of walls encourages people to educate themselves, to find legitimate employment, and to contribute to society, those who follow such a path inside make themselves vulnerable. There is no escaping the perils of the pen. A man must learn to navigate his way through it.

The early decisions of my life dropped me into the viper pit with Crip Tank. He moves like a snake himself, slithering through such an environment with ease. Crip Tank is a hustler. He smuggles drugs inside. He oversees the distribution of those drugs. He stabs or beats those who he thinks have shown him or his homeys disrespect.

Crip Tank capitalizes on his ability to instill fear and extort others. He has no respect for authority or for the values that hold law-abiding society together. Crip Tank is a gangster, a man who has no qualms about being about his business. His business is "gettin' money." He pursues such ends by any means necessary. None of his methods comport with the rules by which most citizens live. Although such behavior is not well regarded outside, through it Crip Tank advances his standing as an important and respected shot caller in the pen.

With different racial, cultural, and geographical backgrounds, Crip Tank and I have nothing in common other than our entry into the penitentiary together. Yet somehow that is enough to open a friendship. That does not mean we eat at the same table, that we exercise together, or that we pass much time in each other's company at all.

Our values differ. Sometimes months pass where I do not see him, as Crip Tank's behavior brings him a considerable amount of hole time. He is a gangbanger, a leader among violent, lawless men. His world is inside. I make mine outside. Most of my interactions with Crip Tank, Choo Choo, Lion, and every other gangster or shot caller in the pen take place in the law library, where I make myself available to help others write, or type, or do research. That is how I come to know so many other prisoners from so many varied walks of life.

"Yo, wussup, muthafucka." Crip Tank comes to me as I'm working in the library, studying through courses that will lead me to a graduate degree. "This my little homey Lunatic. I needs you to look at his case. These people carrying Lunatic real greasy."

Crip Tank introduces his fellow gang member and friend from Compton, his homey. "Talk to a muthafucka and see wussup. I'm a send you five hun'red to fix his shit. Know what I'm sayin'?"

"You don't have to send me any money," I tell him. "I don't even know if I can do anything to help. I'm not a magician. I can't undo the past."

"Looky here, muthafucka," Crip Tank says. "You know what I'm about. I'm a send ya five hun'red. It ain't shit. You just keep goin' school. And take care my homeys. See 'bout yo work. I'm a see 'bout mines."

Crip Tank takes off, leaving Lunatic behind to tell me his story. "So how do you know Crip Tank?" I ask.

"Shee-it," Lunatic says. "Crip Tank my nigga. His set is a few blocks from my hood. We CC Riders, Compton-Crip Riders. Know what I'm sayin'? We been bangin' since way back in da day. I been knowin' Crip Tank since we was both young Gs. Then they locked a muthafucka up. I just come up in here and sees what's up."

"You mean Crip Tank got locked up?" I ask.

"No." He clears up my confusion. "Since they locked me up. I been locked in state joints back in Cali. Pelican Bay. I just got out last year. This here some new shit. Dat's what I needs you to look at for a muthafucka. Know what I'm sayin'?"

Lunatic appears to be in his midtwenties. His head is shaved bald and he wears a goatee. He has numerous welts from scars that did not heal well on his head, neck, and arms. He looks rough. "So what's up?" I ask. "How can I help you?"

"Check dis out," Lunatic says. "I gots to serve eight years with the feds. But I still got some state shit that's gonna fuck me up when I gets out. Crip Tank says you might can help me lift that shit now."

"What kind of problems do you have with California?"

"Man, I been havin' problems fo'eva," Lunatic begins. "I was si'-teen when they locked me up for blastin' a muthafucka. Know what I'm sayin'? I been doin' time ever since. I been in Folsom, San Quentin, Soledad. When they opened that new Pelican Bay joint, they sent me up there 'cause I'm a Crip. When I got out, I was tryin' to do right. Shee-it. I gots me a job drivin' deliveries for the newspaper. I'm doin' real good. Know what I'm sayin'? I was keepin' the parole officer off my dick. Then I got a call from my homey Raven. Some niggas done jacked him for his ride. Da-moo muthafuckas. So he needs me to get his back. What the fuck I'm gonna do? Right? He's my homey, so I'm down for whateva. I ain't been out the joint for mo' than a month or two. And it's on again."

"What is it that you did for Raven?" I ask.

"I'm sayin'," Lunatic continues. "I goes to pick up my homey. When he gets in the ride, he whips out two gats, two foe-fives. He slides me one a da gats. We rollin' lookin' for them muthafuckas, straight up ready to blast 'em if we sees 'em. After a while, I needs some gas. When I pull up to the station, I let Raven pump da tank while I walks back behind to take a leak. I got the gat wit me. As I'm comin' back to the car, I see fuckin' one-time pull up. They lookin' at me, so I throws the heat up over a bank."

"Did they see you throw the gun over the bank?" I ask.

"I don't know if they seen me throw it, but they found it," Lunatic says. "One-time came at me and asked what I was doin' back there. I tol' him I was just takin' a leak. One of 'em gets to snoopin' and finds the gat. They hauls a muthafucka in. But I gots a fake ID so I bails out with the quickness, befo' my parole officer hears 'bout da shit."

I steadily write notes as Lunatic describes his legal problem. From his description, I gather that police officers, whom he calls "one-time," found his gun, which he calls "heat" or the "gat." As a felon, he is not allowed to possess a firearm. Lunatic provides fake identification to bail out of jail before his parole officer finds out about the offense.

"When I woke the next day my parole officer is callin' me on the phone. He's axin' whether I'm the muthafucka one-time caught with the heat. I thinks about lyin', but I know they got a nigga's prints and shit. So I tells him it was me. Muthafucka tells me to come in. I axes him to give me a few days to get my shit straight. Muthafucka tells me to come in now. So I tells him to give me two hours and I'll be there. But fuck it. I wasn't fittin' to turn myself in to no muthafucka. He gots to catch me. Know what I'm sayin'? So I takes off. Go see 'bout my work."

"Is that your problem?" I ask. "Do you have a weapons charge hanging over your head in the state that you want to resolve while you're serving your federal sentence?"

"Dat's only part of it," Lunatic says. Rarely are legal stories so clear in prison. "Ya see," he continues, "after I takes off, I goes to see my homey Criptinite. I needs ta get right. I sees him on Long Beach Boulevard at da Spot Light Car Wash. Muthafuckas pushin' a fi-hun'red Benz. He ballin' out a control. I see my homey's doin' da damn thing. He tells me that he's 'bout his work, slingin' that D. I tells the homey to put me down. Know what I'm sayin'?"

"You're saying that after the police caught you with a gun, and your parole officer wanted to violate you and lock you up, you went to meet your homey, Criptinite, who told you that he was selling drugs." I clarify the events for my notes.

"Dat's wussup," Lunatic confirms the facts. "I tells him to put me down and he says it ain't shit. I follow him out to his crib. We drive all the way down Anaheim. I can see he's the muthafuckin' shit. He stylin' in a fi'-be'room house, pimped out wit marbles and mirrors on da walls. I likes how Criptinite livin'. He takes me in da back and tells me to check out what he's got. Muthafucka's got 'bout fifty birds in there. When I tells him to put me down, he tells me it ain't shit and says to grab three or foe them muthafuckas."

"He gave you four kilograms of cocaine?" I ask.

"You know," he says. "Dat's what I'm talkin' 'bout. I'm still tryin' to get my ends. Shee-it. It don't stop. I gots to keep gettin' money. Make money. Sleep money. Think money. You know how it go. Muthafucka gots ta have all the finest things in life."

Lunatic took his four kilograms of cocaine up north to the Bay Area, he told me. He wanted to avoid local law enforcement who would be after him in Compton. In the Bay Area he was not well known. He had a girlfriend up there, he says, Wanda, and Lunatic moved in with her while setting himself up to sell the cocaine. He sold the first four kilograms without any problem, then returned to Anaheim to pay Criptinite and pick up ten more kilograms. He sold nine of those kilograms easily, but decided to break the last package into smaller quantities. That is where he found another set of problems.

"I sees this muthafucka Smiley," Lunatic says, "dis nigga I knowed from Soledad. He tells me, 'Wussup, Lunatic? What you doin' up dis far north?' I tells da muthafucka I'm up here gettin' paid, dat I'm crackalackin'. Know what I'm sayin'? Smiley tells me he's lookin' for work, for dat real work. He wants Snow White and dem Seven Dwarfs. 'Bout nine zips is what he wants. Nigga tells me he can pay eight hun'red. Shee-it. I wants him ta dump da work quick, so I gives it to him for six hun'red. He says that he stays monied up. So he gives me da chips and I give him da work. I tells him to hit me on da hip when he needs some mo'."

"What does that mean," I ask, "to hit you on the hip?"

"Muthafucka's posed to page me. Know what I'm sayin'," Lunatic explains. "But he don't. He just shows up at my crib. I'm mad as a muthafucka at dis nigga for jus' showin' up like dat. I axes him what he's doin'. He says he just wants to kick it, so I lets him in. We watchin' the Raiders, tippin' back some eights."

"What are eights?"

"We drinkin' ol' English 800s, you know. Gettin' high. Then the muthafucka says he's gonna go hit a few co'ners, see 'bout gettin' some chips from some them young muthafuckas. Says he wants to come back to get nine mo' zones. I'm cool wit dat. But 'bout fi'teen minutes after he leaves, I'm takin' a leak. I hears the knock on da doe. I tells Wanda to gets it 'cause I'm in da bafroom. When she opens da muthafucka, I hears one-time bustin' in. That nigga Smiley done set me up."

"Did they bust you there?"

"I climbed through the window and got away. I was runnin' from dem muthafuckas. I was hittin' gates, jumpin' fences, creepin' behind houses and trees and shit. Just stayin' in da cut. I hear one-time chasin' a muthafucka, but they can't catch me. Not Lunatic! Not no real Crip. I'm the muthafucka. I slides up unda one a dem crawl spaces and hides unda a house. I hear one-time's radio and I hear da fuckin' helicopter up top. I'm cool. When I hears 'em leave, I scoot out. I gets in touch wit my man Criptinite and tells him shit went bad, dat I'm in distress. He has one of his hos pick me up and take me to da airport. I flies out an' meets him. Criptinite hooks me up with a car, some chips, and foe them chickens. I head down south to dump da work. That's when the feds catch a muthafucka and bring me up in here."

"Is that it?" I ask. "Are those all the crimes you're facing?"

"That's ev'ythin'," Lunatic says. "Dat's how I got here."

"So you're facing the eight years with the feds for the four kilograms of cocaine. Then you have possible charges waiting for you for using a fake ID to bail out of jail, for being a felon in possession of a firearm, and for selling those ounces to Smiley. Is that everything?"

"I also gots a problem with my parole violation," Lunatic says.

"Well, I can help you file some papers with the court that might result in the state running the new criminal charges that you're facing together with the time you're serving now. But I don't think you can squash your problems with your state parole so easily. It's possible, but not likely. I can tell you that everything will be harder for you if you get into trouble here. You need to keep a clean disciplinary record, at least while you're trying to persuade the courts to help you. Can you stay out of the hole?"

"Shee-it," Lunatic says. "A muthafucka don't know what's gonna happen from day to day. I gots to be ready for whateva in here."

"I'll help you prepare the paperwork to file all this with the court and with the parole officer in California. Just know you can help your chances if you stay out of trouble and enroll in some programs." Lunatic listens to the advice I offer, but he does not leave me with much hope that he intends to abandon Crip life or the ways of the pen.

After leaving me to my work in the library, Lunatic joins Crip Tank back on the yard. Crip Tank sits on the bleacher stairs outside the gym with about sixty other homeys. They're all wearing sagging khaki pants and laced-up boots. They wear blue sweatshirts under khaki shirts despite the hot sun. Crip Tank wears a blue rag that he ties around his head. He is drinking from his jug of hooch, getting high while toking on a joint that he passes around with his homeys. "Hey you muthafucka," Crip Tank calls to Lunatic. "Let's go hit a couple co'ners. I been waitin' for you. We gots a little work to take care of. Take a hit off dis." He passes the joint.

"Wuss crackalackin', cuzz?" Lunatic asks what's going on.

"I'm a put a little press game down on a muthafucka. Punkass bitch Trick owe da homey fi'teen thousand. We just gonna scare the muthafucka for Gangsta Pimp. I needs you to have my back like we on da streets. I'm fittin' to check a nigga," Crip Tank explains. Knowing that Crip Tank has the power to scare people, Gangsta Pimp promises to pay him 15 percent of whatever money Crip Tank can force Trick to pay.

"Let's do it," Lunatic says.

"First I'm a grab Big Hoover," Crip Tank tells him. He wants more backup before he steps to Trick, the man who owes Gangsta Pimp.

Big Hoover is cranking out push-ups and dips by the weight pile on the yard when Crip Tank and Lunatic approach him. "You is one big muthafucka," Crip Tank calls out between sips from his jug of wine. "I ain't never gonna fight you, big homey. But if you step up to see big Crip Tank, I sho 'nough would let the air ow'chu."

Big Hoover laughs.

"You crazy, Crip Tank," Big Hoover says to him. He's pumped up like a TV wrestler.

"Check dis out, big homey," Crip Tank says. "I needs you to roll wit me. I'm a put da press game on a muthafucka. I jus' need you to walk wit me an Lunatic here."

"Let's roll," Big Hoover says. He stands well over six six, and his biceps are bigger than most men's thighs. With his shirt off, Big Hoover looks more like an animal than a man. The trio walk to the pull-up bar, where Trick is leaning, talking to his partner.

"Move out da fuckin' way, bitch," Crip Tank orders. Big Hoover and Lunatic are standing by his side.

"What did you say?" Trick attempts to stand his ground.

"You heard me, bitch," Crip Tank says while walking up and pushing Trick with an open hand to his neck. "I said move out the way befo' I fuck you up right here, bitch." Crip Tank shows his anger.

"Dat's right, bitch," Big Hoover says. "You move when my homey talks to you. Don't talk back." Hoover slaps Trick across the face.

Crip Tank latches his fingers around the pull-up bar and starts lifting his body up effortlessly while glaring into Trick's eyes. "And another thing, muthafucka," he says while showing off his strength. "You betta get my homey his money or you ain't gonna have to worry 'bout standin' for no mo' counts, bitch."

Trick starts to tremble. He realizes that Gangsta Pimp sent the cancerous group of Crips to collect. "I told him I'm gonna have the money next week. It's, it's all worked out." Trick is scared, caught in the wrong place at the wrong time. He has no backup with him.

"Yeah," Crip Tank says while dropping from the bar. He steps up to Trick's face, mean mugging him, as close as a baseball manager to an umpire in a heated argument at home plate. "Now I'm tellin' you, bitch. Get dat money right by next week or you gonna be leakin'. You don't git dat money, cuzz, you ain't never gonna walk no penitentiary mainline again. And dat's da fuckin' shit. Consider dis a warnin'. You don't want Crip Tank comin' to see you again." They walk off, Crip Tank slamming Trick with his shoulder as he moves.

As the three walk away, Big Hoover pulls Crip Tank aside. "I likes the way you put that down, homey, the way you step to a muthafucka."

"Dat's right," Crip Tank says. "A muthafucka gotta see 'bout his work. It's 'bout bi'ness. We need ta start gettin' mo' money up in dis bitch. Dat's what I'm talkin' 'bout. Pressin' up on all these soft, rich muthafuckas. I gots to git paid. Shee-it. Crip Tank 'bout gittin' money. It don't stop in here. Tic tic toc da block. Know what I'm sayin'?"

"Dat's what I'm talkin' 'bout," Big Hoover says. "We gots ta work togetha. I'm tryin' ta get some a that shit up in here."

"Shee-it," Crip Tank says. "Then see 'bout yo work. Wuss crackin'?"

"I heard you still got mad plugs on da street?"

"Dat's right. What's crackalackin', nigga? Wha'chu need?" Crip Tank asks as the two continue their loops around the track. They walk past a group of guards.

Officer Roosevelt calls out to Crip Tank. "Wha'chu doin' out here, Crip Tank?" the officer asks as he walks toward the two.

"Oh, you know," Crip Tank says. "Cuttin' co'ners with my lo-co."

"You know the position," the officer says. "Spread out and grab the wall. What are you carryin' today?"

Crip Tank has a shank planted in his left boot, but he knows the officer will not find it during the routine pat search. "I ain't got nothin'. Why you fuckin' wit me for?" Crip Tank asks with hostility in his voice.

"Just hold the wall," the officer says while moving his hands down Crip Tank's arms, across his body, and down his legs. It's as if the officer is trying to squeeze pork through a sausage tubing.

"You likes feelin' on a real man. Don'chu, bitch?" Crip Tank says.

"Watch your mouth, Crip Tank."

"Don't get mad at me jus' 'cause I knows wha'chu like. I sees you gettin' yo feel on touchin' on all these mens."

"Get moving," the officer says after he finishes the search, ignoring Crip Tank's taunts.

"Fuck dat punk cop muthafucka. I ain't got time to be fuckin' wit him. Now wha'chu was sayin'?" Crip Tank says to Big Hoover.

"Man, I needs six zones a dat shit, eleven-five. I can get it in here, but I needs a hookup on the street," Big Hoover says, asking for six ounces of heroin.

"Shee-it. Dat ain't no problem. I can ge'chu dat. But you sees how one-time be on a muthafucka. I can't move nothin' up in here."

"I'm a take care a dat," Big Hoover says. "You just get da work to my comrades on da street. I'll take care of ev'ythin' in here. I'm a split it wi'chu thirty-seventy."

"You take care a ev'ythin' in here?" Crip Tank asks.

"Dat's right. I got dat," Big Hoover says.

"Done den. Gimme a hookup," Crip Tank says while they use the Crip handshake, folding their hands over each other together to form letter Cs with their fingers. The handshake seals the deal. "I'm a git you ready by tonight, baby boy."

The following morning, while walking into the chow hall for breakfast, Crip Tank sees his homeboy LaLa arguing with Porkchop, one of the Bama boys. The argument, Crip Tank sees, is heated. So he steps between them. "Hold up, cuz," he says to LaLa. I'll see you right back. You don't need to be talkin' here with all these poe-leases. One-time all over the fuckin' place. Let's roll, homey. Crip Tank drapes his arm around LaLa and leads him away. "Fuck dat muthafucka. Don't even trip, homey. I'm a handle dat for ya."

It's just after three thirty in the afternoon when I leave the library that day. I walk toward the gates with all of my paperwork in hand and join the hundreds of convicts coming off the yard. We all are making our way back toward the housing units.

I see Crip Tank in the center of a pack. They are all wearing the Crip outfit, with their blue sweatshirts and blue rags. "Hold up," I call out to Crip Tank. He hears me and waves me through the wall of thirty Crips waiting to squeeze through the gates. As I make it near him, the line begins to move. We are heading into the madness of the main corridor. "I finished Lunatic's briefs for the court," I tell him. "Bring Lunatic up to my cell and I'll give them to you. I've got team tonight, so I'm going to be in the unit. He needs to mail the papers out now."

"Word," Crip Tank says as we approach D Cellhouse. "You finished that shit already? Dat's love, cuz. Tell me wha'chu need."

"I don't need anything. I told you that."

"Ev'ybody needs somethin', cuz. Just tell me wha'chu need. You know I'm rollin' up in here."

As we're talking, in the midst of hundreds of convicts moving slowly through the long, narrow corridor, I see Porkchop walking toward us. He is on his way out while we're on our way in. I don't notice it, but as we're walking and talking, Crip Tank slides a shank out from the sleeve of his sweater. Without missing a beat in our conversation, just as Porkchop is passing by him, Crip Tank uses his right hand to thrust the point of the fiberglass knife into Porkchop's gut while using his left hand to pull Porkchop into the blade. Then he drives the bleeding body to the ground while simultaneously pulling the knife out of his stomach and passing the weapon back to one of his homeys. The homey wraps the knife in a towel he was holding open, then moves on in the opposite direction.

Porkchop never saw who or what hit him. While he fell to the floor, bleeding, the other Crips passing by pushed him down and kicked him.

"What the fuck," I say to Crip Tank. "How are you going to pull that kind of move when I'm walking with you?"

"Mind yo muthafuckin' bi'ness and keep walkin'. You know how it go up in here. Anyplace, anytime, anywhere, I'm a serve a muthafucka." Then he laughs. "The element of surprise is a muthafucka; it's Crip Tank's best friend. Don'chu get caught slippin'. But anyway, me an Lunatic gonna come holla at you after the count." As he turns into his Cellhouse I keep moving up the corridor toward mine. I hear him holler out, "I got mad love for you, cuz. Keep it movin'."

A few hours later, before dinner, Crip Tank brings Lunatic to my cell. "Don't you ever want to leave here?" I ask him.

"Check dis out, cuz," Crip Tank says. "Dat muthafuckin Bama boy was talkin' shit to my homey in da chow hall. Da nigga ain't built like dat. Dat's disrespectin' da whole Crip car. Crip Tank can't let no kine a shit like dat slide. An anyway, muthafucka, di'n't nobody see me do nothin'. You know how Crip Tank move. I'm a stealth muthafuckin' bomber." He says it with pride.

"We've been behind these walls more than six years already," I tell him. "You gotta think about your life," I say. "What are you going to do when you get out? Remember that you're getting older. You'll be forty when you get out."

"Man, fuck dat shit you always be talkin'." Crip Tank dismisses my advice. "All a muthafucka gotta do in here is stay strapped, stay high, and jack his dick off. I'm not gonna let no muthafucka disrespect da Crip car. A muthafucka don't do right, it always come back to haunt him. I ain't thinkin' 'bout goin' home. This my house. I takes off on a muthafucka at will. 'Cause if I don't, it might be my ass dat's leakin'. No one's fittin' to put Crip Tank in da dirt, takin' me out in no pine box. Fuck all that bullshit," he finally says. "Wha'chu got for my homey?"

There is no sense talking to Crip Tank further about reforming his ways. He's a gangster. I pass the documents I typed to Lunatic and explain what they mean. I tell him to read through the work so he understands what he is requesting from the court. As he comes to words like "background," "petitioner," and "pleading," Lunatic stops reading to ask me a question. "Why a muthafucka got all these B-words and P-words? I'm a Crip. Those are words the Bloods use, from West Piru Street in Compton. We don' use those words."

I look to Crip Tank. "What is Lunatic talking about?"

"Crips try not to use any words that start with B or P. Those are the Blood words." He describes part of the gang rivalry between the Crips and the Bloods, which apparently extends to the alphabet.

"Lunatic," I say. "You can be sure the judge who hears these motions is not going to be a Blood or a Crip. These are legal documents. I wrote them in English, not gang language, cuz. Just sign them and send them to the court."

I walk with the two down toward the door that leads out of the unit. We make it through the crowds to the chow hall. They wait together through the black line, on the left side of the dining room. I pass through the right line. It's noisy inside. There are more than eight hundred people inside, all segregated in various sections of the chow hall according to race, ethnic background, and geographical roots.

At the serving line I hear Crip Tank's booming voice demanding more food from the server. He weighs about 250, and all of that weight projects through his voice. The server tells Crip Tank that he's going to have to come over to the other side of the line and serve himself if he wants more food.

"You think I won't, muthafucka?" Crip Tank says. He jumps over the stainless-steel serving line and takes the serving spoon out of the bewildered older convict's hands.

The guy standing behind Lunatic in the line starts hollering about Crip Tank's not wearing gloves or hairnets. "You're gettin' shit in the food."

Lunatic fires on him, blasting the man in the jaw for disrespecting a Crip. Then two tables of Crips leave their meals to swarm over to the serving line as they "rat-pack," or gang up, on the man Lunatic is beating to the floor. Crip Tank is rushing around the line, trying to get himself into the action. The officers arrive first. They break up the stomping and haul the group of gang members off to the hole. Crip Tank is left standing, angry that he didn't get any punches or kicks in.

The chow hall is madness. I usually avoid it for that very reason. I am there to eat on that evening only because my unit team, which is my case manager and others who oversee my case, scheduled me for a six-month review. The unit teams are usually a routine, perfunctory gathering where the staff members tell me to continue the same program that I'm on. Sitting there at dinner watching a gang of men beat another helpless man on the floor, I reflect on all those years of chaos. I wonder how much longer it will last.

I return to my housing unit after the meal and wait for the team members to call me inside. I'm leaning over the railings of the tier as I listen for my page. Below me, on the flats, I watch as G-Money sits at a table playing cards with three others. His mind is not on the game. He's looking toward the shower, where a new prisoner whom I know only as Steve is standing, waiting for a turn inside. Steve appears naked except for a towel wrapped around his waist.

G-Money yells up at Steve. "How you doin', baby? You aw-ight?"

Steve does not respond but looks down in a blank stare. G-Money puckers his lips while sucking on a toothpick. He blows Stevie a kiss.

"Wha'chu doin' playin' with them punks?" G-Money's partner, Thunder, says to him.

"Man, you live yo life, muthafucka," G-Money says. "Let me live mines." G-Money keeps his eyes focused on Steve. The shower opens and Steve walks in. A steel door with a small window separates the shower from the tier. Soon after the door closes behind Steve, G-Money throws his cards down on the table, climbs the stairs, and makes a line for Steve's shower. G-Money keeps his right hand between his legs, holding his crotch as he walks. He opens the door leading into the small space and steps inside.

In the penitentiary, it's better to shower while wearing steel-toed boots. Steve, I saw, is wearing flip-flops. I am ashamed at myself for not having the courage to stop the encounter. Whatever happens behind that closed shower door, I know, is not welcomed by Steve. Over the years, the penitentiary has conditioned me to mind my own business, at least not to interfere in the business of others.

The unit-team members finally call me inside. My unit manager is there. My case manager is there also, and she chairs the meeting. After the usual talk about my scheduled release date, comments on my quarters, my job assignment, and the academic programs I have completed, my case manager surprises me. "We have submitted you for a transfer," she said. "The penitentiary is crowded. We need to push guys who can leave into medium-security prisons to make room for those who need the pen. You're going to an FCI. You'll likely pack out this week."

My release date is still twenty years away at the time, but the idea of leaving the penitentiary feels like a step closer to home The news lifts my spirits and renews hope. I learn that I am transferring to a medium-security prison in the Northeast. The move keeps me thousands of miles away from my family in Seattle, but it will get me out of the bedlam of penitentiary life.

I want information about medium-security prisons in the Northeast immediately, so I seek Bright out. He lives next to me on my tier of the cellhouse, and we have become friends. Bright is a native of New York, from the Italian American enclave of Bensonhurst. Bright serves a sentence much shorter than mine and began his term in medium security. He is about my age, a tough kid from Brooklyn who courts trouble with authority.

A disciplinary transfer brought Bright inside the penitentiary walls. "There is a lot of dope up at Allenwood," Bright explains to me, "and I'm always lookin' to get high. I caught a dirty and theys threw me in da fuckin' hole for tree months, da cocksuckas."

In an effort to quash the drug problem, the Bureau of Prisons requires each institution to conduct a certain number of random urinalysis tests each month. Besides the random tests, administrators place some prisoners on a "hot list" and test those men as frequently as once each week. When officers call a prisoner for a urine test, the prisoner must urinate into a small plastic tube while a guard stands close beside him, vigilantly monitoring the prisoner's hands and penis, and the urine filling the tube. When Bright told me he had "caught a dirty," it meant that his urine test had revealed to authorities that drugs were in his system. That dirty resulted in a disciplinary infraction and a lengthy stay in the hole.

While serving time in Allenwood's hole, Bright continued to get high and cause commotion. As a lieutenant was walking through the segregation unit making rounds, Bright said, he "had words wid' 'im."

"That fuckin' guy, I'm tellin' ya. A real fuckin' asshole. Fuhged-aboutit. He's a no-good eggplant-lookin' shine who hates Italians. I tells him to fuck hisself as he walks by the cell. He stands there lookin' through the winda at me like I'm the fuckin' asshole. Right? I'm high as a motherfucka, but I'm in the hole already. Right? I'm there for ninety days so I gots nothin' to lose. I tells him to go suck his mutha's cunt. She shits out her cunt and comes out her ass, I tells him. The motherfucka. I tell him if he's got any fa-zools he can un-lock the door and we can handle it like mens. He just smiles at me, the mutherfucka. Before leavin' he tells me, 'We'll see who's gonna get fucked.' Then the cocksucka walks away. The next day I'm on the chain to dis fuckin' hellhole he-ya."

I asked Bright about my new FCI.

"Any medium is better than the pen," he tells me. "But I hear yours is one of the best FCIs. I got some partners up there. I'm gonna give you some solid guys to look up. They'll get ya started." I am so en-thusiastic with the news of my transfer that it wouldn't have mat-tered what Bright had to say. I wanted to go, wanted outside of USP walls.

I packed my belongings the next day. Then I went around to say my good-byes to the men with whom I had been sharing space for so many years. Everyone but Crip Tank wished me luck. When I spoke with him, he said, "What the fuck you goin' to some pussy-ass FCI fo'? Ain't no action up dere."

"I need to get out, bud. This life isn't for me."

"Shee-it," he said. "This the only life for me. This life here for thorough muthafuckas, for real Gs. I likes it."

12

After so many years living inside penitentiary walls, walking onto the expansive green campus of a medium-security prison brought immediate feelings of relief. I was still locked inside fences, and thousands of miles separated me from family. Yet the new scenery of the FCI lessened the severity of my confinement. I could see through the chain-link fences, over the countless coils of glistening razor wire. Instead of a tall, solid, penitentiary-gray concrete wall that obstructs all vision, I saw mountains and evergreen trees. In the FCI I saw and smelled the beauty of nature. Somehow, that brought a measure of freedom.

As I walked onto the compound I sensed a lower degree of tension. It was not absent, but neither was it as pervasive as I had known. Like in the pen, correctional officers controlled the movements of men from one area to another. There was the heavy presence of guards in their gray slacks, white shirts, and maroon ties. Loudspeakers blasted constant institutional announcements. With fifteen hundred prisoners inside the fences, it was crowded. At a glance, the majority of men struck me as being volatile. Yet the FCI did not seem to be heavily dominated by prison gangs. It looked like a place where I could make better progress.

I caught the final months under the leadership of Dennis Luther, a progressive warden. He used the promise of incentives rather than the threat of punishment to control his institution and those of us wearing khaki uniforms. Through good behavior, we could earn our way to honor dorms; that option had not existed in the pen. It allowed each man a measure of control regarding the company he kept. Warden Luther's was a management style I embraced because it allowed more progress with my academic program.

During my years inside the walls of the federal penitentiary I began undergraduate studies. I learned by working independently through courses at Ohio University and participating in courses the excellent professors at Mercer University offered inside. In 1992, Mercer awarded my first degree. Hofstra University then honored me with the privilege of studying toward a graduate degree. While in the medium-security prison I could continue my work.

Rather than obstructing a prisoner's efforts to grow, Luther encouraged us to pursue learning opportunities. In my case he authorized the use of a word processor to facilitate my studies. He allowed scholars from across the country to visit me despite my not having known them prior to my imprisonment—a fact that has always been a stumbling block to such meetings for me in other prisons. When leaders from the American Society of Criminologists invited me to participate in their annual meeting, Warden Luther instructed his staff to provide a video camera so I could film my presentation; he allowed me to send the video out to help me network with other academics. When a distinguished professor from Princeton University offered to bring students of his who were studying corrections on a field trip to the prison, Warden Luther made his conference room available for me to describe my experiences to the group.

As a consequence of the advancement I was able to make under Luther's leadership, I completed my coursework and thesis. Hofstra University awarded my graduate degree in 1995. I then began studying toward a doctoral degree at the University of Connecticut. My good fortune ran out when Warden Luther retired. A more traditional warden replaced him, and with the change came an end to my formal studies in prison. The new warden determined that prisoners should not study at the postgraduate level. He felt that such independent studies interfered with the security of the institution.

Traditional prison administrators, like the bureaucrat who replaced Luther, do not generally support any programs that allow individuals to distinguish themselves formally in a positive way. They prefer rigid, inflexible, and simpleminded adherence to written policies. Such bureaucrats insist on uniformity in every way. They encourage prisoners to adapt to the prison and refuse to acknowledge that in some cases it is in the best interests of society for the prison to adapt to the prisoners. In my opinion, this is the reason prisons succeed so brilliantly in churning out failure in the form of high recidivism rates. Prisons, as they are managed today, have nothing to do with "corrections."

Like Crip Tank in the pen, most prisoners with whom I serve time in the medium-security prison come from backgrounds that embrace a criminal lifestyle and gangster values. Yet a growing minority are like me, with roots in middle-class America. Regardless of background, few of those in medium-security prison settings succeed in overcoming the social structure of the prison; it seems to suck people in, cultivating failure. Rather than encouraging people to grow, it pulls everyone down.

Shamrock, for example, is one of four children reared by loving, supportive parents in a stable New England home. After Shamrock graduated from high school his father opened a career opportunity for Shamrock in a large shipbuilding firm. The high wages he earned led Shamrock toward a gambling problem. And that gambling led to actions that brought him inside prison fences with me. We became friends. Despite our similar family backgrounds, Shamrock did not adjust to confinement in the same way as I.

"It all began for me when I started betting with a bookie." Shamrock describes how he walked into trouble. "The guy saw me betting heavy and living it up at the bar. He thought I was a drug dealer, flush with cash. I was earning sixteen an hour at the shipyard and blowing every cent of my paycheck. It's a lot of money for a single kid living at home, but it's not real money. The guy thinks I've got it, so he gives me a line of five thousand per game. Idiot. I bet three games and I win all three. The guy pays me fifteen grand in cash. I start blowin' it, just pissin' it away."

Two weeks later, the gambling wasn't going so well for Shamrock. He owed the bookie over thirty thousand dollars but had no money to pay the debt. The bookie was pressing Shamrock for the money hard. "When I open the mailbox and see a snapshot of my mom, with a note telling me that if I don't pay the money within a week, my mom won't be able to use her arms or legs, I realize I have to do something." Shamrock started robbing banks.

Never having engaged in crime before, Shamrock turned to the popular television show *America's Most Wanted* for tips. He learned that successful bank robbers hit the banks before they're open for business. The lesson served his needs. Over the next two years he held up twelve banks and made off with a total of over one million dollars. The money paid off his gambling debt and helped Shamrock establish a small business. Good detective work resulted in his arrest several years later. By then Shamrock's money was safely stored away in an interest-bearing account. After a jury trial, his judge imposed a twelve-year sentence.

While we're inside the fences, FBI agents come to see Shamrock. He is not expecting the page to the visiting room. "There's two of them there," he tells me. "I knew them from the trial, Larsen and Kramer. They yip-yap about how they can have my sentence cut down if I give back the money. Imagine that. I tell them if they would've come seen me yesterday I might've been able to help 'em. But last night I had great roast beef for dinner and joined a softball team. The food is okay and I'm getting along fine. That really ticks them off, like they expect me to give a flyin' fuck."

Shamrock has no remorse for his convictions, and authority does not intimidate him in the least. "Larsen's really taking this shit seriously," Shamrock says as he continues to describe his surprise visit by the FBI agents. "You'd think it was his money that was stolen. 'You're about forty, aren't you, Larsen?' I ask him. He says he's forty-two. I tell him that I'm supposed to get out when I'm forty. I tell him, 'Hypothetically, if I did take that money, which I didn't, what kind of interest do you think it would bring me in an offshore account?' Larsen says it probably would earn 2 or 3 percent. 'Try four,' I tell him. The suits are fuckin' pissed. I keep pushin' 'em. 'How much do you think that money would be worth by the time I got out if I took it, which I didn't?' I ask. Larsen says he doesn't know. I tell him two million. 'Did you have two million in cash when you were forty?' I ask. He says no. 'I didn't think so,' I say. 'I'm going to stick around here and play softball and eat roast beef.' As I'm leaving the room I tell them that I've got nothin' to say and that they should leave me the fuck alone."

Shamrock and I spend a lot of time together inside the fences. We exercise, we eat, we play cards. Without access to university programs, I have a lot more time on my hands. I'm doing that time and finding humor in Shamrock's defiant adjustment.

"Swanberg calls me to this joke of a meeting," Shamrock says as he describes his first team meeting. "Four morons sittin' around a table drinking coffee and congratulatin' each other on what a great job they're all doin'. Morris struggles to read from this sheet describing how much time I got to serve and other crap. I don't even know why I gotta be there, but Swanberg tells me to sit and listen. Then he tells me that he wants me to sign up for some of those jerk-off programs they got around here. I tell them I ain't signing up for shit. 'Santos has finished every school program there is and you're holding him three thousand miles from home; you won't even give him a lower bunk. Fuck that,' I tell 'em. 'Let me mind my own business. I don't need a bunch of prison guards telling me how to grow up.' "

"We're correctional officers," the counselor says. "We have training."

"You can be whatever you want to be," Shamrock says. "Just leave me alone."

Shamrock has no interest in signing up for the courses available to him. With more than ten years of prison ahead, he wants to serve his time without being bothered by prison administrators. No such luck. Before leaving the team meeting, Swanberg, the unit manager, hits Shamrock up for a payment toward his restitution. "We want you to sign this form authorizing us to deduct two hundred dollars from your account each month as payment toward your fine."

"You think I'm a moron," Shamrock scoffs after glancing over the form. "There's no way I'm signin' anything."

"If you don't sign the form I'm going to move you into the common area and assign you to the landscaping detail." The unit manager tells Shamrock about the consequences of his refusal to participate in the program administrators call Financial Responsibility.

"Tell you what, pal," Shamrock says. "You do what you gotta do. I'll do what I gotta do."

The unit manager makes good on his threat, sending Shamrock to less comfortable quarters and assigning him to an unpleasant job mowing lawns. Shamrock responds by calling his lawyer. Because Shamrock's sentencing judge clearly ordered that Shamrock's restitution payments were to begin after his release from prison, the lawyer advises Shamrock to sue each member of his unit team for violating his civil rights. Shamrock authorizes the lawsuit.

A processor serves Swanberg and other members of the unit team with the lawsuit papers, infuriating the unit manager. "What the hell is this?" Swanberg asks Shamrock after paging him to report to the office.

"Let me see," Shamrock says. "Huh. I wonder how you got this job. You must not read too well. These papers say you're being sued." Shamrock tosses back the papers.

"You can't sue me! You're a prisoner in a federal institution. I'll lock you in the hole," Swanberg threatens.

"What the fuck . . . not the hole," Shamrock mocks fright. "Is that supposed to make me shake? Let's get something straight right now. I'm not scared. Send me to the hole, send me to some other prison. I don't give a fuck. I'm not the usual bucket of trash that's going to run for cover every time you get a stiff prick and feel like fuckin' someone."

"Go pack your shit. I'm lockin' you up," Swanberg says.

"You pack it. I told you I ain't doing shit. But you'd better think twice. My lawyer says you're already violating my civil rights. He's itchin' to sue you again. You got hundreds of guys in here for extortion. That's exactly what you're trying to do to me. I ain't goin' for it." Shamrock walks out.

When Swanberg checks with the legal department of the prison, Shamrock wins the battle. The way the judge wrote the order, Swanberg can't force Shamrock to pay. Swanberg returns Shamrock to a two-man room next door to me, and changes his job to unit orderly. "I want to keep an eye on you," he warns him.

Swanberg assigns Shamrock to mop and maintain the floors in an area of the unit where counselors offer treatment for substance abuse. Shamrock sees the job as an opportunity to manufacture hooch. He mixes the fruit, sugar, and yeast, then stores it in a bag to ferment. The hallway Shamrock is responsible for cleaning has a drop-tile ceiling. Shamrock stores the bag above one of the ceiling tiles. While one batch of the wine is fermenting in the ceiling, Shamrock keeps another batch in empty cleaning containers behind the locker in his room.

While making his rounds in the housing unit to harass prisoners over such trivial issues as wrinkles in the bedding or the way shoes are lined up under the bed, Swanberg opens Shamrock's door. "What the hell is that smell?" the unit manager asks.

"What do you mean?" Shamrock asks. "You're the one who gave me the cleaning job. I've got to keep the cleaning solvents up here. If I leave them in the supply room someone'll steal 'em. I keep 'em in here so I can use 'em when I need 'em."

"Get those bottles back to the supply room," Swanberg orders.

Shamrock counts his blessings. He pours the hooch into quart jugs and distributes them to friends. A while later, one of the electrical-maintenance workers discovers the wine mixture Shamrock left to ferment in the ceiling. When Swanberg sees it, he rushes back to Shamrock's room. "Where are those containers I saw in here this morning?" the unit manager demands.

"You told me to take them down to the supply room. Someone probably stole them by now," Shamrock says with a smirk. "I told you I should have kept them here."

"Get down to my office. Now," Swanberg orders.

When Shamrock walks into the office, Swanberg stands behind his cluttered desk, bracing himself with his fists on the desktop. "I know those containers in your room were filled with hooch," Swanberg begins. "And I know that hooch in the ceiling belongs to you. Now here's what we're going to do. You're going to admit to it and you're going to do it now."

"I don't know what you're talking about, but I'm not admitting to nothing."

"Oh, you're going to admit, and you're going to do it now," the unit manager repeats.

"What are you going to do," Shamrock asks, "drill holes in my fingernails, pull my teeth out with pliers, squeeze my head in a vise? You got nothin' on me and you know it. Instead of telling me to admit to something, which I'll never do, why don't you go down and say you found buckets of hooch in my room?" Shamrock asks the unit manager. "Tell the lieutenants you saw it and you smelled it. Then tell them how you told me to get rid of it. How you gonna look in front of the Keystone Kops you're supposed to be runnin' around here then?"

"Get the hell out of my office!" Swanberg yells.

"You bet," Shamrock says. "I always follow direct orders, just like when you told me to get rid of those containers this morning."

Shamrock's roommate, Clover, encourages Shamrock's defiance of the system. Like Shamrock, Clover likes to get drunk on the weekends. Together the two lighten my time while I'm inside the fences. I need the entertainment to lift me from the doldrums after the new administration began blocking my access to further study. Guards broke up our trio when an officer caught Clover engaging in a consensual sexual relationship with Ms. Lewis, an officer whose husband works on the compound as a lieutenant. With the discovery, the administration fired Ms. Lewis and transferred Clover to a faraway prison.

Not long after guards take Clover off the compound, they lock Shamrock up for an investigation on another matter. A young prisoner from Shamrock's hometown, Jimmy, arrives in our housing unit. By the luck of the draw, guards assign Jimmy to sleep in a four-man room with Jamal, Smoke, and Dwayne. Those three run as a clique inside, extorting weaker inmates. Small and frail, Jimmy looks as if he would struggle to lift a sack of sugar. He's no fighter, and because he is from Shamrock's hometown, Shamrock feels the urge to help him.

Before sentencing, an officer of the court conducts a presentence investigation (PSI) on all felons. The PSI describes the background of the offender for the judge and system; other prisoners use this information to determine whether a new guy starts in good standing in the convict community. Shamrock's PSI shows that he denies involvement for the bank robberies he was convicted of. It shows that he has no history of offenses against women or children. Most important to other prisoners, it shows that Shamrock has never provided the slightest assistance to law enforcement, that he has never made an attempt to diminish his own exposure to punishment by ratting on someone else.

Shamrock's paperwork is in order. In prison society, he can be as proud of it as a Harvard Business School graduate showing his résumé. His defiance of authority, together with his criminal credentials, boosts his standing among his peers. He recognizes his position gives him responsibility to help Jimmy.

"I'm going to help you change rooms," Shamrock says to Jimmy. "You're going to have problems if you stay where you are. My friend Carlos has an empty bunk. He's a good guy. It'll be better for you. You want me to do it?"

Jimmy is scared. It's his first few days in prison, and he doesn't know what to do. But he accepts Shamrock's offer to help. Shamrock goes to speak with the counselor, who is responsible for room changes. The counselor is more interested in talking on the phone and playing computer games than in responding to inmate requests; although there are exceptions, as a rule, counselors do not counsel anyone. Yet because Shamrock has several years in the prison, and never whines or complains about anything to staff, the counselor agrees to Shamrock's request to move Jimmy into Carlos's cell.

Two days pass and Shamrock sees that Jimmy continues to sleep in the four-man cell with the three thugs. In the penitentiary, predators would already have latched their claws into him. In the FCI, treachery can move more slowly. Shamrock approaches the counselor and asks what happened, why the move is taking so long. "I tried to move the kid," the counselor tells Shamrock while absorbed in his computer game. "He says he wants to stay where he's at."

Shamrock is incredulous at the news from the counselor, angry that he had used his influence to intervene on the kid's behalf for nothing. "Fuck that punk," Shamrock says. "Here I'm tryin' to do the kid justice and he just shits on me."

Later than evening, while Shamrock and I are playing chess outside the tier of our cells, he sees Jimmy. "Look at that little fuck," he says. "It's embarrassing that he's from my town." Jimmy is seated at a table playing cards. The four are laughing, joking, seemingly having a great time, as if they are the best of friends. Shamrock sees through it. Jamal stands behind Jimmy, massaging the kid's shoulders with powerful hands.

After our chess game, just before lockdown, Shamrock pulls Jimmy into his room for a discussion, a "sit-down." "What the fuck is goin' on?" Shamrock demands. "I use my pull to move you and you say you don't want to go? And now I see you playing cards with those pricks. Are you fucking crazy or just stupid?"

Like a wounded and whimpering child, Jimmy cowers in Shamrock's presence. Jimmy goes on about how the group is not so bad, that they all have become friends. "Dwayne," Jimmy says, "is scoring a batch of hooch for the weekend. We're all gettin' drunk after lockdown."

"Look, you stupid little motherfucker," Shamrock tells him. "Do you think they want to drink with you because they like you?"

Jimmy answers yes, that they're all friends.

"You are a dumb fuck. Tell me this, Jimbo, did you ever try to get a girl drunk when you were out there so you could nail her? Did you ever do that?"

The tough guy in Jimmy comes out as he says that of course he did.

"Well," Shamrock says, "you'd better dress real pretty for the weekend. Because in here, if them motherfuckers are drinkin' with you, you're the prom date."

Jimmy tells Shamrock that it's not what he thinks, that everything is going to be fine. Despite Shamrock's vast experience of living in prison and seeing how prison press games are played, Jimmy ignores Shamrock's advice and says that he can handle himself. "Get the fuck out of my room, then, you little bitch," Shamrock tells him. "And don't come scurrying back when you're in trouble."

Less than a week passes before Jimmy comes back knocking on

Shamrock's door, practically crying as he asks for permission to come in. Jimmy tells Shamrock that he is being pressured to send the group a hundred dollars each month. "And I think one of them likes me," he whines. "You've got to help me."

Shamrock is unmoved by Jimmy's weakness, but it is a particular problem for Shamrock because others in the prison know that Jimmy has come from the same New England town as Shamrock. Shamrock does not want it known that he turns his back on people who need his help. The kid is paralyzed with fear and impotent to respond. Having a natural hatred for bullies, Shamrock ignores his better judgment and agrees to intervene. He approaches the predators.

Jamal is a real piece of work, easily as big as Crip Tank and his homey Big Hoover. The guy is dangerous. Somehow, administrators thought it best to lower his security scoring and transfer Jamal from the penitentiary in Lewisburg. They move him outside of walls and inside fences. There is no fighting him. It would be like a normal guy fighting Mike Tyson. Jamal stands six five in bare feet and is as big as a gorilla. When he hits the heavy bag in the gym, the smashing blows shake the building. Shamrock knows the guy is going to be a problem.

Jamal's face and arms are scarred with welts from knife fights. He has a few missing teeth, black holes when he opens his mouth. Jamal has been locked in cages, on and off, since his early teenage years. Shamrock knows there is no taking him on single-handedly, but Shamrock doesn't involve others in his business. He also knows there is no talking to Jamal.

Shamrock instead chooses to approach Smoke, one of the other roommates, with whom he has an okay relationship. They have watched a few football games together, both cheering for the New England Patriots. Shamrock walks to the room and asks Smoke to come out for a talk. Shamrock tells Smoke that Jimmy is from his hometown. As a courtesy, he asks Smoke to lay off the press game on Jimmy.

"Shee-it," Smoke says. "The little bitch is giving us a C-note a month. How the fuck we gonna let dat slide?"

"Listen, man," Shamrock says. "The kid doesn't know nothing about prison. He can't really afford to pay. I'll give you two hundred just to lay off the kid. And I'll get him moved out of your room."

Unbeknownst to Shamrock, Jamal is inside the room standing at the door. He is listening as Shamrock makes the pitch to Smoke. After Shamrock offers the severance pay to cancel the extortion, Jamal throws the door open and orders them both inside. Refusing to show fear, to punk out, Shamrock goes inside. He has no weapon with him. He has no backup. He did not anticipate this turn of events, but his reputation is everything in prison, and he cannot refuse the challenge, even though he knows it may end badly.

Once inside, Jamal starts on about how Shamrock should not interfere in other people's business. "Stay the fuck out my game, muthafucka. Since you put yo badass nose in it, I want the hun'red from the bitch and another hun'red from you. I wants it ev'y muthafuckin' month," Jamal says.

Shamrock is not one to back down when threatened. Although he has had no previous encounters with Jamal, Jamal couldn't possibly have taken Shamrock for a punk. Dwayne and Smoke both know that Shamrock has all the respect in the world from Irish and Italian shot callers in the joint. Still, they are aligned with Jamal and will stand by him to the end, whatever comes. Even so, the two know that Shamrock will not back down like a mouse retreating to its hole.

Thoughts race through Shamrock's mind. There are only seconds available to respond. A solid punch across Jamal's mouth or stiff fingers jammed into his eyes would result in a fight against the three men. They all would jump into the brawl, rat-packing him. Shamrock is angry at being trapped in a closed room. He regrets that he did not bring a weapon. He didn't expect a conversation to explode like this. The wind blew wrong, and he knows that he has to handle it. But Shamrock will do it on his own time. Just to get out of there, he agrees to Jamal's demand. Dwayne and Smoke have to know that Shamrock will not simply roll over like that. A battle is on the front.

"I leave the room," Shamrock says, "just thinkin' what I've got to do. I don't want to tell no one what's goin' through my mind. I just can't believe that I let myself get put into such a pinch. I have a pipe. It's about two feet long, maybe an inch and a half in diameter. Heavy. I painted it white, the same color as the ceiling, and it's fastened near the light in my room. When guards come in to shake down the cell, if they look up and see it right there attached flat against the side of the light in the open like that, they never notice it or make it for a weapon. I stay up all night, knowin' that I have to do somethin'. There is no way I'm gonna send nobody nothin'. With those guys, there won't be no fair fight. This one's for real."

Shamrock does not sleep that night. When he hears his roommate snoring away on the lower bunk, he climbs up onto the desk and pulls down the pipe. His secret weapon. He secured it there specifically to protect himself against men like Jamal. With the pipe in hand, Shamrock climbs back onto his bunk. He waits for morning, envisioning the intended attack with exact precision.

As always, the guard comes around to unlock the steel doors at six. Shamrock's room is one of the first, and when he hears the turn of the heavy steel bolt, he climbs down from his bunk to watch from the door's window. The unit is still dark.

Shamrock watches, looking out to Jamal's room. The guard unlocks the door. Jamal is waiting. He walks out, naked except for a towel around his waist and shower shoes. He carries a shower bag in his hand and moves toward the shower. It's early, and no one else is in the common area. It doesn't matter. Shamrock has committed himself and there is no turning back.

"As Jamal leaves the shower and starts walkin' away, with that towel wrapped around his big ass, I come from behind and bring that pipe down on his skull. Hard." Shamrock describes the assault. "A one-hand overhead swing. I only have to hit him once, because I hear that crack and he·falls right to the ground. But I go ahead and slam the pipe down on his head a second time. He ain't movin'. He doesn't even know it's me that hit him. He's out, and blood is spillin' all over the place. I ditch the pipe and the gloves I wore in a garbage can. Then I go back to my room. I take off my clothes and hop into bed, climb beneath the covers like I've been sleepin' all night. My heart is beatin' a million thumps a minute. I just pretend to sleep. Ten minutes later I hear the ol' compound-closed announcement over the loudspeaker."

Shamrock passes a few days after the assault normally, as if nothing happened. Then the guards lock him up for an investigation. The lieutenants have received a few anonymous notes identifying Shamrock as the assailant. The FBI investigates. Jamal did not die, but rumor has it that he will never walk or talk again.

Guards stick Shamrock in segregation for a year while they and the FBI investigate the attack. While in the hole, he lives locked in a cell. An hour each day he can leave the cell and go to another cage for recreation. "While I'm in the rec cage," Shamrock tells me, "the guards are always pushing me to leave early. I ignore them for as long as I can. This fuckin' Lieutenant Lewis is coming through one day with a tour of morons in their monkey suits. He tries to flex his authority, telling me to cuff up so I can return to my cell. I'm on the pull-up bar, ignoring him." Shamrock continues his defiance of authority in the hole. Lieutenant Lewis's wife is the female officer with whom Clover, Shamrock's former cellmate, was caught having inappropriate relations.

"Lewis can't believe I'm ignoring him and keeps calling out my name," Shamrock continues. "Instead of answering him the way he expects, I call out, 'Hey, Lieutenant Lewis, I hear you're the luckiest guy in the world.' The comment surprises him. He asks me why that is. I tell him it's because Clover said his wife gives the best blow jobs on the planet." For that insolence Shamrock tells me he receives a beat-down from the goon squad in his cell. "But I'd take it again just to see that prick's face."

The prison environment, Shamrock explains, sometimes makes things happen all on its own. On those occasions, a prisoner has only so many options available. Avoiding the guy who brings the problem is not viable, because the space is so confined. Reporting the incident to the guards brings an entirely new set of problems. Shamrock recognizes that sometimes, when a problem in prison unfolds, only an immediate response is feasible. If the response is violent, it can lead to ominous repercussions.

About a year after his being locked in the hole, it becomes clear to both prosecutors and BOP investigators that without a witness who will testify to seeing Shamrock's assault on Jamal, no conviction will stand. Guards release him from segregation and place him back on the prison compound. His friends are glad to have him back. Even Dwayne approaches Shamrock to say that he knows Jamal was wrong to have tried pressing Shamrock in such a way. Shamrock denies that he had anything to do with what happened to Jamal. He is happy to have been released into the general population and wants to settle back into an easy routine.

Perhaps a year passes before Shamrock encounters the next inevitable wreck. Again, it comes as a consequence of his relationship with other prisoners. This time it is Red, from Charlestown, Massachusetts. Like many prisoners, Red is a dope fiend. He injects drugs into his veins whenever he can, notwithstanding his inability to pay. It is a sickness, an addiction.

Red accepts a quantity of heroin from Dre, promising to have his family send Dre payment through the mail. Dre never receives his money. He expects payment from someone. If Red is going to run, Dre intends to make trouble for the whole crew. Shamrock is friends with the guys from Charlestown, but he is not a drug user and is oblivious of any transactions between Red and Dre.

Both Shamrock and Dre work as orderlies in the housing unit. They are responsible for cleaning their assigned areas in the early morning; then they are free to pass their time leisurely. An avid sports fan, Shamrock likes to watch ESPN's *SportsCenter* for hours at a time. He is relaxed, sipping on a cup of hot French vanilla coffee, when Dre steps away from the table where he was watching Snoop Dogg thugging it out on the rap video station.

"Yo, what up, my man," Dre says as he approaches Shamrock's table.

Shamrock acknowledges him with a head shake, still leaning back in his chair, flip-flop slippers on his feet. He doesn't like to take his eyes off the screen as he takes in the scrolling highlights from the previous night's games.

"I'm sayin', holmes. Wussup wit my money? Your boy Red ain't come through for a muthafucka."

That is enough to bring Shamrock to attention. He removes the headphones he uses while watching television, sets them on the table, and brings his feet down. Dre even inquiring about a money matter he has with Red is wrong, a breach of prison protocol. "I don't know nothin' about no money between you and Red. I don't want to know. Whatever you got goin' with him doesn't concern me."

Dre's posture changes. "Ain't you one of them Charlestown muthafuckas? I knows you crackers is into everything together. You in it, muthafucka, believe dat. And I'm a git me my money."

There are seven or eight other people in the common area. Everyone senses the tension. A gauntlet has been thrown. Dre's tone is too hard, a level too loud. The stance isn't right. Although only a few sentences are exchanged, clearly it is not a friendly conversation. Instinctively, Shamrock knows he shouldn't be a part of it. He stands up, gathers his headphones and radio. He is prepared to walk to his room before anything further is said.

Then Dre brings more. He has to say one more word. "It ain't over, bitch."

That is it. Shamrock is already moving away. His back is to Dre. He stops for a second to take in what has just happened, closes his eyes with a wish that Dre had simply kept his mouth shut. Now it is out. The others in the room have heard the killing words that came from Dre's mouth. There is no taking them back. Realizing he can do nothing with flip-flops on his feet, Shamrock continues to his cell.

Allowing such an insult is not an option for Shamrock. Not with the time he is serving, not with the life he lives. He is tough and he is white. He cannot allow someone from another racial group to insult him in such a way. Within hours gossip would spread that Shamrock can be had, that he is afraid, and he would pass the rest of his sentence being tested and exploited by stronger, meaner prisoners. He tried to walk away before it got too late, but Dre made it impossible. If Shamrock lets the remark go, he will not be able to stand himself. Each time he looks in the mirror, a coward is all that he would see. For him, it would be like dying a thousand deaths. Not an option.

As Shamrock has his routine, so does Dre. Each day after lunch, Dre naps. Shamrock waits until just before two, when he expects that Dre will be zoned out in a deep sleep. He walks by Dre's room and hears a roaring, rhythmic snore. The opportunity is at hand. Shamrock takes it.

Shamrock returns to his room to retrieve his weapon of choice. "I prefer a heavy pipe to a shank. If I got a pipe, no matter where I hit him, he's goin' down. You stick some motherfuckers with a knife and they keep comin' at you. I don't want to fight no one. I want him out, want to go about doing my own time. When I connect with the pipe, I know he's in trouble. It don't matter where I hit him." Shamrock slips the pipe inside the sleeve of his shirt, then creeps back to Dre's room.

The unit is quiet. Shamrock takes a look around. He doesn't see anyone. He opens the door to Dre's room and slides quietly inside. The lights of the room are out, but Shamrock can see enough to make out Dre's shape on the bed. A blanket covers his upper body and he has a towel draped over his eyes. Shamrock pulls out the pipe, then nudges Dre in the shoulder to wake him. Dre's hand reaches toward his face to lift the towel. When he looks up, that is it.

Shamrock says he waits for Dre's eyes to open, then he swings. Slam! A direct hit to Dre's cheek. Dre tries to climb up from the bed. Shamrock smashes him again. Two hits and Dre is down, unconscious and bleeding on the floor. Shamrock then places the toilet-in-use sign on the door and walks out.

The two o'clock movement is about to begin. Shamrock slides the pipe back inside his sleeve and walks directly to the guard's station. He requests a pass to recreation. Officer O'Brian signs Shamrock out, and then Shamrock joins the group of other inmates walking toward the gym. He falls behind the group and, before he comes to the metal-detector shack, lets the pipe slip from his sleeve into a shrub. It makes a thump as it hits the ground. Shamrock keeps walking, passing through the metal detector without obstruction.

When Shamrock makes it into the gym, he sees another officer from recreation and asks the officer to sign his pass. Shamrock checks out a basketball, then begins to shoot hoops. He is alone, but right outside a group of officers stationed in the gym.

An hour passes. The three o'clock controlled movement comes and goes. Shamrock wonders why there has not yet been an institution lockdown. At half past three, everything closes in preparation for the four o'clock census count. Still there is no word. Shamrock has the recreation officer sign his pass out, then joins the herd of other prisoners heading back toward the housing units from the gym. Officer O'Brian is standing outside, in front of D Unit. Shamrock hands O'Brian the pass. Nothing is said.

Shamrock walks into the unit, climbs the stairs, and walks down the tier. He passes Dre's room. The toilet sign remains in the window; lights, he notices, are off. Shamrock keeps walking toward his own room, four cells down the line. The factory workers begin pouring into the housing block, and Shamrock hears Rabbit, Dre's cellmate, as he sees the toilet sign in the window of the cell's door. "Why a muthafucka gotta shit now, just befo' the count!" Rabbit yells in frustration while waiting on the tier.

Shamrock waits. It will be only minutes before the guard walks by to lock all the doors for the daily census count. His roommate walks in. "What's up with you?" Shamrock just lies on his bunk, wondering when it will come.

Then it hits. Rabbit, from down the tier, lets out a scream. "Oh shit! Someone done kilt my cellie!"

Guards and lieutenants soon rush into the unit. The prisoners, locked in their cells, are peering through the thin strip of a window in the cell's door to catch a glimpse as Dre is carried out on a stretcher. Speculation runs rampant as to whether a dead body has been found. Cheers go up with the excitement. The unit remains locked for several hours while the staff initiate an investigation. They pull men from the cells individually to conduct interviews, to gather any information on what might have happened.

Later that evening, two guards come to Shamrock's cell. "Cuff up," they tell him. With Shamrock in handcuffs, the guards lead him to the lieutenant's office as the rest of the prison is locked down. More anonymous notes are dropped, identifying Shamrock as the attacker. He is told to sit in a waiting area. "The lieutenant will call you when he's ready for you."

While waiting, Shamrock hears Officer O'Brian's voice. He is arguing with the lieutenant. "Listen. I'm telling you. There is no way Shamrock could have done this. I signed his pass out at two o'clock. He's been at recreation all afternoon. I don't care how many anonymous notes you've got. He isn't your man. He wasn't in the unit when this happened."

O'Brian's assertiveness surprises Shamrock. He doesn't expect it. The two haven't exchanged many words since O'Brian has been assigned to D Unit. But the support emboldens Shamrock. When the investigating lieutenant finally calls Shamrock in, he denies knowledge of or involvement in anything. "I was in the gym all afternoon," is all he has to say. "Every time a guy gets popped, you guys want to blame me. I didn't do nothin'."

The lieutenant strikes out again. Without an eyewitness, and with an officer attesting to Shamrock's story, there is no holding Shamrock. He walks out of the lieutenant's office, unescorted, and back to the unit. The assault goes unsolved, and Shamrock's reputation remains intact.

13

Despite Shamrock's suburban background, he adjusts to prison in the same way that so many other convicts adjust. He has no interest in reconciling with society.

Fox, another prisoner with whom I served time inside medium-security fences, has four years remaining to serve on a 235-month sentence he received for a weapons violation. He began serving this sentence when he was thirty-one, and he is forty-three now. With twelve years in, it is not Fox's first term of imprisonment, but he insists that it will be his last.

Fox was raised in inner-city West Philadelphia, and he has led a life of perpetual crime since he was thirteen. "In my era, when I was a youngsta comin' up, wasn't nothin' wrong with bein' a criminal. Niggas know me as Cooney Fox, from Sixtieth Street in West Philly. Ev'one be knowin' that I been carryin' it like a man from jump. Write it like I lived it."

Coming into his teen years, Fox began earning money by shoplifting. He says that neighbors from the projects in which he lived gave him orders for the size and type of clothing they wanted. Without thinking he was doing anything wrong, Fox would go on a spree through large department stores, stealing clothes off the racks. By taking them to his customers, most of whom lived as hustlers themselves, Fox would receive cash on delivery. His is a background more typical of the men in medium- and high-security prisons.

Between the ages of fifteen and seventeen, Fox says, he began committing robberies on a weekly basis. "One sweet spot was the drop-off box at the bank. People was 'posed to insert they key in the box befo' droppin' they bag of loot off for deposit. I would press some bubble gum or putty into the keyhole, then stand back and watch as a sucka tried to fiddle his key up in the joint. Sometimes a stupid muthafucka would put his bag up under his arm while he was tryin' to open the box. I'd just come up behind and snatch that bitch right up out his arms. It was like takin' candy from a baby."

As a young criminal, Fox says, he never gave a thought to the consequences of his actions. "I'm sayin', I was tryin' to git money. You know what I'm sayin'? My life was just stealin'. I been doin' robberies all my life. Ev'one I knew was robbin'. A muthafucka from my block would just lay down the plan, and that'd be a wrap. We did what we had to do. We just di'n't care."

Robberies gave Fox immediate cash to flash around town. He spent with wild abandon. He says that he also took pleasure in the process. Robbing others gave him a sense of power, a sense of control. The thought of working never crossed his mind. All of his acquaintances were thieves, drug dealers, hustlers. "I ain't never knowed no one with no job. Not back in those days. Workin' was for suckas. I was a playa, know what I'm sayin'? I was tearin' up the streets, a dog for real. Ya heard?"

When Fox was twenty-one, one of his robberies resulted in gunfire and his first stretch in prison. He was accustomed to carrying firearms, and on that occasion he ended up in a shoot-out with a police officer. "I ain't usually tryin' to shoot it out with no po-lease. I ain't tryin' to shoot it out with nobody, not unless a muthafucka gots it comin'. But sometimes shit happen. Usually I just gots to shoot my pistol and it's a wrap. If I gots to fire at all, I could just shoot at the ground, scare a muthafucka. Know what I'm sayin'?

"On that job I was takin' down a drug dealer who had beat a friend a mines out some dope," Fox justifies his actions. "I had my pistol on him and I was tellin' the dude to empty his pockets, to gimme his money.

"The po-lease peeped the robb'ry, and as I was leavin' the scene, the cop tol' me to halt. So I broke out runnin', tryin' to git away to my peoples. As I was runnin', I turned around and fired at him. Po-lease then dived between two parked cars, bitchass muthafucka. He shot at me twice, and I shot at him one mo' time, but kept runnin'. Bullets was flyin' crazy, but neither one of us got hit. I was able to sneak up in one a my partner's cribs and got away."

Although Fox was able to elude the witnessing officer who had been in hot pursuit, within a week he was in custody. An officer identified Fox when he returned to the crime-infested neighborhood where the shooting had taken place. The officer arrested Fox and charged him with several crimes, including attempted murder for shooting at the police officer while he was running away from the scene. Without the weapon or additional witnesses, however, the state's case was not as strong as it needed to be, and the prosecuting attorney elected to accept Fox's guilty plea for robbery in exchange for dismissing the other charges. The judge sentenced Fox to a seven-year term in Rockview Penitentiary.

When Fox went into the prison, he had no skills that could qualify him for employment upon release. Nor did he care about acquiring any. "I knew I was comin' out to hustle. There is no way I was 'bout to do no work." Fox's sentence could have resulted in his serving seven years, but the state of Pennsylvania offered prisoners the opportunity to advance their release dates through parole. Administrators encouraged the men to participate in self-improvement programs to enhance their chances of receiving a favorable parole decision. Fox signed up for a nine-month vocational-training program that resulted in his becoming a licensed barber. "I was likin' the program. It taught me how to cut hair, and that let me get my hustle on in the joint. I earned a few dollars, and that money pushed me through my bid. But I knew there was no way I was gonna cut hair once I hit the streets."

Fox also acknowledges that his having completed a barber VT program and acquiring a marketable skill made it much more likely that he would serve the minimum time on his conviction. The possibility for an early release was a powerful motivator for him to participate in and successfully complete the program. The parole board released Fox from the penitentiary when he was twenty-five. Immediately he returned to the streets of Philadelphia under the lax supervision of a state parole officer. "Parole was more of a hassle in those days than anythin' else. I just had to report in and sign a form each month. There was no drug testin', no pressure to work. I just did my own thing. Within a few days of my release I was back on the move, takin' down scores."

True to his word, Fox never pursued legitimate employment upon his initial release. The thought of a return trip to prison was less important to him than continuing his life as a street hustler. He and his friends lived a life of crime, of robberies and drug sales, for several years. Fox was arrested on numerous occasions, served some brief periods in county jails, and accumulated a string of felonies on his record. When he was thirty-one, in 1991, officers arrested Fox, and he was found to be in possession of a firearm. He was held in Pennsylvania's Graterford Penitentiary while authorities decided how best to prosecute Fox, whom the law identified as a menace to society.

"Graterford was aw'ight. I have a lot of homeys up in there." Fox waited in Graterford for two years while his case worked its way through the courts. He explains his living conditions and frame of mind while being held in Pennsylvania's maximum-security prison. "I live good. The po-lease is bringin' me drugs. I'm havin' sex with my shorty. She comes up for a VI and the po-lease give us some time in a closet to handle our bi'ness. Sometimes they want a ten or a twenty piece, sometimes they just turn they back. Cops is cool up in that joint. The jail is so intense that it might pop off with a riot at any moment. Guards know that a nigga might be one to save his life. Or take it. So they don't sweat no one. I'm lovin' it up there in Graterford. Shit is sweet. Sellin' drugs. Lady po-lease sellin' pussy for a C-note. Buyin' swag sandwiches. Just jailhouse livin', like up in the projects. It's aw'ight."

Fox's story makes it sound as if the inmates were running the asylum. That atmosphere at Graterford changed in 1995, when the state of Pennsylvania launched an offensive to reclaim control of its prisons, sending scores of police officers and dogs into Graterford to seize drugs and weapons, and arresting several staff members, whom the state charged with corruption. While Fox was there, however, he lived as if he were on the familiar inner-city streets of West Philadelphia. "I'm in denial while I'm in Graterford. I figure I might get six months or a year. The state just keeps puttin' it off and puttin' it off. I'm livin' so good in the joint that I jus' don't care 'bout what a muthafucka is gonna do. You know what I'm sayin'? I'm like, 'Fuck it. Bring it.' Then I hear the state is gonna drop my charges and give 'em to the feds. That fucks me up."

Fox knew that his exposure to prison time increased exponentially in the federal system. A federal prosecution and conviction would result in a much longer sentence, no possibility for parole, and time in an austere federal prison. Federal prison is significantly more rigid than the conditions Fox knew in Pennsylvania's Graterford Penitentiary. "I know 'bout the feds, and I know the time in there isn't gonna be no joke."

Being a felon in possession of a firearm usually results in a five-year sentence in the federal system. Without parole and with minimal amounts of time off available for good behavior, such a sentence yields more than fifty-two months in custody. Fox, however, had previously been convicted of six felony crimes, exposing him to the severe sentencing enhancement for being an armed career criminal. He pleaded not guilty to the charge but was convicted. The judge sentenced Fox to a 235-month term. "That sentence really fucks me up. What! I couldn't believe a nigga is gonna have to serve twenty muthafuckin' years. It's a wrap."

Fox's surprise at receiving such a long sentence seems disingenuous to me. Considering the choices in his life, and his experience of an earlier term in confinement, he should have known about the probability of a lengthy term for further convictions. After all, he lived as a violent, predatory criminal in the street.

With a fresh twenty-year sentence to serve, Fox had to accept the inevitable fact that he would remain in prison for at least seventeen years. He would be nearly forty-eight upon his release, and even that would be contingent upon his not losing any good time. He began the term with an aggressive attitude. During his first year he assaulted another prisoner with a chair. Authorities charged him criminally for the attack, and Fox received an additional felony conviction and sentence of one year. "But the dumb judge runs the year with the rest of my time so I might as well've got nothin' at all."

After settling into his sentence, Fox began to review his life's choices. Prisoners convicted under the federal laws with which Fox was charged have no possibility for early release through parole or programs that had existed in the state of Pennsylvania when he served his first term. Fox began to mellow out as time passed, moving into a more structured schedule that he hoped would keep him away from problems. Since there is nothing he can do to advance his possible release date, I ask Fox what motivates him to change his behavior so drastically from the reckless way he lived prior to confinement.

"I'm gettin' old," Fox replies. "I been lyin' up in these steel racks for too many years. And I just realize that I can't be doin' this here no mo'. The feds done pushed me to my limit. When I was comin' up, things was different. I done seen too much now. I don't wanna give these people one mo' day a my life. You feel me? Not one mo' day. Word. This time broke me."

It remains to be seen whether Fox's commitment to live a law-abiding life upon release will continue. What is clear is that he has given thought to the choices he must make inside the fences and to the prospects he will face when imprisonment ends. Rather than running wild in the prison or idling away his time, Fox holds a full-time job in the prison factory sewing mailbags. He has held it for the past nine years. He works as many hours as possible and uses the money he earns to support himself in prison; he has a bank account and mails deposits regularly. It is the first time in his life that he has used a bank for its intended purpose.

The money he saves will help him upon release. Fox earns only $1.15 per hour, but even after monthly expenses for toiletries, food, postage, and phone calls, he still manages to save $50 each month. Fox expects to leave prison with $5,000 in savings.

Besides holding full-time employment, Fox also participates actively in a program to help juvenile delinquents reform their ways. The Save Our Youth program brings prisoners like Fox together to discuss the values that lead to crime and the consequences of such decisions. Fox, being a gifted speaker, always provides a frightening and persuasive reason for the adolescents to make different decisions than he made at their age.

"I ain't tryin' to be no role model," Fox explains. "Ain't nobody ought to model they behavior afta me. You talk about one-time, two-time, and three-time losers. I'm a six-time loser. Alls I'm trying to tell them kids is to stay in school, to stay away from crime 'cause this ain't no way to spend a life. It ain't the same as when I was comin' up and could catch a break. There ain't no mo' playin'. You come up in here and it's a wrap. I'm livin' in a tomb up in here, and I know I'm

lucky 'cause I could've been on death row. I know it and the feds
know it. I'm jus' tryin' to tell the kids to think, to stay outta here."

While Fox says that he never thought about work or the consequences of his actions prior to his imprisonment, now he thinks
about the obstacles he will face upon release. He makes conscious
choices to prepare himself. One way is by laboring in the factory and
committing to a plan that will result in his having a savings account
that he can draw upon to ease his transition. He has ambitions of
working as a guidance counselor for troubled inner-city adolescents.
In prison, Fox says, he learned that there is no way to get away,
nowhere to go. He has begun to evaluate his life in terms of the possible consequences because he knows that any other criminal problem could result in a life sentence.

Rather than returning to his block in West Philadelphia, Fox plans
to relocate to Virginia, where he can establish himself in a new community. Everyone he knows in Philadelphia, he says, has a history of
problems with the law. A new location will bring him new relationships, and he expects that will enhance his chances to savor his freedom. Fox plans to work cutting hair, as a cook, as an orderly, or as
maintenance worker. "I'm a do anythin' I can to keep from spendin'
another day locked up."

14

While locked inside medium-security fences I began teaching classes. I became convinced that I was as ready as I would ever be to leave prison and begin life as a contributing citizen. More than eight years of continuous confinement had passed. I was thirty-one. I was strong and healthy, and held a master's degree. That was when the warden and the correctional system he represented blocked my ability to advance my academic credentials further.

With eighteen years of imprisonment still in front of me, I knew that I could not join my friend Shamrock to live in a constant state of resentment and rebellion. My fear of the obstacles I expected to face upon release drove me. The anxiety of knowing that I would live as an ex-convict with more than a quarter century of continuous confinement tormented my thoughts as I lay in my cell. I wanted some kind of life upon release. I knew that to overcome the stigma of my past, I had to navigate my way around the obstacles that correctional policies present and continue preparations for my life. I felt that leading classes and teaching others could sharpen my skills.

Through teaching, I have come to know scores of prisoners. Many of their backgrounds differ from mine. Like Fox, the men with whom I work were conditioned or predisposed to crime since their earliest years. They did not grow up with middle-class values. Their acquaintances, family members, and community role models all had long histories of confinement. To them, confinement brought no stigma. These people began living in and out of institutions before their teen years. Despite their participation in my classes, I wonder whether they will succeed in breaking the vicious cycle of return trips to prison.

Prince is one of the men I taught. It was not his first time inside. A thirty-five-year-old native of the Duncan Housing Projects in Jersey City, Prince began serving time when he was thirteen. Authorities locked him up for robbery.

"I was big for my age when I was thirteen, and definitely one of the tougher kids in the projects. I was hangin' with this older cat who was about fi'teen or si'teen. I was just as big as he was. We was in the video arcade and saw this old dude, maybe about thirty or thirty-five. He was playin' one of the games. He pulled out a big knot and it was on from there."

Prince describes how he and his teenage friend scoped out their victim after seeing his wad of money. "When the dude walked out the arcade, I just ran up from behind and put his neck in what we called the Duncan Crush, you know what I'm sayin', yokin' my arm round muthafucka's neck in a choke hold and pullin' him down from behind. The dude was a lot bigger than me so I had to jump up to get at him. Once I had his neck in my arm grip, he came right down. My homey put the knife to his neck and tol' him that this was a robb'ry and he better give us the money. Otherwise we'd make it a homicide. We went in his pockets and came up with the cash. Five-O started chasin' us though. They must've saw the whole thing. My man got away. They caught me as I was runnin' toward the grave-yard. They locked me up."

Prince says he learned a lot during that first period of imprisonment. After he challenged the toughest delinquent in the detention center, then smashed a chair over his head, his confinement became much easier. The staff gave him a single cell, and all the other adolescent prisoners showed him respect. They feared him. "After that experience, I knowed that bein' locked up isn't no big thing. I knowed I could do time without no problem."

Prince estimates that after his stint in confinement as a juvenile, he has been arrested on ten separate occasions. Authorities expelled him from school in the tenth grade, and Prince began hustling on the streets full-time. "I was always gettin' my groove on. After the school kicked me out I just stepped my game up." His arrest record is for charges related to drug sales or robbery. Except for one stretch, he never served more than a few months in jail. "It is easier to beat charges in state court." When he turned twenty, a judge sentenced Prince to a year in prison. During his time in confinement he exercised and says that he became more serious about his Islamic studies.

Upon his release Prince knew that he would have to serve a period of time under the supervision of a federal parole officer, but he fully expected to hit the streets hustling again as soon as he got out—his devotion to Islam notwithstanding. Apparently, Prince saw no contradiction between a holy life and the life of perpetual crime. Prince's lawlessness resulted in his supervising officer returning him to prison for violating the conditions of his parole. "I spent my time there exercisin' and hittin' the heavy bag."

Prince never held a full-time job. He never thought about a career or the job market. Not until he was locked up again for this conviction did he begin to think about his future. When he was twenty-nine he began serving this six-year sentence for being a felon in possession of a firearm. "On this bid I realize I have to do sumpin' diff'rent. I just want to better myself, you know what I'm sayin', to do anythin' that can benefit me. I sign up for classes to get my GED. After I pass the test, I sign up for the college courses. I take a course I need to go out and get a job removin' hazardous waste. You know, like asbestos and shit like that. Muthafuckas pay good money for that kind of work. I ain't never done it, but I took the courses and now I got the certificate. I work out. You know, keep myself strong."

After Prince was in the prison for a year, his case manager, Ms. Adams, told him that she was sending him to the minimum-security camp. The camp, however, did not offer as many formal courses as were available inside fences. Prince expected that his preparations for the job market would suffer if he transferred there. Instead of concentrating on the skills-development program he had set for himself, he feared that camp administrators would assign him to a job mowing lawns all day. Prince told Ms. Adams that although most prisoners look forward to minimum security, he wanted to remain inside fences, where he could continue preparing for the job market.

"You don't tell me what you want," the case manager admonished Prince. "We are overcrowded here and need the bed space. Your points are low enough for me to send you to the camp, and that's where you're going."

"Come on, Ms. Adams," Prince pleaded. "Don't do me like that. I needs to stay inside. I'm signin' up for college, tryin' to get a certificate. I'm a have a hard enough time when I get out. If I get the college certificate it might help me get a job."

"You should have thought about that before you got locked up," the case manager told him. "There are plenty of people outside who can't take college classes and don't break the law. I'm not keeping you in here just because you want to go to school."

With the case manager unwilling to listen, Prince returned to his bunk in frustration. The feeling of having no control over his life overwhelmed him. He tried to suppress a rage that he felt coming over him. In reality, regardless of where administrators confined Prince, he could take steps to continue his education, if not formally then informally. In the classes I teach I suggest students study through math and English books. Mastering such basic subjects, I tell them, will broaden employment prospects upon release.

Prince did not recognize those possibilities. He couldn't grasp the

concept of creating opportunities for himself. He was conditioned to
believe that his environment controlled him rather than vice versa.
Convinced that he would meet failure if he transferred to camp,
Prince tried again to convince his case manager to leave him inside
the fenced and secure prison.

"Ms. Adams." Prince talked to his case manager through her open
door while he stood in the hallway, outside her office. "Just listen to
me for a minute. You being a black woman ought to make you know
how hard it is for a brother to make it on the streets. Especially one
just comin' off lockup. I'm just tryin' to finish my time here so I can
work on my education and job skills."

The case manager did not look up from her desk. "I'm just doing
my job, Prince. When your points drop, you gotta go. There is nothing you can say that will change that." She had a job to do, and it did
not include having concern for Prince's anxieties.

"I try to go see her one more time," Prince says. "While I'm there
talking she gets up from her desk and slams the door in my face."

With his case manager refusing to listen to him or consider his
needs, Prince began feeling emotionally unbalanced. He knew that
he was coming close to doing something that he would later regret.
He thought about hurting someone in order to raise his security
level. Instead, he walked to the health services department to see the
psychologist and explained that he needed to talk with her. The doctor saw him right away, inviting him to sit down, to collect his
thoughts and express what was on his mind.

"I tell her how frustrated I am. I'm scared of leavin' prison at
thirty-five, you know what I'm sayin', scared of getting' out there
without no skills. I tell her how good I'm doin' in here, and that I
want to finish my education but that my case manager is sendin' me
out to the camp no matter what." Prince explained to the doctor that
he felt unstable, and worried that if he was sent out there without opportunities to develop skills, he might make a bad decision and do

something that could hurt him even more; he might hurt someone else, maybe a staff member.

The camp his case manager was sending him to had no physical boundaries, no fences or walls. Prince knew he could walk away at any time. Doing so, however, would expose him to escape charges. "I jus' explain that I want to stick with the structured program inside, to work on my education, you know what I'm sayin', and get out when I finish my time." After listening to Prince, the doctor agreed to speak with Ms. Adams.

Soon after Prince returned to his housing unit, Ms. Adams paged him to her office. She admonished him for going to the psychologist, saying that he should not have gone over her head. "But I came back here and tried to speak with you three times," Prince told her. "You wouldn't listen to me. You told me you don't want to hear it." Refusing to acknowledge her previous indifference to Prince's concerns, Ms. Adams instructed Prince to express his feelings in writing. Then, she said, she would issue a management variable to his custody and classification scoring. That would enable him to remain inside the fences and continue with his program. Prince had discovered one of the constants of bureaucratic life: it is the squeaky wheel that gets the grease.

"I ain't tryin' to come back to prison. And I know I need the classes to help me. The little bit of extra freedom in the camp doesn't mean nothin' to me. I want to get my education." Prince was able to remain inside.

When not working toward his educational goals, Prince exercises. He relieves stress through workout routines that consume as much as four hours each day, a combination of weight training, calisthenics, running, and hitting the punching bags. "I ain't lookin' for no problems, but at the same time, I'm not about to be taken lightly by no muthafucka either. The workouts help relieve some a the frustration of bein' locked up."

Those workouts may relieve some of Prince's frustrations, but not all of his anger. "I know I got a short fuse, and I'm not too good with authority. I've had to knock out six guys since I been in this time. They weren't really fights, just one or two solid punches to the head and they'd be out." Prince is a Golden Gloves boxer. "Little things set me off. Like lines for the microwave or the telephone. I don't care who it is. A muthafucka get lippy or disrespect me in any kind a way, I'm a take it to him. Ya heard? It don't matter how much time I got or who he's with. Anyone who messes with me is goin' down."

Prince's unit-team members told him that he had a six-month halfway-house date and that release would come in September. The halfway-house programs provide an opportunity for prisoners to reacclimate themselves to the community after a prolonged period of confinement. Ordinarily, prisoners serve the last 10 percent of their sentence in a halfway house, or up to six months. While there, they live under strict conditions somewhat similar to confinement, but are given the freedom to leave the facility each day to find a job. Once the prisoners in the halfway house locate a job, they may report to their employer each day, but must return to the halfway house under a strict schedule during nonworking hours. Halfway-house administrators require the prisoners to forfeit 25 percent of their gross earnings to pay the cost of confinement. After they find steady employment, the men may receive weekend passes home; several weeks of cooperative behavior qualifies some for a transfer to home confinement.

Although most prisoners eagerly await their release to the community under any conditions at all, Prince's reservations about release from the structured environment that he had come to know so well continued. The uncertainty of the halfway house made him apprehensive. "I'm sayin', prison ain't bad. It ain't nothin' I haven't done befo'. I got my routine, you know what I'm sayin'? I get up in the mornin'. I get my exercise on. I study or go to classes. I run, I hit the heavy bag, the speed bag. I been doin' this thing for a minute already and I'm really not tryin' to change things up by goin' to no halfway house. With only six months left, I figure I can just do it like I been doin' it. But since they gave me the halfway house, you know what I'm sayin', I jus' say fuck it and give it a try."

As scheduled, in early September Prince walked out of the fences. For the first time in nearly six years he was walking in the community without leg irons, handcuffs, or supervision. His mother and sister picked him up and drove him to the halfway house in Newark, New Jersey.

"Man, I'm sayin', as soon as I walk inside I can feel the problems," Prince says. "I'm not ready. I know my problems with authority. Them muthafuckas in there are somethin' else. I'm sayin', rules, rules, and mo' muthafuckin' rules. It's all 'bout how you can't do this and you can't do that. How you have to be in bed by eleven and call in to check in whenever you cross the street. I'm not feelin' that halfway house in no kine a way.

"I have two jobs lined up when I get there," Prince continues. "But because they require me to drive, the halfway-house people say I can't take either of 'em. The owners of the company don't care 'bout me drivin' the company truck. It's the halfway-house rules that stop me. They only let me take a job where they can check on a muthafucka all day. They want me to work flippin' burgers or some kine a place like that, some place for minimum wage. I'm sayin', that shit is beneath me. I ain't tryin' to work for no minimum wage. It's 'bout the principle with me. Why I'm a work for minimum wage when I got a job lined up that's gonna pay me a twenty piece a hour? If I got a job for minimum wage and a partner tries to put me down slingin' that shit, I'm more likely to take it just to come up."

Prince recognizes his weaknesses. "Besides that, the top dog in the halfway house is always makin' those threats 'bout how he can send a muthafucka back to prison. I'm like, fuck it, he can send me back 'cause I ain't really wanna be in the halfway house no way. Prison ain't shit. But when they finally knowed that I don't give a fuck 'bout bein' sent back, they come with all this woo woo woo shit, sayin' they want me to try and make it work out and all that. So I keep with it for a while."

Prince explains that the halfway house required him to sleep in a twenty-two-man room. The staff members rousted everyone out of bed by seven, and they assigned those without a job to a series of chores to complete around the building. There were two hundred prisoners, male and female, in the halfway house. Prince says there was more than enough labor available to maintain the sanitation level. Most of the work, he explains, is just busywork like polishing stainless-steel phone booths or railings.

"They order me to spend hours on somethin' that doesn't even need cleanin'. It's just 'bout harassment, makin' me do degradin' shit that I don't want to do." He says that after completing the chores staff assigned him, he started looking for jobs in the classified ads. But if he remained too long in one place, another staff member assigned some other menial task. When he did go apply for a job, the staff required him to call upon his arrival to check in, and call again before he left from one location to another. They evaluated how long it took him to move from place to place, then questioned him on the minutes in between.

"The whole thing is just too much of a hassle. And I knows my temper. If those muthafuckas keep disrespectin' me any kind of way they want to, you know what I'm sayin', I'm liable just to snap off, to do somethin' I don't want to. I have enough after ten days of that bullshit. I just tell 'em to send me back to prison. I don' need no halfway house no way. I'm a do my last months here, then I'll get out and just be me. Shit will be easier that way."

Prince insists that his decision to exchange the quasi freedom for a return to prison was not irrational. It may have not been the right decision for everyone, he acknowledges, but he did not want to live under such conditions. He worried that remaining under such pressure might push him to violence, creating even more problems than he already had. Since Prince had a higher-paying job lined up, but one that the halfway-house administrators would not allow him to accept, he preferred to finish his term in confinement, then begin his life fresh. Like many prisoners, Prince says he is not willing to compromise his principles by accepting employment that he considers beneath him, even if it means he can partially live in the community. "I ain't workin' for no minimum wage."

Prince believes that the high school equivalency certificate, along with the spattering of college and vocational courses under his belt, have prepared him for the challenges of the job market. He says that there is no way that he will make decisions which can lead him back to prison. At the same time, Prince acknowledges that he has a personal code of principles and beliefs, and he will not compromise those beliefs, regardless of the consequences. An example of that rigidity is his conscious decision to conclude the final months of his sentence in prison rather than accepting a minimum-wage job and adhering to the strict code of conduct necessary for him to live in the halfway house.

Prince still faces three years of supervised release upon the completion of his term. That obligation, together with the sometimes difficult demands of an employer, may present real challenges to Prince that he is not prepared to master. He admits to anger-management issues. Prince's long history of confinement and pattern of responding to frustrations with violence have conditioned him for living inside. Such conditioning, however, presages difficulty come March, when Prince will leave prison to join the job market as a thirty-five-year-old ex-convict who has not previously held employment in his life. Nevertheless, Prince expresses confidence that there will be no more return trips to confinement for him.

My anxiety about what I will encounter upon release is much greater. It keeps me awake at night. Unlike Prince and others with whom I interact, I expect that many in society will see my prison record as an indelible brand. Prospective employers will be suspicious of me. Neighbors may not want me around their families. If I am involved in a traffic violation, I expect officers will see my lengthy prison record and detain me. Although I am certain that I will never commit another crime, I do not know how my past will interfere with my future. Regardless of what efforts I make to reconcile with society, I expect the bad decisions of my early twenties will always be with me.

I learn by listening to the characters in prison with whom I interact. Their stories help me anticipate what more I must do to prepare for the challenges ahead. I know the journey is long, lifelong. Like Odysseus, I must struggle to find my way home.

15

Living for years at a time without access to female companionship—and to sex in particular—is especially frustrating for prisoners. In the penitentiary, and to a lesser extent in medium security, predators make sex available through violence and coercion. But in any prison setting, whether inside fences or inside walls, opportunities for consensual sex sometimes present themselves. When they do, wily prisoners pursue such opportunities like ravenous wolves.

In many ways, prison communities resemble miniature cities. Besides holding thousands of felons, they also employ several hundred staff members. Those staff members, who come from cross sections of neighboring communities, supervise and guard inmates working in infrastructure jobs like food services, landscaping, janitorial, and administration.

Administrators are convinced that inmate idleness represents one of the greatest threats to institutional security. Accordingly, they require all inmates without health restrictions to work on a job assignment. That strategy divides the inmate population into literally hundreds of work details; staff supervisors accept responsibility during their assigned shifts for watching a detail of between one and twenty inmates.

Administrative policies expressly discourage the building of personal relationships between inmates and staff. Such policies lessen the possibility for the introduction of contraband into the population.

Indeed, as a staff member becomes physically closer to a prisoner, as in a supervisory role, the chances escalate that the two may find common interests and develop a friendship. Administrators believe that close relationships embolden some prisoners to entice staff members into ventures that compromise the security of the institution. Flipping staff members is precisely how Lion and other leaders in the pen make their rackets possible and their own worlds more palatable.

Despite the efforts of administrators, such bonds can and sometimes do blossom. After all, inmates report to assigned jobs that require them to spend several hours each day with their supervisors. They interact on a daily basis for years at a time. Two people may pass through seasons and holidays together. Sometimes they share space no larger than a small office. They talk. It is inevitable that at least quasi friendships will develop. When the staff member is of the opposite gender, the relationship can advance to much more than friendship.

Frankie, a handsome Italian American from Philadelphia, is five years into his sentence when he scores big-time with a romance he successfully cultivates inside the fences. He is serving time on extortion charges and enjoys the pride that comes with his reputation of being a rising associate in one of the East Coast organized-crime groups that tabloid newspapers frequently glamorize.

The notoriety gives Frankie a kind of celebrity status inside the prisons where he is held. Other prisoners like to stand next to him, to be seen talking or eating with him. They laugh quickly and easily at his jokes. Some blush with pride when shaking Frankie's hand. Frankie lives as the prison equivalent of an NFL superstar, and many inside the fences want to be in his company, a part of the club. He and his friends are to prison communities what Frank Sinatra and the Rat Pack are reputed to have been in Hollywood. Staff members cut a wide path around him, respecting a tacit deference to wiseguys with Mafia ties. To many, they represent the top of the criminal food chain.

During the early years of Frankie's sentence, he held jobs that required minimal accountability. "Sign in and sign out. That's what I'm talkin' about."

Not needing money from paltry prison wages, Frankie preferred the do-nothing jobs. His goombahs from Philly kept him in commissary money with stipends, a considerable Mafia tithe each month. Soon after he joined me inside the fences, however, Frankie spots Ms. Martin, a department head who works as the business manager in the factory; in federal prison, the factory is known as UNICOR, an acronym with a meaning unknown to this author.

"*Bellissima.*" Frankie nudges me while taking in Ms. Martin's sex appeal. She stands near the center of the chow hall with a small group of other staff members. Frankie takes an audible and deep breath as he fans his face with his hands. "Look at dis woman here," he says. "What the fuck is she doin' workin' in a prison? How 'bout that ass, them legs. Those tits are perfect. I could suck on her for days. Now that's a woman. I'd fuck her on the streets."

Ms. Martin, an attractive, petite woman in her early thirties, began her career in accounting with the Bureau of Prisons years earlier. As the business manager for the factory, she is responsible for financial matters; she oversees an office with a few other staff members and inmate clerks. Ms. Martin dresses in the fashionable good taste of a young professional, wearing clothes that reveal a trim, youthful figure. On the day that Frankie sees her, Ms. Martin is wearing a snug-fitting skirt, blouse, and waist-cut jacket. Her skin has a honey glow.

"I want a piece a that." Frankie can't take his eyes away from her.

Over the following days, Frankie uses his considerable charm to manipulate his way into a job that will place him in direct, regular contact with Ms. Martin. He approaches her and requests an assignment as her personal clerk. The initial interview does not recommend Frankie as a viable candidate for employment. He is a high school dropout (but he has passed his GED in prison). His large hands are more suited to cracking skulls than typing or filing. And over the years, Frankie has worked to cultivate an image that inspires fear in men rather than the easy congeniality most staff members seek in a clerk.

"I appreciate your interest in the job, Mr. Tatino, but I don't employ a clerk. Inmate clerks work in accounting, payroll, or shipping offices. All of those clerical positions are filled. Leave your application on file, and when an opening comes up, in a year or so, we'll consider you." Ms. Martin speaks in precise English, somewhat dismissively, to Frankie.

"No, no," Frankie persists. "I want youse to look at my file. You'll see that I'm really tryin' to turn my life around. I ain't been in no trouble and I could do real good at dis job here. I wanna learn from youse." Her smile and brilliant blue eyes embolden him. "I'm thinkin' a openin' my own business when I get out. A pizzeria. I'm a real ha'd worker and I learn fast. I want to work for youse, to learn from the best. You don't even have to pay me. I can help with all sorts of stuff. Just you watch. Give me a shot, will ya?"

Frankie's adolescent determination amuses Ms. Martin. She gives him some hope. "I've never had a clerk work directly for me. I'll think about it. Come back and see me in a few days."

Frankie is sure that he sees fire in her eyes, maybe even an involuntary wink. She smiles at him as he rambles, almost giggling as he tries to sell himself. It feels to Frankie as if he is pitching a line to an attractive woman rather than humbling himself to a staff member. There is a connection. He is sure of it.

Two days later Frankie hears the loudspeaker page his name. Ms. Martin at the UNICOR business office is directing him to report to her. He notices a new desk directly outside the door of her office. Frankie steps in to see her. "Okay, Mr. Tatino," Ms. Martin says. "I'm going to give you a chance. Don't disappoint me."

"Oh, no. Don't you worry about a thing. And call me Frankie."

She smiles. "I'm making you responsible for cleaning the office, filing, typing simple order forms, and delivering messages to other staff members. You'll work the regular day shift with me." Frankie knows he is in the door.

Over the following weeks the two grow closer. Frankie's desk is positioned in such a way that from where he sits, he and Ms. Martin make direct eye contact through her office doorway. She never closes the door. They are situated far enough away from other staff members and inmate clerks who work in the business office so that they can banter without fear of eavesdroppers. Frankie comes to think that Ms. Martin did not hire him for clerical work.

She tells him about her personal life, that her husband works as a high school counselor. "He's somewhat of a drip." Frankie learns that they had been high school sweethearts before marrying. "He just doesn't have any ambition. He's so provincial," she tells Frankie. "He doesn't ever want to leave these small towns." Nancy—Frankie comes to know her first name—is attracted to the big city. She loves the excitement of Washington, D.C., is thrilled whenever she has to attend business meetings at the BOP central office. "Tell me about New York," she says to Frankie. "I just love watching *Sex and the City*."

A Philly boy all his life, Frankie doesn't know New York. But that has no significance. To this country girl, one big city is another big city. He speaks about the streets, the action, the excitement. His descriptions of New York come from the gangster movies he watches religiously, not from his own experiences. Frankie cannot tell Nancy about the Met, the Guggenheim, Fifth Avenue, the sophisticated sites of New York which she longs to know. That does not matter. Frankie is from a real city, and big-city magnetism has not left him. "I like them big words youse sometimes say," Frankie tells her. She beams.

"I read your file. That's why I hired you. I like reading that you're not in here for drugs, that you're a real man, able to take what you want."

"That's what I'm about. I shouldn't even be in here. I ain't never did nothin' to nobody that didn't have it comin'," he adds. She likes having Frankie around, likes having someone with whom she can talk each day, someone who appreciates her. She has a stale marriage and cannot wait each morning to leave for work. She craves the excitement that comes with Frankie. Nancy tells him that she thinks about him at night.

The electricity between them never stops flowing. They both are looking forward to the inevitable. Then it happens. Nancy asks Frankie to bring her a box of paper from the computer room. She accompanies him to the door to unlock it. After turning the key, she opens the door to the unoccupied dark room; a sign on the door denies access to unescorted inmates. The room is buzzing from the whirring noise of computer equipment. Along the back wall is a steel rack, and on the top shelf, several boxes of paper. She directs Frankie to retrieve one.

As he walks in, Frankie hears the door close behind him. He knows that it locks automatically upon closing. He turns around. From the dim of the computer lights he can see Nancy following him in. She is unbuttoning her blouse as she approaches, revealing her breasts. She embraces him. They kiss with the hunger, the thirst that a prolonged, denied passion inspires.

"Take me now," she says as she turns around and lifts her skirt. "We only have a few minutes." A long, leisurely afternoon in bed is out of the question for the two lovers.

The affair lasts for more than three years. They have sex whenever an opportunity arises, but opportunities are not as frequent as either would like. They cannot cuddle, cannot hold each other. Prolonged kissing is out of the question, and it is essential that they mask their feelings for each other at all times around the office. They begin exchanging gifts. Frankie has his *paisans* from Philly send Nancy a diamond ring, a leather coat, perfume; she gives him her mother's address for mailing. She brings Frankie food, a watch, new sneakers, and anything that does not attract attention. Frankie has no interest in drugs or contraband that can earn him money. Their motivations differ from those of others in the pen. The two are in love.

Because of Nancy's position they cannot exchange letters, cannot visit as lovers, cannot talk on the phone. It becomes torture for both of them. As Frankie moves into the final months of his sentence, he pushes Nancy to leave her job at the BOP.

"Come on, baby," Frankie presses her. "You've gotta leave this job. You can't be with me and work for this lousy outfit. We're gonna have a new life together me and youse. We'll live in Philadelphia, or even New York if that's what you want. But you gotta be with me all the way."

"Honey, I can't just quit now," Nancy says. "I've been working here ten years. I can retire with a solid pension, with all the benefits. We're going to need that security." Nancy is reluctant to extend her commitment.

"You're with me now, baby," Frankie coaxes her. "That's all the security you'll ever need." Nancy is not ready for more.

But Frankie is obsessed, determined to bring her with him. If she will not leave voluntarily, Frankie wants to force her into it. As his release date approaches, he begins bragging to loudmouths in the prison, of which there is no shortage. He tells them that he has been with her. "You know I'm fuckin' Ms. Martin," he tells Karl. "But don't tell no one while I'm here. You just watch. I'm leavin' next month on the fifth. On the day I leave, she won't be here." He knows that such hot news will spread through the prison grapevine faster than multiplying fruit flies.

Sure enough, the entire compound is whispering about the affair. On the day that Frankie is scheduled to walk out of the prison, Ms. Martin calls in sick. The BOP's Special Investigative Services office, having heard of the illicit affair, stations an unknown officer to observe Frankie as he waits for the train that will transport him back to Philadelphia. Nancy is there. Undercover officers snap photos as she bids her lover good-bye.

Days later, Ms. Martin is called in from her desk to speak with the BOP investigators. That is the last any of the prisoners see of Ms. Martin. She never returns to her desk. But talk of the romance lingers on.

Sexual affairs between staff members and inmates do not happen every day. But to the chagrin of prison administrators, they do erupt with some regularity. Any time a man and a woman come together, there is a possibility for sexual energy to flow between them. I know of female guards, psychologists, teachers, nurses, counselors, factory workers, case managers, unit managers, lieutenants, and executive staff members who have pleaded guilty to the federal charges known as the "sexual abuse of a ward," a consequence of their sexual relationships with prisoners. Such convictions end careers and expose the offenders to prison time. Those threats, however, do not stop the passion inside prison perimeters.

While it is against the law for staff members to engage in sex with prisoners, it is a violation of prison rules—but not the law—for prisoners to engage in consensual sex with visitors. Sex between a prisoner and an approved visitor occurs more frequently than sex between a prisoner and a staff member. But again, as there are no conjugal visits for prisoners in the federal system, such encounters are always highly risky, always furtive and tension filled.

Those in federal prison are allowed a simple kiss and embrace with their visitors at the beginning and end of each visit. They may hold hands, occasionally, during the visit at the discretion of the visiting-room officer. Rules in federal prison prohibit any further contact, and those accused of violating visiting-room rules will have their visiting privileges terminated. They will also receive a disciplinary infraction for inappropriate contact with a visitor, serve a period of time in segregation, and likely lose their telephone privileges and commissary privileges for an extended period of time, frequently exceeding one year. One correctional officer gave me a formal warning and told me he could suspend my visiting privileges because, he said, I was looking in the direction of my wife's fully clothed bosom.

Despite the severe sanctions, rules do not dissuade all prisoners from attempting behavior that administrators consider inappropriate. Visiting rooms resemble bus stations or airport waiting areas. Vending machines line the walls, and doors that lead to visitor bathrooms are well within the sight of the ever-vigilant visiting-room officers. Surveillance cameras for off-site viewing are strategically placed in ceiling spots to record all visiting-room activities. Still, many prisoners try their luck.

When visiting rooms crowd, it is not uncommon for officers to catch prisoners whose fingers have found their way inside the clothing of their female visitors, or vice versa. As men spend year after year in confinement, away from the women they love, some revert to the behavior society expects from horny adolescents who try to "cop a feel" in any way possible. Sometimes the sexual tension escalates, and a deprived and desperate prisoner will sneak into the women's bathroom for a quick lovers' tryst with his girl in a stall.

Peter, however, succeeds in finding more regular sexual contact when he seduces an attorney whom he meets in the prison's visiting room. Peter is serving a lengthy sentence for convictions related to the distribution of cocaine. He is in his fifth year when he meets Wendy, a business attorney who has a downtown practice. Peter is visiting with his father when he sees Wendy visiting with Carlos, a friend of his inside the fences.

Carlos is serving a lengthy term for a smuggling offense, but he still controls a thriving retail business outside. Wendy is his attorney. On occasion, she comes into the prison to discuss ongoing business concerns with Carlos. After hearing about Wendy from Carlos for some time, Peter looks forward to meeting her. He is from the West Coast, and not knowing anyone nearby, he rarely receives visits. When Carlos tells Peter that Wendy has recently severed her relationship with her boyfriend, Peter becomes even more hopeful that he can develop a friendship—or more—with her. In his fantasizing mind, she is vulnerable. Peter is lonely, as are many prisoners.

Upon seeing Wendy in the visiting room, Peter excuses himself from his father so that he can introduce himself. He explains that besides serving a lengthy sentence, he is active in independent study programs. When Wendy encourages his efforts, Peter expresses the hope that she might help him overcome some of the obstacles he is encountering. She gives him her card. Peter writes her, and that leads to a correspondence. Before long, Wendy and Peter open a relationship. Being an attorney, she has greater visiting privileges than ordinary family members or friends. The two are able to visit in a small room reserved for legal counsel rather than the general visiting room. The legal conference area does not have the intensive surveillance of the larger room, as staff members do not generally suspect attorneys of wrongdoing. There is no guard watching their every move, no cameras, no one else to listen to what is said.

The room offers the two as much privacy as a prisoner can ever expect to receive, and in that privacy, passions erupt like a volcano.

While talking, Peter looks into her eyes with an intensity of wanting. Five years have passed since he has known a woman. The flirting leads to touching as he reaches across the table to take her hand in his. "We can't do this," she tells him. But there is no strength in her objection.

"I just need to feel you for a minute," he tells her. "All I know is the roughness of prison. Through your skin I can feel your heart. Just let me hold you."

"But someone might walk by a window. What will happen to you if they catch us?" Wendy is weakening to Peter's touch. She knows that guards periodically walk around the visiting room. At any time one can walk past the door. Through the window he could look inside and catch the two in a compromising position.

"I don't care what happens to me," Peter says. "I am in love with you. I need you. We can hear the keys if the guards walk by. They won't catch us. Just let me touch you."

As Peter massages her hand, Wendy closes her eyes. Her head falls back as she lifts his hand to her breast. He leans across the table to kiss her. Despite the risks, Wendy cannot help herself. She stands from the table and crosses the few feet toward the door. She wants to look through the glass to each side to make sure no guards are approaching.

"Baby, don't stand like that," Peter says. "I can't help myself when you're up." Peter stands behind her. He places his hands on her slender waist and kisses her neck. He lifts her skirt over her bottom while unbuttoning his own trousers and pulling himself out. He slides her panties over and enters her from behind while she bends forward, hands against the door, eyes darting from side to side as she watches for approaching officers.

As an attorney, Wendy can visit without restriction. She comes to enjoy several hours with Peter a few times each week. His friends suspect that he is enjoying sexual favors with her. Thousands of eyes are watching in prison. They can smell it. "Why you spending so much time with that hot little attorney?" they ask.

"Come on," Peter says. "You guys know I got a big case. She's helping me consider strategies to reverse it."

"I don't know nothin' about that. A lot of guys in here get fucked by their attorneys. I think you've found a way to turn the tables."

After several months of watching Peter's regular legal visits, guards grow suspicious. Wendy is an attractive young woman, and when each visit ends, both she and Peter leave the room a bit disheveled, perspiring more than is to be expected in an air-conditioned room. Officer Riley begins dropping by a bit too frequently. He once insinuates that he knows something, giving Wendy pause. Riley asks for her card so that he can speak with her away from the prison. He calls her at her office.

Riley tells Wendy that officers suspect that there is more than legal work going on between her and Peter. She feigns outrage at the accusation. They speak for a while longer, and then Officer Riley suggests that they meet for dinner or drinks to discuss the matter. He figures that if she has an interest in a prisoner, she may want to step up to a correctional officer. Wendy declines Riley's crude advance, but it also brings an end to her prison visits, and to the passionate assignations that Peter has come to crave.

As a long-term prisoner, I know that opportunities for sexual intercourse will not open for me until I become eligible for a furlough. As laws currently stand, proclamations about the importance of preserving family values notwithstanding, the BOP does not authorize prisoners for family furloughs until they are within two years of release. Years of prison condition me for abstinence, for this monastic life. What is more troubling is the knowledge that as a consequence of my long-term imprisonment, I also lose the ability to procreate. Other prisoners try to open other options.

Rules not only keep those inside walls and fences from women. They also keep men from bringing children into the world. It is all part of the correctional process.

16

Although many prisoners wish they could open relationships with women, most men inside the fences learn to live without sex. Living with abandonment and the loss of love is much more difficult for these men to accept.

When I began my sanction, I was in love with a woman. The forty-five-year sentence my judge imposed made it impossible for our relationship to continue. We were both young then. We did not share a discipline that would allow us to nurture our relationship despite our physical separation. At that time in my life, losing love hurt more than the lengthy prison term. It was more acute, more immediate, more final. With so many years of confinement ahead, I wondered how I would attract another woman into my life. In time, I grew stronger. But when the loss of love came, prison compounded the pain. I felt it in every cell of my body. It is a stage of confinement through which many prisoners struggle. A man I know named Frank grapples with it now.

Frank is in his seventh year of confinement, and some might think he should be used to living with any type of loss by now. For him, the end of prison is near. He expects to walk outside in twelve more months. Considering how much time Frank has already served, he is a short-timer. He breezed through the first seven years. It was easy for him because he had Sharon, the woman he loves and the mother of his child. Now she is gone, and he is serving the hardest time ever.

Two months ago, Sharon devastated Frank with words no prisoner wants to hear. "I'm sorry," she said over the phone. "I feel that
it's time I move on with my life. I slept with another man last night."

Frank is thirty-two. He was reared in small Montana communities, places where there is little emphasis on grooming young men
for careers. He was kicked out of every school he ever attended for
fighting, selling drugs, or both. Frank decided to quit school alto-
gether at fourteen. He did not complete his freshman year of high
school. Rather than struggle through the structure and demands of
academia, Frank wanted to run free. He supported himself by selling
marijuana, cocaine, and methamphetamines.

The druggie lifestyle suited Frank. Without the accountability issue that comes with employment, he slept late and caroused in the
streets at night. He hit bars, clubs, parties. As the years passed, Frank
knew where to find those who wanted to buy his drugs, and he was
not averse to using them himself.

During those years of his life, every morning began with a snort
of cocaine or a line of meth. He continued to indulge himself
throughout each day with stimulants. After two o'clock, when the
bars began to close and Montana shut down, Frank switched to
smoking pot, a drug that mellowed him out but did not send him to
sleep. "I save the skunk weed for the nighttime, way after midnight.
It soothes me out just to roll the leaves in my fingers, to feel the stick-
iness. I save the best for myself, the Purple Haze or the Thunderfuck
weed. As I load it into a clean glass bong, I see little crystals in the
weed and I know that feeling of lightness is about to come. The pot
evens out my high, gets rid of the twitchings. It is beautiful."

As Frank tells the story, his eyes light up. He relives the experience. Drugs were the center of his life for many years, and when he
was outside, he never allowed himself to stray too far from what he
called home. "Up until the time of my arrest," he says, "I had been
high every day of my life for as long as I could remember. Every day

for at least ten years. I mean blasted. There were times when I crawled out of the shower gripping anything around me for balance. I was vomiting and using the toilet at the same time; it was coming out of both ends of me. I was a mess. Without fail, though, I always found the strength to crawl over to my nightstand or dresser, where I drew out a line of meth as long as a brand-new number-two pencil."

By the time Frank reached his early twenties, he had become one of Montana's premier dealers. He was a sort of neighborhood pharmacy, providing a service almost as if he had a license to sell drugs. Supplying illicit substances to the party people in town filled Frank's pockets with cash. Thousands of dollars came to him in crumpled five-, ten-, and twenty-dollar bills. He spent the money as quickly as it came in.

Gambling is legal in Montana, and not a day passed when Frank was not sitting in front of a keno machine at the Old Chicago Club of Great Falls. He enjoyed a fat cheeseburger and had five hundred dollars in small bills to feed into the machines. "Sometimes I win, sometimes I lose. It doesn't matter. Gambling is just part of my day. I'm like a kid, just about fun." At night Frank moved on to the Little Joker, a popular strip club where Frank's drugs always had a market. "That's where I meet Sharon."

Sharon was then an eighteen-year-old exotic dancer at the Little Joker. Frank saw her dance and was smitten with her beauty. He tipped her high, with fifties and hundreds. "Sometimes I roll a rock of meth into a hundred-dollar bill, then slip it into her G-string. It's just my way of letting her know that I want her."

Frank made inquiries about Sharon. She had moved to Great Falls with her boyfriend from Three Forks, a small town in southern Montana. They were living in the Super 8 Motel. He sold drugs while Sharon performed her nightly striptease.

"The first thing I have to do is get rid of the boyfriend," Frank says. Once he found out the guy was a petty dealer, he says, the rest was easy. Great Falls is small. As one of the main sources of supply for drugs, Frank let all the other dealers know that they could not sell to Sharon's boyfriend. "I'm cutting off anyone who sells to this guy," Frank warned. Before long, the boyfriend's only source of income dried up, and he saw no alternative but to creep back to Three Forks. With a good thing going at the Little Joker, Sharon stayed put.

The high school boyfriend gone, Frank easily moved in on Sharon. He was older than she was, and wired into everything happening in Great Falls. Sharon lusted for the fast, carefree life that Frank lived. The cash. The drugs. The complete freedom from convention. He bought a trailer for her, then outfitted it with furniture and paid a year's rent to the trailer park in advance. "I know the guy who owns it and I pay him off in meth. Sharon loves it. Sometimes we bring in a box of porno tapes and drugs, then just get into each other for three days without stopping. She is a good girl that way, up for anything I want as long as I take care of her. I fall in love."

Frank's arrest came two years after he began living with Sharon. They spent most of that time in a drug-induced blur. He had been traveling west with her from Montana, trying to outrun a series of drug busts that crippled Frank's distribution scheme. Task-force agents rushed into Frank's motel room in Clarkston, Washington. The officers targeted him in an ongoing investigation to purge Montana's drug underground. The arrest led Frank to jail, where his body finally had a chance to recuperate.

"I'm so zoned out when they bust me that I don't even care," he says. "I throw my mat on the floor, pull a blanket over the top of me, and fall into a comalike sleep. I'm out for days. The guards finally wake me for more processing. I am so weak and wrecked that the guards have to hold me up for fingerprinting. My system just isn't used to living without the drugs."

Frank's strength returned to him as he passed those initial weeks with officers shuffling him around various jails, courtrooms, and holding facilities. For the first time in well over a decade he was clean from alcohol and drugs. He had time to sleep, to eat. He agreed to plead guilty to drug charges that required him to serve eight years in prison. Perhaps it would be what he needed to straighten out his life.

Just as Frank was adjusting to the flash that he was about to begin a long stretch in prison, Sharon brought him some tidings in the jail's visiting booth. In order to prevent the passing of contraband, jailers allow inmates to visit only through a glass partition; visitors use a telephone handset to communicate through the glass. When Frank came into his side of the booth and picked up his handset, he saw that Sharon was crying. "I'm pregnant," she said, leaving Frank with a load of responsibility that he was not quite strong enough to handle. He shrugged.

"Man, I'm not ready to have no child," Frank explains. "I'm only twenty-six and on my way to prison, a road I've never traveled. I don't have no money, don't have no plans or no future. And I'm not thinking about nothing else but Frank."

Despite Frank's indifference, Sharon insisted upon bringing their child into the world. Frank's mother offered to help, giving Sharon a place to live and supporting her in every way possible.

Frank was busy trying to cope with confinement, figuring out how to make it through the tough initial months. One thing he came to realize was how lonely life in lockup is. "I'm in way over my head," Frank reminisces about his initial months. "I am overweight, weighing close to two hundred seventy pounds. And I am depressed. I realize how messed up my life was. The guard closes that heavy steel door and I just hear it slam. Then the key and the turning of that large bolt that locks us in. I'm alone. There are four other guys in the cell, and I live right in the middle of the snoring and the farting. But it is the loneliness that wipes me out."

Frank describes how imprisonment trapped and tormented him. He lay on his rack thinking about how he was going to make it through so much time without drugs. The thought of living clean did not appeal to him. A junkie's life was all that he knew. This new phase in prison through which he was about to pass scared him. Others around him were relieving stress by playing spades, pinochle, dominoes, and other table games. Frank wanted no part of it. His head hurt. He didn't want to meet new people. He wanted to get high. He missed the keno games at the Old Chicago Club. He missed the freedom. He missed his trailer. What he began to realize was that he missed his life with Sharon.

Sharon gave birth to their daughter and named the child Jessica. While Frank passed through those months of feeling sorry for himself, Sharon was leaving Jessica with Frank's mother. She lost her weight from the pregnancy and returned to the fast life that she and Frank once shared. It was back to the striptease, the drugs, the drinking, and living without a care in the world. Sharon was only twenty years old, and her life was in a tailspin, completely out of control. Like Frank, she knew that she was lost.

Feeling cut off from the world, totally disconnected from anything meaningful, Frank reached out to Sharon. He wrote a lengthy letter, even though the written word did not come easily to him. He had not read a book prior to his imprisonment, and he certainly had not written anything. While he lay on his rack, Frank poured out his feelings onto the unlined paper. He spelled out the desolation coursing through his veins. He was sick with loneliness. He had been without drugs or alcohol ever since his arrest, over a year, he wrote her. Although Frank still craved the rush, he explained that he knew the criminal lifestyle he had lived for his entire life led to nowhere but misery. Happiness did not come from staying high for twenty-four hours each day, from staying awake, twitching, for ten- and twenty-day stretches. Frank wrote that he wanted to change, to grow into a man who could provide a clean, responsible life for his family. The family he wanted, Frank expressed, was with Sharon and Jessica.

Frank called home several days after he sent Sharon's letter. Surprisingly, he found her there. High on mixtures of cocaine and meth, Sharon had been awake for three days. While Grandma was taking care of Jessica, Sharon did her own thing. But she read Frank's letter. When she heard his voice on the phone, she broke down in tears. "Did you mean all those beautiful words you wrote me in that letter?" she asked while sobbing.

"I mean every word of what I wrote," Frank answered with sincerity. "I mean it and I want it. I know that I need you in my life to help me through this. I can't do anything, not even sleep, without you. I love you."

The lovers made a pact that night on the phone, and they reaffirmed it time and again in months to come with letters they exchanged. Frank and Sharon both vowed to change their lives, to leave drugs and the wild life behind them. Frank expected to serve seven more years, and he gave Sharon his solemn word that he would use every day that he remained in prison to prove himself worthy of the love he wanted to build. He wanted to discipline himself, lose weight and become healthy through diet and exercise. He promised to study, to learn a trade or skill that would help him find employment upon release. Frank began attending church services, grasping the strength that comes through spiritual worship. He sought every crutch that could help him grow into a better man.

Sharon pledged to stop stripping. She promised to abandon the promiscuous life and live as his faithful partner. She was going to wait for Frank. As of that evening's phone call, Sharon assured Frank, she would not touch drugs or alcohol again. She was going to begin living as a mother, a nurturing and loving role model for their child. Rather than live a life that others would look down upon, Sharon said, she wanted to live responsibly, to support Frank through his travails and be a good woman to him, to be strong and welcome him home upon his release. There would be no more day-to-day living. The two of them were going to build a plan to carry them through, and they both expected to emerge from the prison experience as a stronger couple.

With Sharon's love in Frank's life, the prison term became much easier for him to bear. He had a partner in her, a reason to live. Because of her love and devotion, Frank could stand the lockdowns, the strip searches, the deprivations he had to endure. There was no sex between them, but that did not matter. To Frank, their love was something deeper, something more meaningful. He stayed away from the drug element in prison. He no longer craved getting high. He clung to Sharon's love and the hope that came with it. It was his inspiration, his reason for rising each morning. Sharon and Jessica meant everything in the world to him, and he was determined to strengthen his relationship. True to his word, Frank became a model of discipline.

Over the coming years he embraced a pattern of living that led to good health. He stands six feet tall, but had ballooned to obesity during the unstructured haze of self-indulgence and debauchery that had been his life before confinement. Frank never exercised. He regularly passed seven to ten days without sleep. He says that on one occasion he cranked himself up with methamphetamines to keep him awake for twenty-eight days. The drugs did not stop Frank from binge eating, though, as his corpulence proved.

Motivated by Sharon's love, Frank became an exercise fanatic in prison. Over the years that followed his transfer to prison, Frank dropped 80 pounds of fat. Through a disciplined diet coupled with three hours of daily exercise, Frank began to fulfill his promises to Sharon. He combined weight training, bar work, and running to sculpt his physique from a blubbery mass of flesh into 190 pounds of muscle. He looked like a statue, as if a thin layer of skin covered twisted steel. Frank mastered exercise and nutrition books, then advised others on steps they could take to enhance their health and sense of self. Frank attended Bible study and religious services regularly. He studied for and passed his high school equivalency exam. With Sharon to inspire him, Frank felt as though his life had meaning, as if he were on his way to becoming a man of substance.

Sharon, too, behaved in ways that demonstrated her commitment to the relationship. She assured Frank that she was carrying the burden of imprisonment with him. She did so willingly, she said, as a testament of her love for him. Sharon lived with Frank's mother, stayed consistent in nurturing and educating Jessica. She was home each night, and during the day she worked at the various jobs her limited skills allowed. Most important, Sharon abstained from both drug use and the druggie lifestyle.

The cleaner path allowed Sharon and Frank to establish a savings plan. The plan made evident a tangible, measurable progress that would help them weather the storm of confinement and the troubles that would follow Frank's release. With years of consistency, Frank came to rely upon the fantasy that the stable, productive life they were living would continue.

Sharon skimped and saved in order to accumulate the funds necessary for her to make the long trip to visit Frank. He served his time in Minnesota and Colorado prisons, more than a thousand miles away from the small Idaho town where Sharon lived with Frank's mother. She sent him provocative pictures to comfort him and remind him of her beauty. The letters came with perfume and lipstick kisses, flowed with prose promising her fidelity and commitment to their plans. She promised her love, and that was the air that Frank breathed. After so many years of Sharon's steady presence, Frank was happy, eager to move forward, and secure in the relationship that they had built. As he came into his final year of imprisonment, he had reason to believe the love would last forever. He was wrong.

The signs began to show themselves late in the spring of Frank's sixth year. He called home on schedule and his mother told Frank that

Sharon had left the night before and had not come home to sleep. She had not been drinking for the previous five years; now Sharon told Frank that she had made some friends with whom she liked to party and get high. When she drank too much to drive, she said, she slept over. Despite the change, Sharon continued to pledge her fidelity, her love, her commitment to the relationship.

"But you're killing me in here," Frank pleaded. "I'm feeling that we're going sideways, or backward. Just tell me if there is something going on."

"There's nothing going on. I love you," Sharon replied.

But the all-nighters continued. Finally, she told him. Sharon had met another man and had been sleeping with him. The news crushed Frank. For years he had depended on Sharon. He had allowed himself to build his hopes and dreams around the possibility of a life with her, his stripper girl whom he thought he had turned into a woman. Her betrayal sent Frank over the edge, dropping him into a depression from which he has not been able to emerge.

"I call her numerous times, humiliating myself with pathetic pleas for her to stay. I don't care. I tell her that I will overlook an indiscretion if only she will stay with me. She has taken Jessica and moved out of my mother's house. Suddenly, I feel alone in the world, craving the woman I love like I used to crave the drugs I was addicted to."

Frank changes his routine in prison. He begins running twelve- and sixteen-mile distances, lifting heavier and heavier weights. He exercises until he breaks himself with pain. He needs to bust through the heartache somehow. No matter what he tries, the memories keep him sucked in. Each night he lies on his bunk, staring at the steel springs on the bunk above him, wondering about the life she is living. He wants to hate her. But he can't stop wanting her.

Months pass after Sharon moves out of his mother's house. There remains so much for Frank to grow through, so many feelings for him to shed. He hasn't been able to let go. He realizes that although he is in the final stretch of his imprisonment, the loss of love has knocked the life out of him.

Frank begins keeping a journal to cope. The lines he writes alternate between love and rage, pleadings for her to return and invectives that send her to hell. "I wrote her a three-page letter today," he tells me. "Three pages describing how I feel. I tore it up after writing her. It's an exercise of will I use, forcing myself not to communicate with her."

Frank had to send his photo album home because he could not stop himself from looking over the pictures. "I can't even watch television anymore," he says. "Every time a slender blonde with big breasts comes on, I want to swing at the TV. I'm sick."

Like tens of thousands of prisoners, Frank is sick with unrequited love.

17

When I advanced to within eighteen years of my scheduled release, administrators transferred me again. This time I walked inside the fences that enclose the low-security prison south of New York City. It is still thousands of miles away from my family in Seattle, but I'm used to being locked away far from home. It is not my location that concerns me. I cannot control where this system locks me up. My focus is on initiating strategies to ensure that I do not leave prison weak, afraid of the obstacles that are certain to follow a quarter century of confinement. The more stories I hear from long-term prisoners, the more projects I realize I have to complete before my term expires.

During those earlier years of my sentence, while progressing through academic courses, I made a habit of keeping extensive journals and notes. As a prisoner, my survival depends on knowing everything going on around me. I live like a submarine, progressing beneath rough surfaces with my periscope up to maneuver my way around the constant calamity and confusion. The transfer to low security results in a reduction of tension equal to what I felt when I left walls behind and walked inside medium-security fences. My progress inside is certain to continue.

Instead of locking the men in cells, guards assign those in low security to open cubicles or large dormitories. The prison confines nearly five thousand men in three separate compounds. Officers direct me to begin my time there in a twelve-man room. The arrangement bothers the strangers around me. I welcome it. Unlike them, I know worse. Now I feel fewer restrictions, more freedom to walk around, less open hostility. The time is at hand to reflect on what so many years of living inside higher security has taught me.

With the drop in my security scoring, I am around a less volatile group of men. There is talk about extortion attempts, press games, and gang activities in the low, but it is more hype than reality. People in prison want others to perceive them as being bad. In higher security the threats are real and constant. Crip Tank and Lion, Choo Choo and KooKoo and Lunatic and Speedy, do not hesitate. Inside lower-security fences the men cheer for the villains on television and talk about how bad they are; few are packing knives and pipes to put in work. It's like a decompression mode. More people are coming to the end of their term. They have an eye on release, or on a transfer to a minimum-security camp. Their willingness to pay lip service at least to the values of society makes it easier to avoid conflict.

From my experience of living among and talking with thousands of prisoners over the years, I knew that during the eighteen remaining years I had to serve I needed to focus on release. I had to build resources that would help ease my transition into society. I could not allow myself to leave prison like Prince or Fox or others who have so little to draw upon. I am not like Shamrock, without a care in the world and millions collecting interest in an offshore account. The onus was on me; I had to make the transition to low security a positive step in my life, leading to greater independence. In the less tense environment I would master the adversity of my life as a prisoner. My hopes were that low security administrators would prove more receptive to my continuing education efforts.

"Good morning, Mr. Creackle," I say upon introducing myself to the supervisor of education in my new institution. "I've just transferred here, but I've been locked up since 1987. My record shows that opportunities to educate myself carry me through. In previous institutions I earned an undergraduate and a graduate degree. I am hoping you will authorize me to continue studies here."

The educator doesn't look away from his computer screen. "We offer GED, English as a second language, and a few courses from a local community college. See Ms. Barker to sign up in the next room."

"I'm interested in continuing coursework I've begun at the University of Connecticut. It is a doctoral program. The university has made exceptions to its residency requirement for me to work through independent study. I have already completed part of the coursework and would like to resume my work here."

"My staff doesn't have time to oversee special projects. You'll have to work with the programs we have available here."

"You don't have anything that I haven't completed. I've been in for ten years already. All I need is permission to receive books from the university library. The rest of my work is research and writing."

Creakle still refuses to look up from his screen. "We've got plenty of books in the library downstairs. The rest you can get through appropriate channels, either through interlibrary loans or directly from the publisher."

The educator shows no interest in my studies or the specialized types of research books I need to progress through the work. I try again. "It's not likely that the local library will carry the scholarly books I need to further my work. You certainly do not have them in your collection of westerns and romance novels. In order for me to complete my coursework I must commit to deadlines and will need access to the university. The librarian will send the books to me, and I will pay the postage to return them. I only need permission from you to receive books from the library."

"We don't make those kinds of exceptions here. The university could be sending drugs inside those books for all I know. The rules exist for a reason. If you're so interested in working with libraries and universities, you shouldn't have come to prison."

Although I welcomed the privilege of living with less tension from other prisoners around me, I soon realize that the transfer to low security was not going to open my access to educational opportunities. The news frustrated me, but it was not the first time the system would block my progress. I ordered a book on independent-study programs and learned of a few schools in California. Some of them make law school available through independent study. The American Bar Association does not accredit the programs, but that did not trouble me. I had other plans and discussed them with my mentor, Dr. R. Bruce McPherson, with whom I had been corresponding and visiting since my time inside Atlanta's walls.

"What do you mean you want to enroll in one of those independent study schools?" Bruce asks. "You've worked hard to earn degrees from respectable universities. Nobody will recognize a degree from a law school that the ABA doesn't approve. That's why we have accreditations. As Shakespeare would say, those types of schools are like two grains of wheat hidden in two bushels of chaff; you work all day to find them, and when you have them they're not worth the search."

"But I can't focus on degrees anymore," I explain. "The prison system isn't going to make the arrangements I need to advance with any more university studies. I can't sit here and vegetate for eighteen more years. I need to look at where I am and figure out a way to make this time productive. At the California school I do not need access to the research library. I can buy my own books and use the prison's law library to supplement my needs."

"And how is studying through one of those diploma mills going to help you? That law degree won't be worth a thing on your résumé when you get out of here."

"I'm not thinking about my résumé, Bruce. I'm thinking about something I can be useful at. And this is my world inside these fences. The degree itself might not be worth anything. But if I study through the books that come with the course, I can learn how to argue the law.

Although I'd like to work as a lawyer in your world, I can't. What I can do is become a skilled jailhouse lawyer in mine. There is no shortage of guys who want help with their appeals or preparations for relief."

"How are you going to file appeals or papers with the courts on behalf of other prisoners if you're not a member of the bar?"

"I won't file the papers," I explain. "I will help the other prisoners prepare the necessary paperwork. I'll do the research, the writing, and the typing. They will file the papers, but they'll compensate me for my time researching, writing, and typing."

"Won't that violate the prison rules?" Bruce asks. "What about this commitment you've always told me about not breaking any prison rules? You can't tell me the system approves of your charging other prisoners money to perform a service for them."

"I have a new commitment. I'll still exercise discipline to keep a clean record. But my first priority is to make sure that I leave prison with the strength and resources necessary to succeed. The prison system doesn't care about me. It blocks every type of progress that I strive to make. This so-called system of corrections breeds failure. Look around. It conditions anyone who serves ten or fifteen years to fail. I am living inside these fences for twenty-six years. I need to build resources so that when I leave I can start my life independently. Otherwise I will face a new kind of prison. The prison of dependence and vulnerability."

Bruce contemplates my argument. I sense him coming around to supporting me. "How much do you suppose you can earn through such a venture?" he asks me.

"I can finish the course in three years," I explain. "With that experience, together with my knowledge of the system, I can provide a valuable service. It is whatever the market will bear. But I intend to do good things for the men around me while I do well for myself."

"How are the men going to pay you? Won't the staff become suspicious if your account starts receiving money from different sources?"

"I won't. Nobody is going to pay me anything. Not directly. If I help a guy with his case I'll tell him that he doesn't owe me. That way I avoid breaking any prison rules. But I will provide him with an address for one of my family members. The prisoner will have someone else send a check. My family will hold these funds for me to help my transition when I get out. If I can save ten thousand a year for fifteen years, I'll be in a lot better position when I leave prison than others who walk out of these fences with nothing."

As I proceed with my plan, I see it coming together well. In addition to studying through first-year law, I am helping the men around me. "I can't undo the past," I tell those coming to seek my assistance. "Every day that passes after law enforcement targets a man for prosecution, he falls deeper into the pit. It's almost impossible to find relief when litigating from prison. Fewer than one out of ten find anything but frustration once they jump on the roller-coaster ride seeking judicial relief. I'll help you if you want, but you've got to know the odds are against you." Most of the men want hope and proceed through litigation for therapeutic reasons. They have to create a stir in the courts to lift their moods.

I'm carrying my food tray to the dishwasher when Lieutenant Prickster stops me in the chow hall. "How's the law business, Santos?"

His question surprises me, as I haven't had any previous interaction with the lieutenant. "You mean law school," I say. "I'm making great progress. I just finished first year."

"Let me share something with you, convict," the lieutenant says. "I know what you're doing. You're charging guys who haven't got a snowball's chance in hell to do legal work. I'm gonna catch you. When I do I'm gonna lock you up and ship you to a higher-security institution."

"Thanks for sharing, Lieutenant. Now let me share something with you. I'm sleeping on the top bunk and I'm three thousand miles away from home. Anywhere you send me puts me closer to my family. Do me the favor because I've been trying to move closer to home since 1987. I'm preparing myself for the future. And I'm quite sure guys in high security need legal work too, your legal opinions notwithstanding."

"You've got a smart mouth," he tells me. "I wonder how smart it's going to be if I lock you up."

"I haven't raised my voice or said anything disrespectful or inappropriate. You know I've been in a long time and I've never had a problem with staff. I'm living inside, trying to prepare myself to live outside. You've got problems with knives, drugs, and gangs. Why are you looking to create a problem for me?"

"I'm not picking on you," the lieutenant says. "I'm giving you a heads-up. I know what you're doing, and I won't let you run a business in my institution."

With the work I am doing for the men inside, my access to capital is increasing. Family members receive checks from others for anywhere between several hundred and a few thousand dollars. Through my family I am paying taxes. I feel proud of the work I am doing, as if I am making a tangible contribution to the world. I am carrying my own weight and deriving a sense of worth, of satisfaction from being something more than a prisoner, even if it's only in my mind.

"Captain," I call out to the head of security forces inside the fences as he walks toward the chow hall. "I need to ask you a question."

"What is it, Santos?"

"You know I'm serving a long sentence. I want to invest some of the money I have in the stock market. Before I do, I want to know whether my doing so would violate any rules of the institution."

"You can't trade stocks from my institution," the captain says.

"What do you suggest I do? You're not going to deny my request to prepare for a law-abiding life upon release, are you?"

"Buy a mutual fund. Give power of attorney to someone else. I don't care what you do. But you can't buy or sell from here."

"So if I give power of attorney to my sister, will it be okay if I tell her over the phone how I want her to invest the money?"

"As long as you're not buying or selling securities yourself, there's no problem," the captain tells me.

In addition to my academic work, I had been studying business publications for several years. In the late 1990s the Internet was making promises to revolutionize the world with a new economy. I was reading about it. It fascinated me even though I could not access a keyboard. I wanted to participate.

The only avenue available to me was as an owner. With the information I received from the captain, I instructed my sister to open a brokerage account. "I want you to use all the money you receive to purchase positions in Yahoo! and America Online. Let's start building a portfolio of stocks. That way my money can grow while I serve out my sentence."

"I'll do whatever you want," my sister said. "Just tell me how to do it."

As time passed, the market bubble propelled the equity in my account like rocket fuel. I quit spending my time on legal work and focused exclusively on market research. I instructed my sister to pledge the equity to buy more stock through margin loans from the broker, increasing exposure to the volatility that came with the Internet stocks in the account. The more stock I instructed my sister to buy, the higher the equity would grow when the market went up. The positions started to increase in value by thousands per day. Then tens of thousands per day. In 1999 I filed a tax return from prison declaring over $150,000 in income; the account began with a $2,000 deposit. By moving in and out of high-flying stocks, I directed my sister in trades with a cumulative valuation of over $20 million. The experience taught me that although borrowing money through margin can accelerate growth, when market forces turn the other way, the equity deflates more quickly than a balloon meeting a pin prick.

The inmate telephone system records every call that prisoners make. Correctional officers monitor the telephone calls of men who they suspect are violating prison rules. As Officer Schreeve listened to the conversations I had with my sister, and especially when he heard of the dollar amounts we discussed, he became certain that I was breaking rules. In his eyes, prisoners should not advance themselves while serving time. He ordered me to the lieutenant's office so he could issue a disciplinary infraction.

"I'm charging you with a violation of the disciplinary code. On March 29 you used the inmate telephone system to instruct your sister to purchase stocks. That is a violation of Code 406. Unauthorized use of the telephone. Your call also violates Code 408, which prohibits an inmate from conducting a business. How do you plead?"

"Are you suggesting that it's against the law for me to recommend stocks my sister should buy or sell?" I ask.

"Don't play games with me, Santos. You know the rules."

"Yes. I do know the rules. It surprises me that you would call me down here to bother me with this nonsense. I didn't violate any rule by calling my sister. Her number is approved on my list, so it's not an unauthorized call. I can give her my opinion on what I think she should do."

"We provide those telephones for inmates to maintain family ties. Not for inmates to run businesses."

"What kind of business are you suggesting that I run?"

"When you buy or sell stock you're running a business."

"First of all, Officer Schreeve, I didn't buy or sell anything. Your report says that I called my sister and instructed her to buy stock. If you play back the tape you'll hear that I told her I like Microsoft."

"And from the rest of what you said I can infer you were telling her to buy the stock."

"According to your inference, does that mean I am running Microsoft? Would I be running the Mariners if I told my sister I liked the team?"

"We consider buying and selling stock running a business. It is an unauthorized use of the telephone. How do you think taxpayers would like it if we allowed prisoners to earn money from prison?"

"I am a taxpayer, Officer Schreeve. My thoughts are that if prisoners are able to prepare themselves for the obstacles that follow confinement, fewer prisoners would return to confinement following the completion of their sentences. That might not be good for your job security, but it would serve the interest of taxpayers. Don't you think?"

"How do you plead to these charges?" he asks.

"Why don't you hold off on those charges, Officer Schreeve. Talk with the captain. I did. He told me that as long as I don't buy or sell stocks directly, I am not in violation of any prison rule. In fact, it is the captain who instructed me to give power of attorney to a family member."

Officer Schreeve checked with the captain. Upon doing so, he was forced to expunge the infraction he wanted to impose. A few weeks later the warden posted a memorandum advising inmates not to discuss stock transactions or any form of business over the telephone. Those who did would face penalties that included loss of telephone and visiting privileges for one year. I spoke with the captain and he instructed me to heed the warning of the memorandum.

With the correctional system closing my access to stock trades, as it had with my access to academia, I was forced to switch focus again. I still had thirteen years remaining to serve and considered a return to legal work. As my investment success grew I lost interest in the law. It is difficult to explain to an individual that no relief is coming, that he must develop a strategy to carry him through two more decades of confinement. I searched for something more fulfilling and in doing so I committed to developing my writing skills. By refining my craft, I could work to help others understand the American prison system, the people it holds, and strategies for growing through it. Using the Internet, I began building a forum that could help me expand my reach outside of prison boundaries.

Knowing the viper pit in which I lived, I first wrote to my unit team. I asked whether my writing articles for a Web site would violate any prison rules. After checking with the regional counsel, my case manager provided written verification telling me that as long as I did not incite others to rebel, writing was within my constitutional rights. Writing, I realized, would bring me an activity I could pursue that correctional officers could not stop. It would take me out of these communities with the promise of connecting to millions in the real world. Good things began to happen for me as I refined the use of the pen.

Carole, a friend from high school, surprised me with a letter. I had known Carole since the fifth grade, but our paths separated after we graduated from high school. We had no communication until her letter. With our correspondence Carole became supportive of my strategies to grow through the adversity of confinement. She opened www.MichaelSantos.net, a Web site to publish my work. Our constant interaction enabled us to discuss and share the visions and values by which we lived our lives. As Carole brought the Web site together, ours grew from a working relationship to romance. She lived in Oregon, too far away from the prison where I was held to visit regularly. Our courtship was like those of times past, where a couple comes to know each other's mind and soul through the written word before they share a single kiss. It inspired love, and that love made me want to reach higher, to become more productive, to prove myself worthy.

Over three centuries ago, George Herbert wrote that for want of a nail the shoe is lost. For want of a shoe the horse is lost. For want of a horse the rider is lost. It is a warning that we must pay attention to all details in order to avoid disaster. That prudent message, I realized, is not only a warning. It is a recipe that can lead to success. It is because I made a commitment to educate myself during my first decade of confinement that I was able to build a network of support.

That network made it possible to overcome the obstacles wrought by confinement and to earn my degrees. The knowledge that came from my studies opened opportunities for me to earn an income. The skills I developed in seeking to earn an income gave me the resources to publish my thoughts for communities outside of prison fences. Those writings were the seeds from which my relationship with Carole grew. I am in love with her. Despite the decade of imprisonment I have remaining, she is in love with me. She joined her life to mine by moving to be near me and becoming my wife. We married in the prison visiting room on June 24, 2003.

With a loving partner in my life I am able to transcend these boundaries that will hold me until 2013. "You may as well tattoo the word 'idiot' in large uppercase letters across your forehead," Lieutenant Marts told me on the day of my wedding.

"I guess holy matrimony didn't work out so well for you," I responded.

"That's right. And I didn't marry from prison."

"I appreciate your observation, but I think I'll look outside the corrections profession for guidance as to how I should pursue happiness in life."

Carole's love and the commitment we make to each other open additional paths to freedom for me. Not only do we establish clearly identifiable goals and plans that enable us to nurture our relationship now while planning for our future. She also acts as an intermediary between the publishing world and me. Although corrections professionals make all the recreation equipment in the world available, they prohibit inmate access to word processing, e-mail, or the writing tools of the twenty-first century. I write in longhand, but through my partnership in marriage, Carole transcribes my work for publication. Because of the love I share and build with my wife, I have a life inside prison boundaries.

Corrections professionals continue to make efforts to block my work. They do not want an inmate describing life inside these closed communities. Professors in universities from across the United States use my work to help students of corrections, criminology, sociology, and social work understand the life of prisoners. Those who work in corrections, however, tell me that my work interferes with the security of the institution. They intercept my mail and hold it for weeks at a time. They deny journalists access to interview me. They refuse visitation privileges to those who may help further my writing or learning opportunities when we do not have a relationship that preceded my confinement.

"We don't want you writing," my unit manager tells me. "That's why we place you on mail-monitoring status. As long as you write books about the prison system you will never have regular mailing privileges. Your work interferes with the security of the institution."

"But how can my describing life inside these fences, telling taxpayers what happens inside these institutions from a long-term prisoner's perspective, interfere with security? This is still the United States. I am striving to give Americans a look inside. And at the same time I am working to prepare for my future. What is wrong with that?"

"We don't care about your future," she tells me. "You're an inmate, and all inmates are the same."

"Are we all the same like all staff members are the same?" I ask.

"Get out of my office," she orders.

It is in this restrictive environment that I work hard to grow. It is in this environment that so many other prisoners choose paths differently than I. I have no anger or resentment toward it. Instead, I invest my energy in striving to understand it. In doing so I hope to help other prisoners join me in navigating through the obstacles of America's system of corrections toward a positive, law-abiding, productive life outside.

18

In August 2003 I advanced to within ten years of my release date. With more than sixteen years of imprisonment behind me, I began to feel as though I was much closer to release. As odd as it may sound to others, I felt wonderful knowing that I had only nine more summers to pass inside. Soon thereafter administrators dropped my security level again and initiated a transfer to minimum security. I learned that I was finally on my way to camp.

For those who live inside of fences over prolonged periods of time, a transfer to camp comes as a welcome relief. News of the transfer lifted my spirits to a level unknown since my confinement began. In higher security, camps have a mythical aura. Those inside associate violence and tension, hatred and animosity, with prison. Camps are said to be without those dimensions, and so they hardly seem like prisons at all to men who live through worse. The news that I could expect to spend the rest of my time in such an environment thrilled me.

Any camp brings a precipitate drop in tension from life inside fences. Whereas a high percentage of prisoners inside fences have twenty or more years remaining to serve, no one in minimum security has more than a decade of confinement before release, and the majority of men have much less time to serve. With release pending, prisoners tend to be on better behavior in the hopes of finding the earliest release date possible. I know the culture is different. Men in camps think of going home. They are not thinking of gangs, shot callers, weapons, or violence at all. In fact, there may be more volatility in a corporate office park than in a minimum-security camp. I breathed easier just knowing that I was heading to a minimum-security prison camp.

In preparation for the necessary admittance procedures, guards unchained me. They removed my manacles and leg irons. I allowed myself to hope that no one would ever bind me in steel again. After fingerprinting, a new mug shot, and other processing, guards instructed me to walk from the secured receiving area to the open camp. It was real. For the first time in more than sixteen years I walked unshackled outside of prison fences. An amazing feeling came over me. I knew I was making significant progress on my journey home.

Like low-security prisons, camps hold men in dormitories and cubicles. But there are no controlled movements, no double fences surrounding them, no coils of glistening razor wire. Depending on the time of day, there are between three and twenty staff members who oversee more than five hundred men in the camp. The entire atmosphere is more friendly, less confrontational. That is how I see it. Those without experience in low-, medium-, or high-security prisons have different perspectives.

David, for example, has a successful career as a real estate developer and financier in the real world. He is a typical white-collar offender. Prior to receiving this forty-eight-month sentence for fraud-related convictions, David had no experience with the criminal justice system. "I've dealt with lawyers and courts for the past thirty years. Litigation is part of my business. I've just never been involved with criminal matters before this problem," he says.

David is the father of three adult boys. In his second marriage, he enjoys a wonderful relationship with his wife. His family and background are in Chicago, but like hundreds of other white-collar offenders, David serves time with me inside the boundaries of the federal prison camp.

Inside secure prisons, men with gangster values like Crip Tank, Lion, KooKoo, and other gangsters define the culture. It is a primitive, tribal culture driven by immediate gratification. Even in low security, where prisoners who are within twenty years of their release dates serve time, there are predatory offenders. With each drop in security level, a layer of tension lifts.

With the majority of men coming from traditional middle-class American backgrounds, there are no weapons in the camp. A higher percentage of the population understands and embraces protocol for appropriate social behavior. People welcome each other with good-morning greetings. They say "Excuse me." They smile. Language is less vulgar, if only slightly.

Of course it's still prison. The difficulties of being separated from family and community remain. Those in camps live the open plan with strangers. They share tight quarters and bathrooms with others they have never met. There is no privacy. With few exceptions, camp prisoners handle differences or disagreements among themselves in the same way as those in the broader society.

"After a few days," David says, "a guy calms down and gets used to the other men in the camp. It's not the other prisoners who are a problem. It's the crazy rules. It's the guards trying to punish us. That is what makes time in here hard."

Like many prisoners who begin their term in minimum security, David did not arrive through the prison transit system. There were no chains, handcuffs, or leg irons. His judge issued a time for David to report. His wife accompanied him for the drive. They passed a few days in a local resort, enjoying dinners and acclimating themselves to the environment where David would meet the ends of justice by serving his time. At the appropriate moment, David surrendered himself to camp authorities.

"Like anyone else, I suppose, when I first walked in I was overly cautious." David explains his first impressions of the camp. "I didn't know anything about living in prison. I develop real estate. But it didn't take long for me to understand that in here I'm nothing more than a criminal." David objects to the constant and continuous attention to security. Even in camp there is a measure of the us-versus-them culture that's rampant in the higher-security institutions.

"The staff members don't know me and don't care who or what I am in the real world," David says. "They don't care about my education or my businesses. These guards processing me in don't have the people skills to work as a janitor in one of my companies. Over the course of my career I have employed over a thousand people. Not one of them would last a day if I caught him treating others in the demeaning way that staff members here treat us. Everything is about degrading a man, taking away his dignity, breaking his spirit."

Living in prison is the only life I know. I have passed my entire adult life as a man locked inside. After so long, the treatment that David describes is normal to me. I no longer even recognize it. I expect that I must ask a guard permission to urinate. If he is busy talking on the phone or playing with his computer, I expect that I must wait until he finishes before I can use the bathroom. I expect that an officer may order me to strip naked for a search, may kick my bed while I am asleep, and may reprimand me as if I were a naughty child if I do not tuck my T-shirt into my pants. For David, such experiences are not normal.

"The problem with you," he tells me, "is that you don't know any better. It's a travesty of justice that our system locks you up for twenty-six years. But this isn't the real world. It is a disgrace to our country that we treat people like this. I would never have believed it unless I came in here myself. I still can't believe how long you've been inside. I can't even imagine getting through this four-year sentence I've got. You have more than nine to go and don't seem to care. This place is ruining you. It's ruining me."

As I listen to David and others describe how little I know about the world, I feel as though I am one of those people Plato describes in his famous passage from *The Republic,* the allegory of the cave. I have seen so much of prison that any other type of life is inconceivable. When I try to explain to some white-collar offenders how good we have it, mentioning my former associates Crip Tank and the other violent, hopeless men I have known, they look at me as if I were crazy.

I ask David to describe what troubles him most. "It's everything. I never know what's going to happen. Last week Frank was talking to his wife on the phone. She told him that she had sent a hundred dollars to Frank's cellmate. They are Christians. The kid doesn't have any money and Frank wants to help him out. After he hangs up, a lieutenant locks Frank in the hole. The guards put him in handcuffs and take him to the bucket. He serves a week over there. What's that about? When he comes back, he learns that the guards have taken away his phone and visiting privileges for six months. What kind of crap is that?"

David is talking about a sanction Frank received for violating rules. Public statements about the importance of maintaining family and community ties notwithstanding, prison administrators are quick to suspend privileges for the slightest violation of rules. One rule prohibits inmates from giving anything of value to another inmate. Because Frank's wife sent money to another inmate, administrators punish him. Frank no longer has access to telephone or visiting privileges; his children do not understand.

"Ever since that happened," David says, "the phone gives me anxiety. It is my lifeline, my connection. Yet I never know when someone to whom I'm talking is going to say something that can land me in the hole. Apparently there is a rule against discussing business on the phone. I don't get it. How am I supposed to have a conversation without talking business? I am a businessman. It's like asking me not to speak English."

David says that it is not the hole so much that concerns him. "It sickens me to think that these people can block me from communicating with family members for six months. I've heard that some lose privileges for years. It's bad enough being here. To think that these people might arbitrarily stop me from reaching out makes me feel as if I must walk on eggshells. I don't know whether I am going to make it through this sentence."

David is convinced that judges send offenders to prison as a form of punishment, not for guards to punish men further. Many who make their careers in corrections see their function differently. Years of exposure to the explosive volatility that exists inside higher-security prisons condition those who work inside to see all prisoners the same. I am used to the disparagement. The time conditions me to expect it like I expect winter to follow autumn. David and many others whose only exposure to prison is the camp find it harder to adjust. It is a lesson in humility.

"Another thing I don't like are these ridiculous classes these people expect me to attend," David complains. "I hold a master's degree in business from a top university. The revenues of companies I built exceed forty million per year. I have more employees than I can count. Yet I'm supposed to participate in these release-preparation classes to learn how to balance a checkbook, to learn how to participate in a job interview. It's absurd. Some people need it. I do not. What's worse is that the morons who teach the classes are completely incompetent."

Besides the classes correctional administrators require those approaching release to attend, guards make it difficult for David to adjust because they frequently punish everyone in the camp for the misbehavior of a few. They close television rooms down for weeks at a time if guards discover contraband. They prohibit access to recreation when someone runs to chow.

"I don't smoke," David says. "I can't stand smoke. Yet when guards find matches or cigarette butts thrown in nonsmoking areas, everyone in the camp pays. Last week, after I finished six hours on my job, the guards ordered me to join everyone else in the camp as they walked around picking up these matches and cigarettes. Guards are the only people I see throwing cigarettes on the ground. They walk across lawns and then order inmates to rake up behind them. It's as if we're their slaves, feeding their sense of power."

David's job assignment is to work as an orderly for Ms. Hefty in the education department. He begins his workday immediately following the early-morning census count at five. His responsibilities include clearing and folding tables to make way for his sweeping, mopping, and buffing. He must maintain the floors, keeping them shined to a high gloss. Ordinarily, each morning requires a solid two hours of work, with another two hours throughout the day to maintain the room. On the occasion of outside inspections, David's job requires more than labor.

"We've got the American Correctional Association coming through for an inspection next month," Ms. Hefty tells David. "This room had better be immaculate. I don't want nothing going wrong in my department."

"I'll do my best, Ms. Hefty. When would you like me to strip and wax the floors?"

"The inspectors will be here during the week of the twenty-third. Do the floors on the Thursday and Friday before they arrive. If anything goes wrong," she warns him, "it'll be on you."

David tells me that he doesn't mind working for the institution. But he doesn't like being treated as if he is less than a man. He especially hates the bureaucratic red tape he must negotiate in order to complete his job. Ms. Hefty does not give him the supplies he needs to do the job well, so David uses his own resources to purchase mop heads and scrub pads from other orderlies. Besides that, other teachers in the prison use the room which Ms. Hefty requires him to clean and maintain. Yet Ms. Hefty does not coordinate the cleaning schedule with anyone else.

While making inspection rounds early one morning, Mr. Dicker, an associate warden, sees David working alone in the room. As directed, David applies stripper to remove the wax from the classroom floor. "What the hell is going on here?" Dicker demands. "Why haven't you stripped and waxed this floor yet? I've got an important inspection next week." The associate warden doesn't bother to introduce himself to David, makes no effort to acknowledge their common humanity.

"I'm just doing what I'm told, sir. Ms. Hefty instructed me to begin the job today. I've started, but I'm a little concerned because Ms. Castro's class is scheduled to begin at nine. In order to finish this job right I'm going to need all of today and tomorrow."

"Forget about Ms. Castro's class," Mr. Dicker says. "This job is way past due. You better get it done."

David continues his work. "I'm angry with what I'm doing," he tells me. "This guy Dicker talks to me like I'm some kind of servant. First of all, I'm not the one who sets these schedules. If Ms. Hefty tells me to do the job on this day, what am I supposed to do? Argue? Tell her she's wrong? Forget it. To her I'm not even a man. As far as these people are concerned I'm a wet rag for them to use for cleaning up a mess. I'm something to use and throw away. Dicker knows this. Yet he talks to me as if I'm supposed to coordinate the whole thing."

"What in the world are you doing to my floor?" Ms. Castro screams at David as he is running a stripping machine. The floor is covered with a soupy layer of solvents to remove the wax. "In one hour I'm teaching a class in this room."

"Ms. Hefty told me to strip the floors in here today. I'm supposed to have it done by tomorrow so that I can wax it."

"I don't care what Ms. Hefty told you. Clean this mess up. I've got to teach my class and I can't do it in this mess."

"But Mr. Dicker was just here too. He told me to finish the job."

"I don't care who told you what," Ms. Castro tells David. "This is my classroom today, and I'm going to use it. Now mop all this up and dry the floor. Have it ready by nine."

The staff mix-up puts David in a bind. Mr. Dicker is angry because he believes the floor should have been finished earlier. Ms. Hefty orders and expects David to complete the job according to her schedule. Ms. Castro wants to interrupt David's work so that she can teach a two-hour class on family values that certain prisoners are compelled to attend. If he doesn't successfully negotiate this situation, he faces much more than a dock in pay or even being relieved of his duties: the perceived transgression could result in the administration taking away the last vestiges of dignity and personal responsibility he has by throwing him in the SHU. These are the consequences David will suffer for failing to complete a floor-mopping assignment that has been doomed by administrative miscommunication. And the end result could be a longer stay inside.

"I can't win," David tells me. "No matter what I do somebody is going to come gunning for me. My biggest threat is Ms. Hefty, since she is my direct supervisor. If I don't complete the job she'll fire me and throw me in the hole. That results in a loss of good time and a longer stay in this hell. I know there is nothing more important in this place than shiny floors. Neither the staff nor any of the inspectors are going to care whether anyone is educating himself in here. All that matters is the facade. Can you imagine Ms. Castro teaching a class on values? A piranha has more compassion and understanding than that woman. Teaching is the last thing she wants that room for. She just needs to flex her power."

David walks over to Ms. Hefty's office. Through the window he sees her lounging in the high-back chair. She sucks on a cluster of her disheveled hair while gazing at the office ceiling. David is reluctant to knock. He knows the patronizing ridicule he will meet. He has no choice. Clearly disturbed at David's interruption of her daydream, Ms. Hefty waves him in after making him wait a few minutes. "What is it now?" she asks.

"I just want to clarify that I'm supposed to finish this floor job by tomorrow."

"Didn't I clearly tell you to do it today and tomorrow?" Ms. Hefty speaks to David as if he should complete the job without annoying her.

"Yes. I began work on it at five thirty this morning. Since then Ms. Castro came by to insist that I have the room ready for her class at nine. I already have stripper down and it needs to work through. I can't both strip the floor and have it ready for her class."

"If Ms. Castro says she needs the room, then you'd better hop to and get it ready for her to use. You can continue with your work after her class."

"That means I'll have to mop up and waste all the stripper I already poured on the floor. Then I'll have to start over again completely when she's finished."

"If you know what you have to do, then why are you here wasting my time? I suggest you get back to work," Ms. Hefty tells him.

David returns to the room and restores it to order. After Ms. Castro completes her class, he has to remove the tables again and start the job from scratch. He began his workday at dawn. Because of the interruptions, he does not finish until nine in the evening.

The following day, after applying the wax and buffing it to the high gloss necessary, he asks Ms. Hefty to come inspect his work. She takes her walk around the room. She runs her fingers over the windowsills, picture frames, and any ledges that might collect dust. They come up clean. When she finishes there is no expression of appreciation for a job well done. Instead, Ms. Hefty issues a warning. "Next time you better get the job done without the confusion."

"Every day I'm here I feel myself getting closer to exploding," David says. He struggles to handle the dismissive and degrading ways staff members respond to him. "Later that afternoon, as I'm putting the tables back in order, Mr. Dicker returns. He goes over the room together with Ms. Hefty. When he finishes he shakes her hand and tells her that she has done a fine job, that the floor looks better than ever before. Neither one of them pays any more attention to me than if I were a dirty mop. These people boost their self-esteem by putting us down. I don't know what it is that makes a prison guard tick. Maybe they're so used to working with the criminal minds you describe inside fences. These staff members don't see us as being any different from them."

David objects to staff members diminishing his status as a man. "Last week I'm sitting in my drug-treatment class. I've never had a drug problem in my life. I only participate in the class so I can get time off my sentence. My teacher talks to me as if I'm a terrorist. 'You're not a caring person,' she tells me. 'I've read the file on every man in this program. Not one of you is a caring person. You're all abusive, self-indulged individuals. I'm prescribing an individual treatment plan to help you with your issues of anger and resentment.' This woman doesn't know anything about me. This place is a bigger scam on the taxpayer than anything I've ever known. I have no idea what justice is being served by my being here."

The drug-treatment class in which David participates is a five-hundred-hour program through which qualifying individuals can advance their release dates by a few months. For nine months, those in the class meet four days each week for four hours. While in the class, staff members with the title of drug treatment specialist pigeonhole each individual; to them, every participant is abusive, selfish, and artificial, and struggles with issues of resentment. Anyone who expresses disagreement with the treatment program risks expulsion and in turn the loss of the good time he may receive by proceeding with the charade.

"It's completely different when people from the community come in to address our group," David says. "Last week the teacher brought a guy in to talk with us about his spiritual beliefs. He is humble, gracious. The guy actually thanks us for giving him an opportunity to speak with us. He tells us his name and his story while addressing us as if we are fellow human beings. What a change from the way the staff members talk to us here. They have their handcuffs hanging from leather belts and make it clear that they have the power to lock us away, to separate us from our family members for longer periods. To them we're nothing but registration numbers. It's as if we've made them angry by being here, as if we've done something to them. I just don't get this place."

Some staff members in the camp resent people like David who enjoy wide support from people in the community. "I don't understand why any inmate should receive more than one piece of mail," the correctional officer says to him while passing David his correspondence. "If I had my way criminals wouldn't get mail at all. This place does nothing but coddle you." Another guard objects to David's owning three pairs of sneakers. "You've got more shoes than I have," she tells him.

Because of my long-term experience, the tension in the camp seems like nothing at all to me. Every day is easy. I know how to find jobs that keep me away from both inmates and staff, to keep to myself. The camp frustrates white-collar offenders and others who do not know worse. For them, what I consider minor trivialities that I can easily maneuver around are major obstacles to their peace. They have a hard time with the pettiness, with the seeming senselessness of this particular form of justice. It's true that administrators and prisoners in camps can be much more petty than those in higher security. But I prefer them.

Gerald, a banker who has been here for a while, has learned how to play the system and navigate his way around the problems. He understands how things work and takes advantage of the freedom that his job assignment provides. He is responsible for driving to local communities to make institutional deliveries. As a cigar smoker, he uses his connections outside to arrange his access to choice cigars that he brings back inside the perimeters for him to enjoy with his friends. He hides the cigars on the recreation yard in a case he stashes beneath the bleachers.

"Dagger found the Cohibas I stashed under the bleachers," Gerald tells me. "He calls one of his leg humpers to the office and asks who smokes cigars. Preston names five guys and Dagger calls us in. I'm the last man for the inquisition."

"I hear you like to smoke cigars," Dagger tells Gerald. The ten barrel-wrapped Cohibas are lined up on his desk.

"Yes sir," Gerald says. "I enjoy cigars very much."

"Would you say these are good cigars?" the officer asks Gerald.

"Absolutely, sir. The Cohiba is one of the finest cigars in the world. Although I like the Montecristo, I prefer the Cohiba. It is my personal favorite. It's smooth and rich. An excellent smoke, sir."

"It sounds like you know a lot about cigars."

"Oh, yes sir. I am a connoisseur."

"Would you smoke these cigars?" the officer asks.

"Yes sir, I would. I would be honored and delighted to share one of those cigars with you right now."

"Are these your cigars, inmate?"

"Mine? Oh, no sir. I haven't smoked a fine cigar like that since I arrived here three years ago."

"Uh-huh," the officer grunts. "Well, I'll tell you what I'm going to do. Since they're not yours, and I found them, I'm going to take these cigars with me and smoke every one of them. What do you think of that?"

"I think that is exactly what you should do, sir."

Like the boys inside fences, Gerald has learned to make his time a little easier.

19

During my time in the camp I am in the company of many white-collar offenders like David. They intrigue me, as many of them led lives of distinction prior to confinement. While I work to teach them about the abnormal world we share as prisoners, they help me understand the world that I have missed.

Not only do these men come from different backgrounds and with different values than did those with whom I have served most of my time inside of fences, but the crimes for which many white-collar offenders serve time frequently seem much more complicated. During my early years of confinement I came to know many Mafia chieftains, drug barons, murderers, and armed robbers. Their crimes are rather straightforward and easy to understand.

In the camp I came to know men serving lengthy sentences for violating tax laws, for engaging in fraudulent Ponzi schemes, for violating securities laws, for check kiting, and for failing to disclose personal assets on government forms. One of the most bizarre crimes I came to learn of is a violation of the Lacey Act, a crime for which my friend Arnie was sentenced to four years.

I met Arnie while I was seated in the camp barbershop one Friday morning. He had arrived the day before. As the barber clipped away at my hair, Arnie walked into the small room. With a population of five hundred, the camp has a single barber's chair, so Arnie took a seat as he waited his turn. He is a distinguished-looking man with a healthy, fit appearance that suggests he is much younger than his actual age of sixty-eight. His precise diction and patrician bearing reveal that he is an educated man.

"Where did you fly in from?" I ask as a way of opening conversation with the new camp gentleman.

"Oh, I'm from several ports of call," he says with his elegant South African accent. "This is the eighth prison I've been to in the past eleven months. Most recently I come from the camp at Terre Haute, Indiana, by way of a delightful stop at the prison in Oklahoma City. I'm hoping that I can finish up here. But one never knows where these scales of justice will take me."

"Where is home?" I ask.

"Manhattan," he tells me. "I'm originally from Cape Town, but home has been the United States for the past fifteen years."

"And for how long can we expect the pleasure of your company?"

"Oh, I have a ways to go yet, a couple of years anyway. In addition to the time I serve, I have a complicated restitution matter. It seems the government demands more than its pound of flesh from me."

Restitution is a thorn for many offenders. In addition to prison time, courts frequently augment sentences with monetary sanctions. All felony convictions result in one-hundred-dollar criminal assessment fees. Those funds pass into a pool of money that the government disburses to crime victims. Other offenders receive additional sanctions of criminal fines, forfeitures, and restitution. Some must pay for the cost of their incarceration. In my case the judge not only imposed a forty-five-year sentence; he also levied fines that now exceed two million dollars.

"What did they stick you for?" I ask Arnie about his restitution problem.

"It is most complicated, as it involves the South African government. After a year the restitution is still unresolved. The prosecutor is totally belligerent, asking for over a hundred million dollars. It is absurd, a matter of continuing litigation. I serve time for a unique environmental offense. It is the first case of its type ever heard of in the USA."

Arnie's environmental offense, I learn, has its roots in the South African business he founded over three decades ago. He is a pioneer in the rock lobster industry. In fact, Arnie's company, Hout Bay Fishing Industries Ltd., was one of the largest suppliers of lobster tails to world markets. Through his fleet of enormous oceangoing trawlers, each nearly two hundred feet long, his company hauled in over 140 tons of rock lobster tails each year. That is the quota the South African government allotted Hout Bay Fishing to reap, and Arnie built his business over the years in accordance with that license. Under Arnie's leadership, his company became South Africa's largest privately held fishing business.

With the government's new policy of empowerment and redistribution of wealth following Nelson Mandela's release from prison, the government began to reduce the quantity of lobster tails that Hout Bay Fishing could legally extract from the ocean. Each year the new government would restrict allotment further by tens of tons. By the late 1990s, Hout Bay had lost one hundred tons of its original lobster tail apportionment. Although the South African government restricted it to catching forty tons, it did not compensate Arnie's company for the loss in revenues such a retrenchment would cost him. An analogy would be for our government to limit the quantity of automobiles that a manufacturer could produce, but not compensate the corporation for the losses it would sustain as a consequence of reduced production.

"I employed over three hundred people in Cape Town alone. Besides my specialized vessels, each of which had its own processing and packaging factory on board, my plant and facilities commanded nearly one hundred thousand square feet of waterfront property. The entire operation was geared up to produce a hundred and forty tons of lobster tails, as had been my licensed quota for three decades. It could not sustain itself on a mere forty tons of lobster tails."

Rather than suffer the enormous financial loss, Arnie and his directors chose to ignore the reduction in quotas the new South African government imposed. Hout Bay Fishing continued operations as always, harvesting enough lobster to keep its employees working and its business afloat. In late 2001, the South African government charged Hout Bay Fishing Industries, the corporation, with violating the license by catching more than its share of rock lobsters in the ocean.

The South African case against Hout Bay Fishing Industries resulted in enormous fines and penalties, but no criminal charges against Arnie Bengis or any of the corporate officers personally. As a consequence of his willful disregard for the reduction in allotments, Arnie agreed to a full settlement with the government. He forfeited the business he had built over the course of his lifetime. In addition to losing a business that he says had a conservative valuation of twenty-five million dollars, Arnie paid a personal fine of seven million dollars; it was the largest such fine in the history of South Africa.

In paying such an enormous penalty Arnie was certain that he had put the matter behind him. Not so. As a consequence of Arnie's using his lobsters to supply world markets, including the United States, a prosecutor in New York had an interest in prosecuting him and other members of the Bengis family. This time, the problems for Arnie were not corporate. They were personal and in the criminal courts.

"I do not even understand America's interest in this case. Neither my company nor I committed a crime in this country. There is no victim here. In South Africa I was not personally convicted of a crime, yet I satisfied the government in full with the settlement we agreed upon. Lobster is a legal product all over the world. It is not an endangered species. It is absurd that I am serving time in an American prison for overcatching lobster in the Indian Ocean. South Africa did not deem it necessary to prosecute me in the criminal courts, but in his arrogance, a United States prosecutor deems himself better suited to enforce South African laws."

The crime for which Arnie stands convicted and serves time with me in the camp is a violation of the Lacey Act. This obscure law forbids the importation of endangered species into the United States if the wildlife is caught in violation of any foreign or state law. Traditionally, federal authorities use the act to prosecute people who bring rare plants or animals into the United States unlawfully from places like South American or African jungles. Governments in those jurisdictions may lack the resources to prosecute such crimes. That is not the case in South Africa; that country is second only to the United States in the number of people per capita that it locks in prison cages. Had South Africa wanted to prosecute Arnie criminally, it had the resources and wherewithal to proceed.

The lobsters Arnie imported are neither a rare species nor unlawful to catch. Countless fine restaurants around the world serve them every day. The lobster tails Hout Bay Fishing sold are not illegal in any jurisdiction. The company's biggest customers included Red Lobster restaurants and Costco supermarkets. Yet because the company exceeded the reduced quota imposed by the new antiapartheid government, a portion of the lobsters Arnie's company caught was in violation of the law.

Though Arnie's primary residence is in Manhattan, he and his wife often spend time in the Hamptons, a hundred miles from the city. It is there that law enforcement officers brought a convoy at the break of dawn one summer morning with lights flashing through the quiet Bridgehampton neighborhood. Arnie and his wife were alone in the home when federal officers woke them by using the butt of their firearms to pound on the residence's door. When the couple looked outside the window, they saw the large black sport utility vehicles and blinking lights. "Open up!" the officers yelled to announce the law-enforcement raid. When Arnie's wife, opened the door, the agents showed their force and demanded that Arnie submit to the arrest. They locked the sixty-seven-year-old man's wrists behind his back in steel handcuffs while his wife stood beside her husband astounded and frightened.

The officers marched him into the backseat of one of the large vehicles, guiding Arnie inside with a hand on the crown of his head and a push to his shoulder. Officers sat on each side of Arnie. Communication radios were blasting out directives. With Arnie in the backseat, the driver of the vehicle confirmed that he was in custody. "Ten-four," the officer said into the mike. "We've got the big guy." The crackling *k-k-k-k* followed the announcement, then, "Go get the others. Out." To Arnie it felt as if apprehending him, an elderly businessman, was equivalent to catching one of America's most wanted.

The officers drove him from his home to the federal courthouse at 500 Pearl Street in lower Manhattan. They escorted him into the caverns beneath the high-rise building where he awaited his bail hearing. Officers crammed him into a small cage that was filled with prisoners. The noise of so many men yelling in different languages split his eardrums; the stench of dried urine made him gag. He could not sit, as there was no space in the cell, so he stood shoulder to shoulder with others for six hours while awaiting a bail hearing. During that time jailers were exchanging prisoners. It felt as though each time they pulled two men out they locked three others inside the cage. It was madness, bedlam.

The docket was so crowded that Arnie was not able to see a judge for his bail hearing until nearly four that afternoon. The judge ordered Arnie to post a twenty-five-million-dollar bond to guarantee his freedom. It was too late in the day for Arnie to raise such an enormous amount of money. Officers then took Arnie with a pack of heavily shackled prisoners off to the detention center in Brooklyn.

They locked him in a cell with twelve others, many of whom had just come off the streets. The cell was all concrete and steel. A stainless-steel toilet with a sink bowl attached stood in one corner. Arnie passed sixteen hours crowded in that cell, nearly collapsing from fatigue. He passed through the night and into the morning on the floor with his head leaning against the toilet bowl, his hands holding his folded knees to keep his legs from touching one of the other prisoners squeezed in the cage.

The following day, jailers transferred Arnie to more permanent quarters. They locked him inside a general housing unit of concrete and steel that was bursting with pressure from the angry congregation of men inside. There was no telephone. No writing paper. No place to sit. Arnie saw a well-dressed woman walk in and felt a measure of hope. He pushed his way through the crowd to talk with her. She was a representative of psychiatric services.

"I need to see a physician," Arnie told her. He hoped that he could transfer from the disorienting insanity of the general housing unit to a medical ward. It was a game he must play. Only those who genuinely suffer from dementia or those with good wits about them can move into the better conditions of the infirmary.

When Arnie met with the doctor, he described how two months previously he had shared a stage with six other distinguished gentlemen in Israel: Ben-Gurion University had recognized him and the others with an honorary doctorate of philosophy for their contributions to science and the advancement of humanity. "The fall from that place of honor to this deplorable predicament is too much for me to bear. I do not have the balance or equanimity to endure this struggle." The doctor agreed to confine Arnie in a hospital ward that at least offered the comfort of quiet.

A couple days later, Arnie's lawyers were able to schedule a second bail hearing. Arnie hoped for an opportunity to post a bail that would allow him to return home until he could resolve the charges.

The lawyers argued for a reduction in the huge amount, but the judge would not release Arnie on less than fifteen million dollars. A few more days must pass before Arnie could raise those funds. Finally Arnie's wife and network of support managed to raise the bail. Although Michael Jackson, the internationally known pop star, was freed on a five-million-dollar bail for charges related to the sexual molestation of children, the New York judge presiding over Arnie Bengis's case required the businessman from Cape Town to post a fifteen-million-dollar bond for overcatching lobster in the Indian Ocean in violation of another country's laws. He posted the bond and was released from the Manhattan detention center to home confinement for ten months while the case proceeded through the courts.

"I had no defense against the charges," Arnie explained. "By reducing my allotment, the South African government authorized my company to extract only forty tons of lobster tails from the ocean. We brought in and sold substantially more than that. It was a clear violation of the Lacey Act, although we certainly did not even know the obscure American law existed. Indeed, even South Africa, a country well known for its punitive nature and tough criminal laws, did not consider my violation worthy of imprisonment.

"I had no choice but to enter into a plea agreement with the United States. I agreed to pay additional fines of nearly eight million dollars, believing that in doing so I might avoid imprisonment. The judge imposed a term of forty-six months for me, and additional time for my son and nephew. But the government was not satisfied. In addition to the prison term and the fines, which I paid in full, the prosecutor continued to argue for the imposition of this enormous restitution order."

Unlike a fine, which judges impose to punish offenders for wrongdoing, and forfeitures, which allow the government to seize ownership and control of ill-gotten gains, judges impose restitution orders to compensate victims for their loss. Without a victim there can be no restitution. The American prosecutor used every resource at his disposal to find a victim for Arnie's violation of the Lacey Act. He spoke with creditors, customers, and business associates, but without an obvious crime in this country, not a single victim emerged from the prosecutor's search. Not to be outdone in his passion to punish, the prosecutor contacted the South African government. He offered to go after Arnie's personal estate to compensate the government for its losses. Those losses, he argued, came from Arnie's company's overcatching lobster in the ocean.

The South African government had completely settled with Arnie through an agreement that resulted in substantial forfeitures and fines. It had chosen not to prosecute Arnie criminally, nor had it ever considered a demand for restitution to compensate for the lobster Hout Bay Fishing caught in excess of its licensed quota; the large settlement satisfied South Africa in full. But the New York prosecutor had other ideas. The issue remained unresolved. Because of the complexity of the case, the sentencing judge allowed Arnie to begin serving his sentence while the attorneys continued to argue the merits of the restitution order.

Following the imposition of Arnie's four-year sentence, the prosecutor asked the judge to amend the conditions of Arnie's bail. The government considered this senior citizen a substantial flight risk. Among other new restrictions, the prosecutor insisted that Arnie must change the locks to his apartment, disconnect phones, pay the wages of a twenty-four-hour government surveillance team, accept no visitors, and agree not to leave his apartment for any reason. The new restrictions were to supplement the fifteen million dollars in assets Arnie had posted for bail. Rather than submit to the new terms, Arnie submitted to fate and agreed to the immediate forfeiture of his freedom. The Bureau of Prisons took Arnie into custody, transporting him to the detention center in Brooklyn, where he awaited transfer to prison.

While Arnie languished in the detention center, he became friendly with Sam, a contemporary who obviously had influence over the New York wiseguys in the unit. "We were the same age," Arnie says, "and enjoyed conversations about our family, our grandchildren. He walked paces with me around the pod. I am a Jewish boy from Cape Town who became an honorary member of and got protection from the New York mob."

A migraine headache troubled Arnie as the days in the detention center turned into weeks. In accordance with established medical procedures, Arnie submitted a request to see a representative from health services. The request resulted in an appointment with a physician's assistant ten days later. By then Arnie's migraine had subsided. It was replaced with bronchitis, a condition he recognized from previous experience.

"You're here for a migraine," the medical representative said to Arnie. "I issued a prescription for ibuprofen. That should take care of your problem. You need to report to pill line for pickup." The health care professional hardly raised his eyes from the desk when speaking.

"Right, sir," Arnie began. "But as more than ten days have passed since I submitted my request for medical attention, my migraine has abated. It has been replaced with the onslaught of bronchitis. Please provide me with the appropriate medication." Arnie spoke in a hoarse voice between deep coughs.

"I'm sorry." The physician's assistant dismissed Arnie as he wrote on a pad. "You'll have to submit another request for any new medical issues. I am only able to provide you with treatment for the migraine you reported."

The response astounded Arnie. "But I need medication. Indeed, I am a senior citizen with an asthma condition and a serious illness."

"Your time is up. Report to pill line for your ibuprofen. Submit a new request if you have additional medical needs."

Arnie's experience as a white-collar offender in custody did not become any easier. After six weeks he joined a group of prisoners for the bus ride to the Allenwood camp. Allenwood is a prison complex, with prisons of different security levels. It has a penitentiary, a medium-security facility, a low-security one, and a camp. On the day of Arnie's transfer, prisoners in the detention center launched a disturbance. Puerto Rican toughs were fighting with Dominican thugs. The men refused to disperse and return to their cells when ordered.

Instead, they tangled with the officers. Arnie was nowhere near the disturbance; he was crowded with others in a holding tank awaiting transfer. Furious with the disturbance on another floor of the detention center, the guards punished the men they were transporting to the Allenwood complex by "black-boxing" them.

The black box is a rectangular steel case that clasps over the small chain between the two cuffs. Guards usually reserve it for the most dangerous offenders, those serving life sentences and those they want to punish. The black box renders free movement of the wrists impossible. The cuffs are locked around the wrists and fastened to the steel chain around the prisoner's waist. It was Arnie's first experience with blanket punishment. As a minimum-security nonviolent offender on his way to camp, it was as unusual as snowfall in Miami for Arnie to suffer the black box. It was a consequence of volatile behavior by others with whom he had no more connection than readers have with the pen I use to write this chapter; he endured the pain of the black box for the eight-hour trip to Allenwood.

Although weak from the bronchitis, upon arrival to the Allenwood camp Arnie felt an enormous sense of relief. Time in the detention center meant no fresh air and no outdoor exercise. It was confinement inside a concrete shell of a building, with little opportunity for movement. It kept Arnie in the constant company of felons from every security level. Many murderers and other violent criminals mixed with the few white-collar offenders.

In the camp, Arnie had the freedom to walk outside, to play tennis, to socialize with others who do not embrace the criminal lifestyle or present a threat to him. Correctional officers assigned him a job in the sewage treatment plant. While not an easy assignment, it was not unbearable.

Six weeks after Arnie's arrival, he was told that he must transfer to another facility, as the camp at Allenwood is downsizing. He spoke with the warden of the camp in an effort to ascertain where he was going. The warden told Arnie that it would violate the security of the institution to provide such information; it is the default response staff members give to all questions from prisoners. Another officer ordered Arnie to pack his belongings and report to the discharge department, where he packed for transit. His first stop on the journey was a holdover section within the United States penitentiary at Lewisburg, about thirty minutes away from Allenwood.

"My worst experience in this ungodly system has been the transfer from one camp to another," says Arnie. Many prisoners who transfer between camps do so through a furlough, without escort by staff members. The high profile of Arnie's white-collar offense, however, resulted in his being moved through the prisoner transport system, known as Conair. "In Lewisburg I was stuffed with forty-two other men in a small area. The bed frames were triple decker. Despite oppressive heat there was no window, no air-conditioning. There was no way to see outside. After a period of time I became disoriented, not knowing whether it was day or night. There was no clock. No phone. No chair. The room was infested with mice and cockroaches large enough to riot. Guards would not tell us anything. They would not tell us the time of day, much less when we would resume our journey. They did not provide toilet tissue, so we used pages from paperback books. It is a horrible memory, my time in that dreadful dungeon."

The time as a holdover required Arnie to proceed through chaining and processing and waits and lines and admittance procedures at every stop. Every day was long and exhausting. The transfer kept the gentle senior citizen shoulder to shoulder with rough men. Think of a refined and primped poodle crammed into a cage with Dobermans. It was intimidating, frightening for him. Some of the men had shaved heads tattooed with swastikas, demons on their arms and chests. Some were from penitentiaries and loathed those who served time in minimum security. There was no medical attention; he was without any personal belongings and could not communicate beyond prison boundaries.

In time Arnie's journey continued. He eventually made his way to a camp in the Midwest. It is adjacent to an infamous penitentiary, the site reserved for all federal executions. The culture, he says, is one of cultivated hatred. "I never looked in the eyes of a Nazi until I arrived at that camp." His trouble began soon after his arrival, when a team of lawyers flew in from South Africa, London, and New York to see him.

"The people in charge of authorizing my lawyers to visit felt threatened with my access to the world. They used their power to intimidate me. One woman whom I liken to Eva Braun told me that I had committed a very serious offense because my wife mailed me legal papers in the same envelope as a personal letter. She told me if I received any more such mail she would lock me in the hole."

Arnie believes that staff members singled him out for harassment at the camp because of his ongoing litigation and his interaction with powerful lawyers who visited and corresponded with him. The guards frequently searched him and assigned him to difficult jobs, one of them under the direct supervision of a man he describes as a sadist who took pleasure in assigning meaningless, labor-intensive jobs to demean Arnie.

"I am in my late sixties and this Heinrich Himmler–type fellow ordered me to lift heavy stones into a wheelbarrow. He instructed me to move them from one end of a field to another. There was no purpose in the work. When I complained of searing back pain, the man told me that I had nothing wrong with my back. He accused me of malingering and filed charges that sent me to the hole for four bloody days. I heard him refer to me as a fucking Jew who was either very old or very stupid."

Arnie believes that many of the staff members at the camp come to work with the ambition of hurting others, of making men suffer. They do not hide their contempt for the men in the camp, saying that they are criminals who have life too easy.

After Arnie had endured seven months at the camp, administrators moved him again, farther away from his family in New York. He joined me at a camp in the Rocky Mountains, where he awaits his turn to participate in the drug-treatment program that may result in extra good time and a few months advance toward the completion of his sentence. At present he sleeps in a four-man bunk, close enough to the bunk beside him that if he stretches his arms while sleeping he touches the flesh of one of his cellmates.

For Arnie, his term in prison as a white-collar offender is a severe change from the lofty levels of society that he has known all of his life. As an international businessman and philanthropist, he traveled widely around the world in ultra-first-class accommodations. Now he holds a job where correctional officers require him to rake parallel lines across a rock patch. To sustain him through the ordeal he engages in an extensive correspondence with beloved friends from around the world.

"Each month I receive at least sixty letters. I feel honored with this extraordinary showing of support. Each day I look forward to mail with great anticipation. Yesterday I received fourteen letters. It warms my heart, brings meaning to my life at a time when I need it most."

While Arnie takes satisfaction in the support he receives from so many friends, his true strength comes through the relationship he has with his wife. "The time has been horribly hard on her, especially since guards have moved me so far away from home. There have been times during my transition when my imprisonment broke our communications for over a week. She suffers because she has no way to reach me. When I am locked down, in transit, or unable to call, it strikes her particularly hard. This sentence has been as hard on my wife as it has been on me. Perhaps harder. Yet together, I am sure that we will pull through."

20

After I had been in the camp for several months, Counselor Brotler switched me to my fourth job. Some staff members do not want a writer working in their department. My correctional counselor assigned me a job in food services. The position made me responsible for collecting the dirty rags and mops. I washed them, dried them, and stored them. As far as prison jobs go, mine was not bad. I liked it because I knew exactly what my supervisors expected of me and I didn't have to work with anyone else. When I completed my duties I found space where I could sit and write. Since I was in the dining room during the early-morning meals, I was available to talk with other men who served time inside those perimeters. It was a good spot for me to gather information for stories I write.

As I sat writing at a corner table one morning I heard a familiar voice. "Wussup, you square muthafucka?" That was not a greeting I was accustomed to hearing, especially not in the camp. But I recognized the tone and turned to look. It was Crip Tank, the Compton gangster with whom I first entered the penitentiary so many years ago. He was in a wheelchair and smaller than I remembered from the last time I saw him, more than a decade ago when I left the walls of the USP.

"Crip Tank, is that you?" I ask in astonishment. "What happened? Why are you in a wheelchair?"

"These people done fucked me up," he says. "That's what happened. But fuck all that dumb shit. Where you been, nigga?"

Hearing his voice makes me laugh. Ten years may have moved him closer to forty, but at first glance he seems as committed to gangster life as ever. "I've been a few places," I tell him. "I went to one FCI, then to another. After my level dropped again they sent me to the low outside of New York. As soon as I came to within ten years of going home they sent me out here to the camp. I'm finally getting close to the West Coast. But how did you get to the camp?" As the shot caller for the Compton Crips, Crip Tank is the last person I would expect to leave the penitentiary. I can't believe he is in minimum security.

"Wha'chu think, they only lettin' drug dealers up in these muthafuckas? Think they ain't got room for no real thorough OGs?" His mannerisms, his loud I-don't-give-a-fuck voice, remind me of the penitentiary.

"I just got here before Christmas. You must be on your way out. I can't believe you left the pen. It's good to see you."

"I been in the kizzamp for three years," he tells me. "You ain't gonna believe this, but check this out. I ain't been in no trouble since 1998. That's wussup, muthafucka. Think Crip Tank can't change? Shee-it. I ain't that muthafucka no mo'."

He joins me at the table and we talk for hours. Crip Tank is only months away from freedom. It astounds me to hear Crip Tank—one of the most terrorizing prisoners in the pen, a hard-core gang leader who made some hardened criminals shake—even talk about change. "Tell me what happened," I say. "The last time I saw you, you were leaving a guy's guts hanging out of his stomach in the corridor. It's not so easy for my mind to make the transition of seeing you in the camp."

Crip Tank has the strength to lift himself out of the wheelchair and slide into the swivel chair attached to the dining-room table. "Man, that wasn't nothin' but some penitentiary shit," he says. "You know how it go up in there, how us block boyz carry it. A muthafucka gots to serve somebody or he goin' get served. But I ain't with that no mo'."

"Yeah, I can see that," I say. "Otherwise you wouldn't be here. What I want to know is how you got here. Why did you change?"

"It's a long story."

"Then start talking. You're the one who's going home in a few months. I've still got years."

In 1998 administrators gave Crip Tank an opportunity to move closer to home. With only seven years remaining, they transferred him to a medium-security prison in the Southwest. "My mama was gettin' sick. I kept stayin' on the warden about how I needed to get back to Cali so I could see the fam. It took three years of cussin' that muthafucka out, but he finally sent me out to the desert."

"Yeah, so what happened then?" I asked. "I'm sure FCI has no shortage of gangbangers. Crips are everywhere. The camps are the only places without gangs."

"Shee-it," Crip Tank says. "We got homeys ev'ywhere. Don't get it twisted, cuz. We just layin' low up in these spots. But you right. I got mad homeys down there. They showed me love as soon as I hit the pound."

"And you were able to stay out of trouble in Phoenix? I can't believe that."

"I ain't sayin' I stayed out of trouble. In fact, it was gettin' in trouble that finally got me right." Crip Tank proceeds to describe the disturbance he walked into at the FCI, which led to his change.

"I'm working in the kitchen out there on the early-morning shift. That way I can steal all the food I want and get out to the weight pile and buff before that desert sun starts bakin'. C-low comes in talkin' about how Meat wants to holler at me. 'Yo, check this out,' I tell C-low. 'If Meat wants to talk tell him to come in here.' C-low says that Meat can't come inside with one-time all over the place. He says I needs to go outside. He's in the shit. So I step out to see Meat."

"Yo, we gots to go put in some work," Meat tells Crip Tank when he sees him outside the chow hall. "Da-moo muthafuckas tried to serve us in the cell this morning. They thought we was slippin', but we jumped up to handle our bu'iness." Despite the heat, Meat wears a jacket and a skullcap. When he lifts the cap over the side of his ear and lowers the collar of his jacket, Crip Tank sees pink welts. There are burns on Meat's face, ears, and neck. He uses the cap and jacket to hide the discoloration.

"What the fuck happened to you?" Crip Tank says as he takes in the horror of Meat's skin.

"I told you. Da-moos. Muthafucka creeped in the cell while I was sleep and throwed that shit on me. Nigga had that Darth Vader shit on, but I know who it is." Meat explains his assault by saying a member of a rival gang slid into his cell. The assailant wore a skullcap pulled over his head and face. He had cut owl eyes into the cap so he could see through the holes while disguising his face from cameras and anyone else. While Meat lay sleeping, his rival threw a cup of boiling baby oil on his face, then ran out of the cell after Meat and his cellmate jumped up to attack with knives they had hidden in their pillowcases.

"Where them niggas at?" Crip Tank asks Meat.

"On the yard."

"Yo, let me go get suited up. We goin' handle this shit," Crip Tank says.

"I got you, homey," Meat says. He passes Crip Tank a knife carved out of Plexiglas.

"Lil-G's ridin' too. He waitin' for us by the flag pole."

"Let's roll," Crip Tank says. Crip Tank, Meat, and Lil-G walk through the metal detectors on their way to the yard. As they round the corner they see a wall of thugs from the Bloods street gang. With his reputation of being a Crips shot caller from the pen, all of those rival gang members standing beside each other in a show of strength or solidarity does not intimidate Crip Tank. "Look at all them Da-moo muthafuckas. You see the bitch who hit you?" Crip Tank asks Meat while he walks with his hard grit face, holding his crotch with one hand, his knife tucked inside the sleeve with his other. He stares down the line of men as he approaches.

"Meat gestures to Snake, and Crip Tank confronts him. "Yo, wussup, muthafucka? Why you did that to my homeboy?"

"That nigga done broke in my locker and stole my shit," Snake says to Crip Tank.

"I told you last night that I didn't take yo shit, man," Meat says.

"Nigga, you lying," Snake says. "I know you ain't got no money. You gettin' high on my shit."

"Didn't the homey tell you last night that he didn't take yo shit, muthafucka?" Crip Tank asks. But he is not certain of Meat's honesty. When Meat answered his voice sounded shaky, as if he was hiding something.

"So wussup, muthafucka? Wha'chu got?" Lil-G lifts up his shirt to reveal the shank he carries, infuriating Crip Tank, who prefers action to threats.

"That ain't shit, nigga. Wha'chu think you goin' do? Scare me?" It is not the first time Snake has seen a shank. "I did that to your homey. Now wha'chu goin' do with yo bitch ass? Bring it."

Crip Tank is angry with Lil-G for stepping into the conversation, and especially upset at him for pulling out the knife. He sees no choice but to respond when Snake throws out the challenge. Crip Tank blasts Snake in the jaw and the three Crips begin to rumble with the group of Bloods. They are slashing and battling, firing punches, connecting with elbows and knees, using the guerrilla tactics the gang members practice while locked in cells. Within minutes officers rush to the yard and take the group into custody, locking the combatants in the hole. The guards cram Crip Tank, Meat, and Lil-G in the same cell.

"What the fuck is this shit about?" Crip Tank corners Meat inside the locked cage. "What that nigga talkin' about stealing out there?" Crip Tank did not have the story from Meat over what initiated the conflict. He was only responding to a fellow Crip in distress. He does not condone stealing and does not want to involve himself in defending a thief.

"Who the fuck is you talkin' to, nigga, axin' me about my business?" Meat speaks in a defiant tone. "You know how we do up in forty-eight hun'red," referring to the gang unit of the Los Angeles County Jail, where gangbangers resolve all disputes with battle.

Crip Tank flares up at the disrespect. He grabs Meat's jumpsuit in his fists and pulls him close. Then he head butts him twice before smashing Meat's body into the concrete wall. The instant attack dazes Meat and he cannot find his footing to defend himself. Crip Tank pummels him with his fists from one end of the cell to the other. Blood is splashing out of Meat's mouth with every connection. When Meat falls to the floor, Crip Tank starts kicking him in the head, in the ribs. Meat curls up in a ball. He is unable to stop the 260 pounds of fury that Crip Tank uses effectively to smash him. It is a volcanic eruption of temper. Guards rescue Meat when they hear the commotion in the cell as Crip Tank tries to beat the life out of his homey. It takes four officers to pull Crip Tank out of his frenzy. They lock him in a single cell and take Meat to the infirmary.

Members of the Bloods gang who guards have locked in a nearby cell watch as orderlies carry Meat out on a stretcher. The Da-moos start communicating with Crip Tank. Snake tells him that one of his homeys had seen Meat walk into Snake's cell when no one else was on the tier. "That's a violation right there," Snake says. "When I checks my stash, I see all my loons is gone. Later I heard that your homeboy is axin' around for a rig. So I knows it's him."

Many of the problems in prison have their roots in drugs. Snake is active in the trafficking of heroin. He uses his old penitentiary tricks to smuggle the drugs inside. His girlfriend packs colored balloons tight with a fingertip's portion of heroin. She triple wraps each balloon. She then coats the outside of the balloon with a lubricant. Those balloons fetch five hundred dollars apiece inside federal prison; the heroin that fills the balloons costs about fifty dollars on the street.

To transport the balloons inside, she opens a yellow M&M's Peanuts candy package. The mule then removes enough of the chocolate-covered candies to make room for a few heroin-stuffed balloons. When she walks into the visiting room, Snake's girlfriend carries the package of M&M's in the pocket of her jacket. She walks to the vending machine and purchases several new packages of M&M Peanut candies that come in the same yellow package. She drops those in her pocket as well. When Snake comes into the room, the two kiss lightly to avert suspicion from the guards. Officers who roam around the room and observe visiting interactions through surveillance cameras expect drugs to transfer through open-mouth kisses. Snake's plan keeps him from being a suspect.

As they sit, Snake's girlfriend lays the candy packages on the table. While under the guard's direct observation, Snake swallows the tiny balloons that look just like M&M candies. He uses his body to smuggle the heroin into the institution. In the privacy of his cell, the lubricated balloons pass through Snake's system and increase his fortune. Ten of the tiny balloons bring him five thousand dollars; it is a profit of well over four thousand. In a population of nearly two thousand felons, his homeys move the eleven-five in a matter of hours.

When Snake hears through the prison grapevine that Meat is asking for "a rig," he knows that Meat has heroin. A rig is a needle and syringe that prisoners pass around to shoot the drugs into their veins. In years past, medium-security prisons had problems with only weed and cocaine; with the crowded system, as administrators transfer prisoners from the pen into lower-security institutions, drugs of every kind are a problem. The possibility of passing the

AIDS virus, "the blickie," is less threatening to some prisoners than living through confinement without drugs.

"Man, I don't condone no shit like that," Crip Tank says. As an OG, he despises any gang member who shoots heroin. It is a violation of the Crips code. Further, although he has no problem with a straight-up robbery, taking another's possession by force, Crip Tank does not tolerate a member of his gang stealing from another con on the sneak. "Hey, homey, I was flyin' blind on this shit here. I didn't know nothin' about no stealin', know what I'm sayin'? That's why I had to put hands on a muthafucka when he showed his true colors."

"It's all good, homey. I'm a catch that muthafucka at the next stop," Snake says, affirming his insistence that Meat pay for the breach of gang protocol. The crowded prison system has turned medium-security facilities into minipenitentiaries.

While locked in the single cell, Crip Tank experiences his first pangs of consciousness over his actions, over the life he lives. As a gang leader, his allegiance is to every member of the Crips gang. Meat was in the wrong when he came to Crip Tank seeking assistance to retaliate against Snake. Crip Tank did not take a second to reflect on what he was doing. Just as in my last encounter with Crip Tank a decade ago, he came without thinking or question to the defense of another Crip. That is his loyalty, his allegiance to the gang. With Meat, he learns, some actions are not worth defending.

"I'm lying up in my cell, know what I'm sayin'," Crip Tank says. "It's good to be alone, to think. A nigga gettin' older and I'm thinking about my sons, Rick and Steve. I ain't seen 'em in so long and my mama's bringin' 'em to the FCI for a visit. While I'm in that cell I'm just thinkin' about how much I want to see my kids. Now, with all this bullshit that muthafucka Meat got me up in, I'm thinkin' the man might send me back east, to Leavenworth or Lewisburg. I'm fucked up about this shit, especially since it all started because this muthafucka been stealin'."

But Crip Tank does have his visit with his mother and Rick, one of his sons. "Daddy, why we got to sit up here in front of the po-lease?" Crip Tank has to tell his son that he had a problem and that everyone with problems has to sit close to the visiting-room officer. "Why is you wearin' a orange jumpsuit and ev'one else be wearin' khakis?" The perceptive six-year-old boy continues to ask Crip Tank questions about his status.

"Daddy got into a fight," Crip Tank levels with his son. "They caught me, so I have to wear different clothes and sit next to the po-leases."

"But Daddy, why are you fighting? Why are you always telling me to do good in school, to stay out of trouble, and to walk away from fighting? Why are you tellin' me that and then you fightin' in here?"

The question stuns Crip Tank. For the first time he realizes the hypocrisy of his giving the boy fatherly advice while he lives as a gangster in custody. Before the visit ends, Crip Tank promises his son that he will stay out of trouble. "Daddy, I don't want nothing else but for you to come home. I'd give up all my toys and ev'ything else if you could just come home with me."

"I'm a come home, champ," Crip Tank tells him. "You just be good at home and I'll be good in here. I'm a come home."

Crip Tank's eyes well up with tears as his son sends a strike that triggers his emotions. "I realize how much my son needs me," Crip Tank says. "He's living with my mama and she's not doing so well. My baby's mama died from cancer, and if anything happens to my mama, my son ain't gonna have no one. I realize that I got to come home, that I gots to make a change. When they leave and the guards take me back to my cell, I'm thinkin' real hard about what I'm a do when I get out. That fucks me up. I don't know how to do nothin' but sell drugs and fuck muthafuckas up."

Crip Tank is alone, locked inside his cell, when the first signs of his illness strike him. "I don't know what it was that hit me, but I felt something attacking my whole body. I'm shakin' ev'ywhere. My back is completely froze up and it's hurting me like I can't even describe. I can't move at all by myself. My legs won't lift me. My body is sweatin' like a muthafucka, soakin' my blankets. But I'm still cold, so muthafuckin' cold it feels like I'm lyin' in a bathtub full a ice. I'm vomitin' right there in my cell from the bed 'cause I can't even walk, can't move. I'm thinkin' that I'm dyin', but I don't know from what. It hit me all at once."

Crip Tank finally gets the attention of guards because he is not collecting his food trays. When they unlock the door and come inside, the guards see and smell the vomit on the floor. They see Crip Tank lying helplessly in his rack, covered in blankets soaked in sweat. The prison doctor comes and prescribes Crip Tank some ibuprofen.

"I spend another two months wastin' away in that cell," Crip Tank says. "I just can't get well. I feel myself gettin' weaker and weaker. I can't eat nothin'. The doctor won't give me nothin' but aspirin and ibuprofen. The muthafucka keeps sayin' that I'm fakin' and shit. I can't even stand up from the bed and he's sayin' I'm fakin'. My back is hurtin' so bad I have to sleep with my knees on the floor, just kneelin' over the bunk. It's the only way I can lessen the pain. I lose forty pounds over the next couple weeks. Muthafuckas won't treat me. They don't give a fuck about Crip Tank. Then they give me my disciplinary transfer."

Crip Tank had been worried that administrators would discipline him with a return to transfer to one of the eastern penitentiaries, far away from his family. Instead, they left him in medium security, with a transfer to another FCI in the Northwest. The unknown sickness remained with him. At times it was so bad that he felt certain death was around the corner. During those times, he said, while struggling to remain conscious, he made promises to himself that if he could pull through the illness he would start living for his children and family instead of living for his gangster values.

"At the new FCI I started doin' better. Instead of givin' me ibuprofen and tellin' me that I was just fakin', the doctor started givin' me some other kinds of medicine that eased the pain some. I started gainin' a little bit a weight back. I'm still cock diesel, liftin' weights and shit. But I'm sick all the time. I can't even go outside without catchin' a cold or the flu. The doctor says he is goin' to schedule me to go to a real hospital for some testin', but before it happens they transfer me again."

Upon a review of Crip Tank's disciplinary history, administrators at Sheridan decide that he is improperly classified. They reclassify him as a high-security inmate. Without prior notice, guards lock him in chains and transfer him back to the federal penitentiary. "Man, that transfer fucks me up," Crip Tank says. "Ever since that visit with my son I was doin' good. Know what I'm sayin'? I'm stayin' out of trouble. But they send me right back into the jungle. There's about three hun'red homeys inside the USP. It's where these muthafuckas send all hard-core gangbangers. As soon as I step on the pound, muthafuckas passin' me the shit. Niggas is gettin' high and smashin' shit up. I'm tryin' to stay right, know what I'm sayin', but you know how it go up in the pen. Muthafuckas be wildin' out. Those first days I'm smokin' blunts every day, gettin' my drink on, callin' dogz for the Compton car. Then I see my team. The case manager tells me that I'm still misclassified. She tells me that I should be in the medium. If I can stay out of trouble for six months, she says, she'll send me back."

For a man with ties to prison gangs, it takes discipline to avoid infractions. There is regular pressure to violate rules, to engage in disruption and mayhem on behalf of gang interests. With the case manager's promise that six months of clear conduct will result in a return to medium security, Crip Tank hopes that he may arrange a transfer to another FCI on the West Coast. It is an FCI in Los Angeles that would make more visits with his sons possible. That is the motivation he needs to lie low, at least low for Crip Tank.

While in the USP with me, Crip Tank still had nearly two decades of prison ahead of him. With so much time, he saw no reason to live according to any rules other than his own. His allegiance was to the penitentiary life, to the Crips. Listening to Crip Tank tell me that he passed through six months at another USP without hurting anyone, without engaging in the smuggling operations or efforts to dominate, I felt as if I were listening to a different person. After six months his transfer came through, but not as he had hoped.

Although administrators were willing to transfer Crip Tank out of the penitentiary, they were not ready to transfer him back to a prison near Los Angeles. They sent him to an FCI in the middle of the country. That turned out to be a good move for Crip Tank. During the first years of Crip Tank's confinement there, his illness was in remission. Those thoughts about contributing to his son's life, of living as a better role model, kept him going.

"When I get there I know I'm out of the pen for good," Crip Tank says. "Ever since that shit jumped off down in the Southwest, I thought they might be sending me back inside the wall. I never felt too sure about being in the Northwest. When they sent me to the USP I just figured that was it, know what I'm sayin', that I'd be inside the walls until I'm out. If I'm in there with all the homeys, I know what time it is. A muthafucka got to stay strapped and suited up, ready for work. When they tells me I might can leave in six months, I just say fuck it. I'm out."

As one of the original gangsters from the Compton Crips gang, Crip Tank has respect. Those who pledge their lives to the street gang hold him in high regard. They admire his reputation for fearlessness, for loyalty, for living as the embodiment of everything a gangster stands for in life. When he is inside the USP, Crip Tank has over a decade of continuous confinement behind him. During that time he enhanced the savage reputation he brought into the pen from Compton's most well-known sect, the Santana Block of the CC Riders.

The words "Santana Block Boyz" are inked in large letters across Crip Tank's back. His shoulder has another tattoo that extends down his arm. It is a mural of symbols including demons and prison gun towers and weapons and clocks representing the passing of time inside bars. Crip Tank lives the gangster life to the fullest. He is that thug younger prisoners aspire to grow into. Yet when he learns that he can leave the penitentiary behind, he chooses behavior that will keep him out of the mix.

"Yo, check this out, cuz," Crip Tank says to One Punch, a Crip who calls dogz for another one of the gang's sects inside USP. "I'm almost up outta here. Case manager told me that if I stay out the shit for a minute she's gonna let me bounce back to Cali."

"Word," One Punch says. "So what you sayin', OG?"

"You know how we do," Crip Tank says. "I'm a ride till I die. Always gonna be there for the homeys. But I can do a lot mo' for a muthafucka if I can head back to Cali. I'm a get out in oh-five. Then I'm back on the block, holdin' shit down. Know what I'm sayin'? I'm a fall back some in here so I can get out."

"That's what the fuck I'm talkin' about," One Punch says. "You been doin' the damn thing all yo life, homey. It's time to let some these young niggaz carry the weight around here. You got to take care a you now, OG. Get the fuck up outta here, cuz. We gonna hold it down."

It was that conversation with One Punch, a fellow OG, that led Crip Tank to step away. Since that day, he says, he has refrained from smoking weed or drinking wine. When the bus dropped him off at his most recent stop, he did not set out to find a weapon. Instead, he made a purposeful decision to stay away from problems. "As soon as I stepped on the compound the homeys came up to me, know what I'm sayin'?" Crip Tank explains. "I'm holdin' rank over all them muthafuckas. We all flyin' under the blue flag. But I let 'em know that I'm on my way out. I got less than five years to go and I ain't tryin' to fuck that off."

Because he is one of the gang's elder statesmen, the others respect Crip Tank's retirement from day-to-day chaos. Whereas Crip Tank immediately established his seniority upon entrance to the USP and the earlier FCI, in later institutions he tries to lie low and to take affirmative steps. As a consequence of his decisions, Crip Tank's disciplinary record begins its string of years without infractions.

"But then, this illness starts attackin' me again," Crip Tank says. "I mean it's worse than ever, somethin' terrible. It's so bad that I can't walk. My back is in so much pain. It's like I'm gettin' stuck by knives all over the place. The shit is tormentin' me. I can't stand up straight. I can't lie down flat. And the first attack comes at the worst time. It hits me just as I'm about to get some pussy when I'm in the visiting room with one a my homegirls."

Crip Tank walks into the visiting room feeling normal. He and Booby are seated at an outside table, exchanging kisses and feels whenever they're out of the officer's sight line. "Baby, let's stand over there by the picture line," Crip Tank woos her. "Then we can slide in behind the vending machine and do our thang thang." He convinces Booby to have sex with him in the cramped spot between the wall and the Frito machines.

"Shee-it, nigga," Booby tells him. "You been down too long for that."

"I can still tear that pussy up, baby girl."

"Let's go then," Booby says. "You know what I'm about."

When Crip Tank stands up from his seat, his legs fall out from under him. He collapses to the floor and begins convulsing, shaking everywhere, as he did while he was locked in the FCI cell. It's as if he is a cripple, or enduring an epileptic seizure. The guards terminate his visit and order a few other prisoners to carry him to the health services department on a stretcher. A doctor is not immediately available, so Crip Tank receives nothing stronger than ibuprofen, which he says is the prison system's response to every medical problem. The seizure eventually subsides, but the illness grows progressively worse as time passes.

"I start getting sick every day," Crip Tank says. "The pain is like nothin' I've ever experienced. I'm hurtin' all the time. I go to see the doctor and that muthafucka says I ain't got nothin' more than muscle spasms. If he ain't sayin' that he sayin' that I'm fakin'. The muthafucka takes an X-ray and thinks he can see what's inside me. This shit is real, man. I feel like I'm gonna die. I'm losin' weight fast and there are days when I can't walk at all. I keep tellin' these muthafuckas I need to see a real doctor but they keep bullshittin' me, tellin' me there ain't nothin' wrong with my back. When I say I need a CAT scan or an MRI or some other test, the muthafuckas tell me there ain't nothin' in the budget for that."

As Crip Tank struggles through his illness, he simultaneously advances closer to his release date. As a consequence of his refraining from disciplinary violations, his security level drops low enough for him to qualify for camp placement. "Hey, Warden," Crip Tank says to the man in charge. "I'm ready to head out to the camp. I only got five points."

"You don't have five points." The warden doesn't believe Crip Tank. "How's a hard-core gangbanger like you going to have five points?"

"I'm telling you I got five points. I ain't had no problems since 1998. My record is cleaned up."

"Let me look at your file," the warden tells him. "If you've got five points I'm going to send you out to the camp."

The warden checked Crip Tank's record and saw that he had told the truth about his security points. The warden then called Crip Tank into an office to speak with him directly. "I've read through your file. It's true that your points are now low enough for the camp, but you've got this history. It's bad. You got weapons charges, drinking, drugs, gambling, extortion, disturbances. There's not one rule you haven't broken in prison. Why should I send you out to the camp?"

"Yo, check this out, Warden. That's been ten years ago. My priorities are not the same. I'm gettin' old. I ain't with that no mo'. Shee-it. I ain't got but three years left. I ain't thinking about nothin' but my sons and my mama. Know what I'm sayin'? You can see I haven't had no problems since I left the FCI. That ain't no accident. And I'm sick. If I get to the camp it might make it easier to get me outside to a hospital for some testing."

"We've never put a hard-core gang member like you in the camp," the warden tells Crip Tank. "But I've discussed it with the region. We're going to give you a chance. Don't fuck up. I'm putting my reputation on the line for you. You can either open the doors for others to make it into the camp, or you can screw it up for everybody."

That day, Crip Tank left the security portion of the prison and walked into the camp. He adjusted easily to the complete absence of tension among other prisoners and even volunteered to participate in a public speaking program.

"The counselors bring in these kids from juvenile hall, kids who fucked up in school, got caught stealing, fighting, or selling drugs. I could connect with those kids, explain how fucked up life is inside. I tell them that they need to stay away from a life like I lived, and because I've got the street credibility, they listen to a muthafucka when I talk. I found out that talkin' with kids is something I can do. It's one way that I don't have to hide my background. Instead I use it to help them youngsters make better decisions, to stay in school and shit."

With his health continuing to deteriorate, Crip Tank began filing grievances against the prison system. The health services department refused to acknowledge his perpetual pain. They accused him of malingering, of faking his illness to avoid work. Eventually they began to refuse him ibuprofen, telling him to purchase aspirins from the commissary. By filing official grievances, he succeeded in pressuring a trip from the camp to an outside hospital, where specialists used nuclear medicine to diagnose his illness. Those doctors who reviewed the test results immediately admitted Crip Tank and kept him in the hospital for three months as they performed four surgeries.

He had contracted a severe case of desert fever that attacked his spine. He says the doctors told him that if prison officials had authorized medical treatment of Crip Tank's conditions years previously, at an earlier stage of the illness, the disease could have been cured. By denying him treatment for several years, the desert fever grew worse. The disease shattered parts of his spine into fragments and created numerous tumors, necessitating the surgeries.

"Man, they had me laid up in that hospital for months while they cut into me. After the surgeries the doctors sent me down to the medical center in North Carolina for six months of rehabilitation. Now I'm stuck in this wheelchair for the rest of my life. I'm in pain all the fuckin' time and I don't know how much longer I'm going to live. Half the time I feel like dying, this shit is so bad. When I get out I'm a sue they muthafuckin' ass. Believe that. Muthafuckas gonna pay for what they did to Crip Tank."

Following his release from the medical center in North Carolina, administrators transferred him to the camp. After twenty years of imprisonment, Crip Tank will finish the confinement portion of his sentence in two months. He is returning to Compton. Rather than running the streets as a veteran original gangster, "a vet OG," Crip Tank intends to use his leadership in a more positive way.

"When I was lyin' up in that hospital cell, all fucked up and hurtin', I seen a movie about my homeboy Tookie's life. Tookie is one of the founders of the Crips and he's now up on death row. From inside the cage Tookie been writin' children's books, tryin' to help the kids stay away from violence. Someone nominated Tookie for a Nobel Peace Prize. That's what I'm a try and do," Crip Tank says. "I wanna do somethin' for the kids."

Because of his illness, Crip Tank does not expect to live much longer. The surgeons who operated on him said that they believe the disease will take over his entire body in time. When Crip Tank asked his life expectancy, the doctors did not answer with a promise of hope. They left him to believe that he should not expect to live much longer.

"Some doctors say I shouldn't even be alive right now. These muthafuckas put me on my own death row. Like my homeboy Tookie did, I'm a use this time I got left to go from negative to positive. I don't want my mama and my sons to have only bad memories of me. Shee-it. These muthafuckas the ones who put me in the pen. It's their jungle. I just did what I had to do to survive inside. But I'm goin' home and I'm a use the rest of my time to lay the game down for the youngsters. I'm a tell them the real about what's up in the streets and in these penitentiaries. That's what I can do with my life. I seen that I can connect with them. By talkin' 'bout my experiences, 'bout what I seen and done, I know I can change some this crazy shit in the world. We ain't gotta be killin' and slingin' dope. Muthafuckas need to stay in school. That's what I'm a tell them when I get out."

There is no doubt that Crip Tank expresses different values from when we first walked inside penitentiary walls. He no longer packs heat; he refrains from drugs and violence and rackets. He may have

Michael G. Santos

the exact credentials necessary to communicate with adolescents who are on their way to prison. That same aggressive comportment, however, threatens the more docile white-collar offenders with whom he shares space in minimum security.

21

I am beyond eighteen years into my sentence now. Every day teaches me something new. More than anything, I have learned that it is my responsibility to create opportunities. I must overcome the stigma that will accompany my lengthy record of confinement.

In eight more years I am scheduled to leave these perimeters behind. I will return to a community much different from the one in which I have lived since 1987. I am committed to finding ways to grow and contribute, and I will use every resource available to me as I continue these preparations for release.

Working to understand the choices other prisoners make is an integral part of this strategy. It carries me through the seasons. It is equally important for me to observe and interpret the ways that rules, policies, and the culture of corrections influence the decisions and behavior of prisoners, guards, and administrators. Only by seeing myself in the law-abiding role I commit to leading, and working constantly to understand the world in which I have passed decades, am I able to discipline myself, to do what I believe is necessary to overcome my adversity. I must set priorities in order, must evaluate obstacles and navigate around them. Success requires constant preparation. Through this pursuit of it I hope to bring value to the lives of others and meaning to my own life.

Early in my sentence I walked in the yard at the USP with a man named Brett. He was the picture of a convict, with arms completely

sleeved in tattoos; his nickname, Viking, was inked in large letters
across his forehead. Viking was then in his early forties and nearly
two decades into his sentence, as I am now. I asked Viking whether
he had done anything to change his life in preparation for release.
"There ain't nothing a motherfucker can do from in here. I'm just
jailing, holmes, staying in shape and shit."

With his prison-marked body, lack of skills, and lengthy history
of incarceration, it is likely that Viking finished his term less able to
create a place for himself in society than when he began. Instead of
working for the future, he lived his life and served his time in the
present. Most prisoners make the same decisions. The system itself
influences them. As a consequence, many leave prison without hope
or confidence. Through my work I hope to help those with whom I
connect see other options.

As it exists today, the corrections profession extinguishes hope
from those it locks inside. That loss of hope, I am convinced, is most
responsible for the adjustment patterns of the men it holds. Administrators do not encourage prisoners like Viking or the others I have
written about in this book to prepare themselves for the future.
There are infinite combinations of actions that can result in harsher
living conditions, but few prisoners understand how they can distinguish themselves formally in a positive way.

As soon as gates lock a man inside, the prisoner learns that the
goal of the corrections system is to store his body until his sentence
expires. There is no mechanism within the system to recognize efforts a prisoner may make to redeem himself. Consequently, few
commit to such a path. Prisoners learn to live inside and forget, or
willfully suppress, the characteristics of life in normal society. In so
doing, they simultaneously condition themselves further to fail upon
their release.

The system of justice expects finality. Each man has been convicted. A judge imposed a sentence. Correctional officers consider it

their mission to ensure that the man serves his time. There is no interest or concern for what the man will do upon his release, only that he does not leave prison before his term expires. The prison system has become a machine, and the machine functions best when all the cogs are the same.

Thomas Jefferson wrote that all government institutions should exist only to serve the needs of the citizens. Those who govern the prison system have lost sight of that noble perspective. From the director to the prison guard, the mantra has become to *preserve the security of the institution.* That translates into governing by policy rather than common sense, to implementing and enforcing a rigid culture of us versus them that stymies individual growth. Rather than encouraging the growth of citizens, the prison system has become a thoughtless beast that many unthinkingly and unquestioningly fight to preserve.

Despite intentions to reduce all men to sameness, prisoners remain human beings. Some lead and some follow. Each, however, adjusts to his environment. Each has a human need for an identity, for self-actualization. Recidivism rates show that few prisoners overcome the many obstacles in their lives. Only a small percentage of prisoners create niches for themselves and make progress through their terms. Those who lack a complete commitment to abiding by society's values, and the discipline to grow and develop despite extreme adversity, may acquire their sense of identity through violent or otherwise criminal behavior that does not prepare them for success upon release. On the other hand, disruptive behavior will lift them in the eyes of their fellow convicts. To them, that reputation is essential. These men learn to live in prison. They affiliate themselves with gangs; they engage in the drug rackets; they resist authority as a matter of course.

Men locked inside of cages resist the machine's efforts to weaken them. In their efforts to establish some kind of identity, many prisoners continue the cycle of behavior that brought them to prison in the first place. In response, the machine applies more pressure, creating greater hostilities and distancing offenders further from the values of society. The cycle never ends. Like Viking, many prisoners leave prison even less prepared to function in society than when they began serving their terms. Taxpayers receive an unbelievably poor return on the incredible investment they have made to fund the American prison system.

There is an interesting contrast between the incredible progress our society has made in areas of science, technology, medicine, and other disciplines and that of the correctional system. Our response to criminal behavior has not changed much throughout our country's history. We punish. We build prisons and lock people inside of them. Sentence lengths may change with different generations of judges and legislators, but the principle of locking men in cages has remained the same for hundreds of years. I wonder how far our society would have advanced in other areas without the entrepreneurial spirit, without the willingness to consider change. Our nation is simply stuck in a dark age when it comes to corrections.

Unless the prison system is operating as it is intended to function, those who devote their careers to managing institutions that confine people ought to consider a new approach. Extinguishing hope and suppressing individuality may serve the immediate security needs of the institution, but not the long-term needs of an enlightened society. Perhaps the time has come for change.

America may need to confine a segment of its population as a response to crime. Instead of warehousing all offenders and waiting for calendar pages to turn, however, administrators ought to implement policies that would encourage inmates "to earn and learn their way to freedom," as a former justice of the Supreme Court suggested.

On December 16, 1981, then–chief justice Warren Burger delivered the commencement address to the graduating class of Pace

University. Justice Burger titled his speech "Factories with Fences." As Justice Kennedy would do again in his 2003 address to the members of the American Bar Association, Justice Burger recognized the problem of imprisonment as one that has an influence on all Americans, one that has an impact on society in its entirety. Justice Burger recommended a system through which felons could earn freedom through merit rather than strictly the passing of time. More than a quarter century later, legislators and penal administrators have yet to implement Justice Burger's sage advice. We are a nation that pontificates about compassion but cannot suppress its lust to punish.

Bringing such a change to life would require a paradigm shift for those who govern prisons. It would require them to accept stoically the brutal facts of reality. Namely, people respond better to the promise of incentives than they do to the threat of punishment. This truth represents one of the foundations of our thriving capitalistic society. In contrast, we oppose those societies that treat all individuals the same, that stifle freedom. Prison administrators should acknowledge this truism. They should use incentives creatively to introduce prisoners to new values. Instead of stymieing hope, they should encourage it. Instead of erecting barriers that separate prisoners from society, they should offer bridges that will allow individuals to work their way to freedom.

Despite what corrections professionals may publish or profess, those of us who live in prison are convinced that administrators implement few programs with the interest of preparing offenders for law-abiding lives upon release. There is no authentic interest in motivating or encouraging prisoners to distinguish themselves with excellence. Programs exist purely for inmate accountability. They are tools administrators use to maintain security. To believe otherwise is akin to believing that the tobacco companies have an interest in helping people to stop smoking.

Even in years past, when prisoners had opportunities to advance their release dates through parole, the process itself was more subjective than objective. A panel of law-enforcement officers determined who was eligible for release. Decisions were often governed by political considerations, budget issues, and the impulsive will of whoever happened to sit on a given parole board. Merit was not something an individual could count on; no prisoner could work toward an objective and clearly defined path to freedom. Yet that is the system my experience suggests would work best.

I recognize that every felon who returns to a life of crime after release and falls into a subsequent term of imprisonment makes this concept harder to sell. Some people return to society without the skills or commitment to make it. Listening to Fox's story, for example, discourages me. His is the kind of story that strengthens the case against prison or sentence reform.

Fox admits to having lived a life of predatory crime since he was a child. He received numerous sentencing breaks that kept him out of prison until he was twenty-one, when a judge finally sentenced him to seven years. By completing a nine-month vocational-training program, however, he was able to persuade a parole board to authorize his release after fewer than four years. That time in prison did nothing "to correct" Fox; he admits that he returned to preying on society within days of his release. Fox had no intention of holding a job, and he saw no stigma attached to living a life of crime or serving time in prison. In fact, living as a hustler, for him, was a badge of distinction, an honorable vocation.

Fox now says that he is too old to spend any more time in prison. His lengthy sentence in less comfortable prisons played the deciding factor in changing his willingness to continue living as a predator. While he waited for a disposition at the Graterford Penitentiary, thinking he would receive a term of a year or two, Fox expressed no inclination to change his behavior. He lived in the loosely managed prison just as he lived on the streets. After the case transferred from the state to the federal court, and his exposure to prison time increased, Fox's predicament began to weigh on him. And after he adjusted to the barren cells and lack of privileges in federal prison, he acknowledged that he would have to serve seventeen years. That sobering fact inspired the change in his behavior.

Unlike his first term of imprisonment, where Fox was given every incentive to reform, this time administrators warehoused him for nearly two decades. After twelve years of what he calls hard time, Fox is working. He is saving money. He is making plans to relocate in order to lessen his exposure to criminal influences. He is making realistic goals for accepting employment as a barber, cook, or janitor. His decisions are quite different from those of others, who say they will need to find a high-paying job in order to stay away from crime.

The incentives of his first term did not change Fox's behavior. In fact, it seems that had Fox been able to play the federal system in the way he had the state's, there would have been no change in his plans to avoid crime upon release. He has had no fundamental shift in his thinking: he freely admits that the reason he commits himself to avoiding crime is not because he recognizes it as being wrong to prey upon others. Fox is changing his behavior because of the threat of further long-term imprisonment. It is that risk, together with his maturing years, that convinces Fox he must avoid crime.

In Fox's case, the prison system works in the way legislators intend. It has punished him, a six-time felon, and broken his criminal spirit. At least that is what Fox says now. It is a criminal history like Fox's that makes it so much more difficult to validate the concept of earning freedom that I am trying to exhibit and promote.

Although I would welcome an opportunity for citizens to review the continuous efforts I have made to redeem the criminally wrong decisions of my early twenties, I expect no relief from my sentence. I am committed to using the time I have remaining to contribute to society and to preparing in every possible way for the law-abiding life I will lead upon release.

Specifically, I intend to use the Web site that others sponsor on my behalf to offer free content that will help those looking for information about prisons. I will also contribute work to a nonprofit organization that will distribute advice for others looking to grow through adversity. I will continue writing about the men with whom I serve time. This work will both educate and entertain. It will help others understand the pathways to prison and suggest adjustment patterns for emerging through it successfully.

Yet these commitments I make do not matter to the system of corrections. And that is the reason so few people with whom I serve time make similar commitments themselves.

Afterword

A month has now passed since my transfer to the federal prison camp in Lompoc, California. It is the nineteenth separate institution in which I've been locked up, and the sixth federal prison to which administrators have designated me to serve this sentence. There is no telling how long I will remain here; two groups of administrators already have admonished me about my writing.

They have not accused me of wrongdoing. They cannot. The First Amendment makes clear that even prisoners have the right to express themselves.

After having passed my entire adult life inside, I am convinced that these places of confinement only condition people to fail. It is my responsibility as a citizen of this republic, then, to write about the prison system. I hope my work will persuade taxpayers, legislators, and administrators to consider a new approach to corrections, as it is clear that the current model is a failure.

Through my writing I strive to bring readers inside. I want to help them see the shoots branching off from the American system of confinement as it currently operates. High recidivism rates are well documented. Seven out of ten prisoners return to confinement upon their release. Those deplorable statistics are not enough, however, to convince the correctional complex that the eradication of hope and identities, the dehumanization of men, is a failing recipe for conditioning offenders to live in society.

My literary contributions may result in retaliation from bureaucrats who have an interest in the status quo. That is a risk I willingly take. Despite the perils of my work, I must not stop the effort. Through it I hope to convince others that offering offenders opportunities to *earn* freedom, rather than simply warehousing them like so much inventory, is more consistent with American values and an evolving, enlightened society.

This work gives me a real motivation and valid reason to abide by all prison rules. Since I am striving to build a career as an author and spokesman upon my release, I will not engage in behavior that administrators could use to discredit me further. Because they rely on the bad decisions I made in my early twenties to evaluate and classify me, it is crucial that I strictly obey the rules so as not to give those whose philosophy I challenge additional ammunition to fire at me.

I have never written that it was the "mistakes" of my early twenties that brought me to prison. There was no mistake. In distributing cocaine I knew exactly what I was doing. I was wrong, immature, driven by greed and inappropriate values. That is what led to my convictions and the predicament I endure. Similarly, the course I have taken since my time in confinement began has been no mistake. I have found it crucial that I stay busy and keep focused. The work not only brings meaning to my life, it also spawns hope. Empirical evidence suggests that prisons are masterful at extinguishing those essential components to personal success. It is the reason so few emerge successfully from this vicious cycle of failure.

My assigned work detail at Lompoc has me up at four each workday to arrive at the dairy in time to begin milking cows by four thirty. Early mornings and long, laborious hours with cows do not make the dairy a desirable job. But I take it seriously. I am always punctual. I neither possess contraband nor engage in unauthorized activities. I am appropriately respectful to staff. After completing my assigned duties at the dairy, I spend my time writing, reading, or exercising. Visiting hours are available each Saturday, Sunday, and federal holiday, and I pass those hours with my wife, Carole, who has relocated to this community. Administrators, however, consider my strategy to prepare for the future a threat to the security of the prison system.

My time here at FPC Lompoc, as it has been wherever I've served this sentence, is quite structured. The discipline is part of my commitment to reconcile with society, to earn my own freedom. Administrators are perfectly well equipped to respond to weapons, gangs, and disruptions inside. To them, it is the reaching beyond these boundaries with the written word that causes alarm.

The great majority of the corrections professionals with whom I have come into contact make it clear that they have no regard or appreciation for efforts I—or any other prisoners—make to reconcile with society or prepare for a law-abiding life upon release. As has been the case in every prison where

I have been held, even here at Lompoc the administrative focus is only on the time a prisoner spends inside. Therein lies the crux of the problem. The system locks the offender away from society and implements a repressive social structure that breeds failure and resentment.

Those in prison have no model for exemplary behavior toward which they should strive. If it is a correctional system, then how can a prisoner demonstrate that he needs no further correcting? There is no formal vehicle through which those inside can work to redeem the bad decisions of their past; the system does not allow prisoners to distinguish themselves in a positive way. Consequently, few try. An individual may prove himself informally over time to specific staff members, but no amount of effort can change his formal classification for the better. Only the turning of calendar pages makes a difference in that regard.

Any time the prisoner transfers from one place to another, those charged with classifying him will look only to the time for which he was committed and any negative behavior that his record reflects during confinement. No consideration is given to a prisoner's rehabilitative accomplishments. Gang leaders like Lion and Crip Tank, for example, will receive choice jobs and quarters assignments wherever they go; administrators try to appease and monitor them. A prisoner whose record reflects that he has worked consistently to educate himself or prepare for the future, on the other hand, will receive no personal consideration. That man will start at the bottom and must work to prove himself again and again. The message that comes through, of course, is for prisoners to adapt to the ways of the prison—which do not in any way conform to societal norms.

My written work provides example after example suggesting that the harder a prisoner works, the more susceptible he becomes to attack from the system itself. There are valid reasons why so few inside commit themselves fully to the struggle of overcoming the preprogrammed adversity of confinement. Rather than encouraging prisoners to prepare for law-abiding lives in society, the complex conditions them to fail. That is the culture inside America's prisons. Ironically, the more exposure a man has to "corrections," the more struggles he will face upon release.

Others frequently complain about prison inefficiencies, waste, and corruption. In my opinion, those who voice such platitudes ignore the obvious. They accept the stated goals of the complex. They buy into the delusion that

"correctional officers" actually "correct" behavior in these correctional institutions. In reality, life in prison is punitive, repressive, and degrading. If
preparing people to live as contributing citizens were an actual goal, the use
of incentives would replace the threat of punishment. The system is built for
corruption, a scheme with an exquisite design to self-perpetuate.

Prisons remove hope. They create resentment. They thwart family relationships, degrade each individual's sense of self, and separate offenders *in every
way* from society. The system fosters unnatural us-versus-them, Orwellian
worlds. Exposure to such conditioning for years or decades at a time severely
handicaps prisoners and so makes them unlikely to find a place for themselves
in the merit-based society they will encounter upon the completion of their
sentences. Like Prince, many prisoners become comfortable in the Marxist
communities inside, where each is given according to his need and not recognized for personal growth or accomplishment; the need to preserve and per-
petuate the institution surpasses the need to reform the individual.

This cycle of failure continues as if a closed loop, justifying the need for
more prisons and all the billions of dollars in expenditures that keep the system
alive. Neither those in corrections, nor those benefiting from the enormous
capital disbursements—like prison towns, suppliers, contractors, et cetera—
want to see material changes. Why would they? Doing so would be akin to
those in Las Vegas making a call for an end to gambling.

The corrections complex does not exist to prepare people for law-abiding
lives. Its growth depends strictly upon a culture of failure and high recidivism. The corrections complex has become one more classic example of the
governmental tail wagging the dog. Corrections professionals, oxymoron
though the term may be, want more people serving longer sentences. Con-
versely, they do not want people earning freedom, or preparing themselves to
succeed in or contribute to communities outside.

Until taxpayers demand more from this twisted value system, the prison
boom will continue in perpetuity.

Notes

Introduction

Since my status as a prisoner limits my access to news and world events, I rely upon my wife, Carole, to keep me informed. She scans the Internet regularly and sends me the articles that relate to our nation's prison system. In the summer of 2003 she sent me a copy of a speech Justice Kennedy delivered to the American Bar Association on August 9 of that year.

In his speech, Justice Kennedy made such statements as "We should know what happens after the prisoner is taken away," and "We should take special care to ensure that we are not incarcerating too many prisoners for too long," and "Our resources are misspent, our punishments too severe, our sentences too long," and "A people confident in its laws and institutions should not be ashamed of mercy."

These are not the rantings of someone on the lunatic fringe. They are courageous observations by a conservative member of the United States Supreme Court. It is Justice Kennedy's speech that inspired me to write this book. I strive to help Americans understand this system that locks more than two million human beings away from society. I recognize that my status as a prisoner may cause some to question the veracity of my work. Those who live through the system, along with the high recidivism rates our nation suffers, will verify its authenticity.

The statistics I cite are from the *2004 Sourcebook* that the United States Bureau of Justice Statistics publishes. The direct quote of my then unit manager took place in the office and in the presence of the federal prison camp administrator in the early months of 2004.

Chapter 1

All of the information I provide in chapter 1 comes from the journals I kept that detail my initial exposure to confinement and from the memories of my personal experience.

Chapter 2

Ronald MacLean is the pseudonym of an actual prisoner who sat for several hours with me as I interviewed him specifically for this chapter. After recording notes and writing the content, I read the work back to Ronald to ensure that I had captured his voice, and told his story exactly as he wanted it told. The prison nicknames of the other characters in this chapter have been changed as well in order to protect identities.

Chapter 3

Crip Tank is the pseudonym I gave to a long-term prisoner with whom I served several years of my sentence. Woo Woo, Gangsta Pimp, and Junebug are pseudonyms for other gangbangers with whom I interacted in the penitentiary. I helped them file administrative remedies and with other writing projects during the early years of my sentence. Through those interactions, I developed a familiarity with them. I was present for some of the dialogue, such as when Crip Tank was addressing the officer as we were advancing toward the main corridor. I have used my early notes to reconstruct other dialogue for which I was not present, like the conversations between Crip Tank and Woo Woo, Gangsta Pimp, and Junebug. I base those reconstructed conversations on lengthy interviews I conducted with Crip Tank, and from journal entries that record my early years in the penitentiary.

Chapter 4

To corroborate the information I present on supermax prisons, I direct readers to *Supermax Prisons: Overview and General Considerations,* by Chase Riveland; it is a 1999 publication of the National Institute of Corrections. For validation of the Marion murders, I direct readers to the following federal cases; *United States v. Fountain,* 642 F.2d 1083 (7th Cir., 1981); *United States v. Silverstein,* 732 F.2d 1338 (7th Cir., 1984); and *United States v. Fountain,* 768 F.2d 790 (7th Cir., 1985).

Besides relying upon stories from other prisoners, I turned to law books to help me detail abuse at Pelican Bay State Prison. I direct readers to *Madrid v. Gomez,* 889 F. Supp. 1146 (N.D. Cal., 1995).

The case of abuse at USP Florence is documented at *Turner v. Schultz,* 130 F. Supp. 2d 1216 (D. Colo., 2001). The Commission on Safety and Abuse in America's Prisons, chaired by a former U.S. attorney general and a former chief judge of a United States Circuit Court, document the statement of Charles A. Graner Jr. Also, his statement appeared in the *Washington Post,* on page A1 of the June 5, 2004, issue.

Lunatic is the pseudonym I have given to a man with whom I served time in USP Atlanta. I reconstruct my dialogue with both him and Charles Harrelson from the notes of my early penitentiary journal entries.

Chapter 5
The names Little Mick, Buzzard, Beast, Rock, No Good, Pig Pen, T-Rex, Dice Man, Bug, and Little Man are all pseudonyms I have assigned to actual men with whom I served time inside the USP. They all serve lengthy sentences. I am not at liberty to reveal their true identities. I reconstruct the quoted dialogue from recollections and notes of my direct conversations with them. The individuals I quote were housed in cells adjacent to mine.

Chapter 6
Paulie is an actual person in the penitentiary with whom I was close during my confinement inside the walls. His real name is not Paul and he is not from New York. He frequently spoke with me over meals about his acceptance of the life he chose and the consequences of his choices. I reconstruct the dialogue I quote with him from my journal notes.

"Big Country," a shot caller with the Bama Boys, lived on the same tier to which I was assigned in the spring of 1993. I interviewed him for a paper I was preparing on violence in the penitentiary during my graduate studies at Hofstra University. My quoted dialogue comes from that interview.

"Scotty Black" is a friend of mine from one of the prisons in which I served time. He described parts of his life as an associate of the Lucchese crime family, and I base my dialogue with him on those conversations. "Black" is not Scotty's actual last name; "Gaspipe" is the known name of the former leader of the Lucchese crime family, as Scotty told it to me.

"Louie" and I served time together inside the penitentiary. We would exercise on the weight pile at the same time and frequently ate lunch together at the same table. I recorded his dialogue in my notes before he ran to the lieutenant's office for protective custody.

My knowledge of Anthony Battle comes from several sources. Jerry the Jew, a jailhouse lawyer of some repute, but whose name I have changed to honor his request for anonymity, told me about his interactions with Battle while at USP Lewisburg. Lucky is a pseudonym for a member of the gang that Crip Tank led inside the penitentiary. Crip Tank described Lucky's interaction with Officer Tucker—a pseudonym for the officer that Battle actually killed. Neither Hester nor Boone were charged with any wrongdoing in the murder of Officer Tucker. Through my interview with Crip Tank and C-Loc, another penitentiary prisoner with a direct involvement in Lucky's penitentiary drug trafficking, I reconstructed the dialogue between Lucky and the officer that preceded the officer's interaction with Battle. The case, which is public record and published at *U.S. v. Battle,* 173 F.3d 1343 (11th Cir., 1999), does not address Crip Tank's claims concerning "Officer Tucker's" alleged relationship with Battle. According to the published decision, in a confession made to federal agents, Battle claimed only that he had decided to attack the first correctional officer he saw because he was frustrated with prison life and tired of being bossed around.

Chapter 7

In October of 1998 administrators temporarily returned me to the USP where I had previously been housed, as I was transferring from one federal prison to another. While locked in a cell for thirty days, I had a cellmate who was a ranking member of the Mexican Mafia prison gang. I have given him the name Speedy. Speedy and I spoke for hours each day as we waited for time to pass; both of us were in transit. We discussed prison experiences and common acquaintances. It is through those conversations that Speedy described, in detail, that I learned about his integral involvement in the murders I describe in this chapter. In order to protect identities, I have changed the names of each of the characters that Speedy described to me. Further, based on my interview with him, I reconstructed the dialogue of the violent episodes that allegedly took place inside a special-housing unit.

Speedy told me about Toker and how the original plan was to kill Puppet in the bathroom. Speedy told me about Smoke delivering the message that Puppet had been locked in the cell with KooKoo. Speedy told me how he had used mail to deliver his message to KooKoo about the hit he wanted carried out on Puppet. Finally, Speedy told me about KooKoo's return to the yard, and how KooKoo had told him of how he killed Puppet, then kept the guards from discovering the murder of Puppet for several days.

I have seen transcripts of the federal cases that were prosecuted which appear to validate the stories that Speedy told me.

Chapter 8

As a consequence of his response to Stump's assault and attempted rape, Todd received a disciplinary transfer to USP Atlanta. He and I became friends. Todd described his experience with Stump, and from his descriptions I reconstructed the dialogue between Todd and Stump.

The men whom I call Satyr and Wolf transferred to the federal penitentiary where I was housed at that time. I shared the same tier with those men while we were in the USP. I also knew Turd, who shared the cell with Satyr, and Stink, who shared a cell with Wolf.

After officers removed Satyr, Wolf, Caspar, and Bird from the USP general population, I spoke with both Turd and Stink. They described to me what Satyr and Wolf had said about their "party" with Caspar and Bird. From the descriptions I received while living in the pen, I constructed the dialogue to describe Wolf and Satyr's rape of Bird and Caspar.

All of the characters in this chapter are real, but all of their names have been changed to protect identities.

Chapter 9

All of the dialogue I present in this chapter has been reconstructed from interviews I conducted with the men to whom I have given the names Lion, Poo, Woodpecker, Crip Tank, Stick, and Choo Choo. Each of them being members of active prison gangs, they spoke with me and provided information on condition that I not reveal their identities. Accordingly their names, as well as the places, names and identifying features of every character and event in this chapter, have been changed. I did not speak with those I call

"Officer O'Dell," "Scooter," or "Cadillac." Instead, Lion, Poo, Woodpecker, and Crip Tank, who were actual participants in the quoted conversations, helped me to reconstruct all they claim was said in those exchanges.

Chapter 10

The names of all the characters in this chapter, including Officer Nelson and his wife, have been changed. My relationship with Lion and Stitch, pseudonyms for gang members with whom I was confined in the USP, grew from a network inside. I was assigned to a cell directly above Lion. Stitch lived directly across from Lion.

I was present in the housing unit on several occasions when Officer Nelson ordered the unscheduled census counts, requiring us to lock inside our cells. During one of our conversations, Lion asked me whether I wanted to buy time with a woman. Without resources, and with a motivation to leave a high-security penitentiary, I declined to engage in anything that could result in lengthening my prison sentence.

As an aspiring writer, though, I asked Lion to elaborate on his offer. With my assurances to protect his identity, he agreed to provide details about his relationship with the Nelsons. Proud of his exploits, Lion brought Stitch into the room during our conversation to verify the arrangement. I did not speak with either of the correctional officers, the Nelson team. Lion and Stitch gave me the information. From my interviews with them, I reconstructed the dialogue. Neither Lion nor Stitch was present when the male Officer Nelson described to him how he convinced his wife to participate. According to Lion, Nelson and his wife are swingers and engage in spouse swapping with strangers. Because I was not present, I cannot vouch for all of the details of the alleged sexual encounters portrayed in this chapter. However, in my direct experience, inappropriate sexual activity between inmates and prison staff, and even prostitution, does in fact occur in prisons across this country. Indeed, within the past few years two women at a major USP were prosecuted and convicted for engaging in sexual relationships with members of the Crips street gang. One of the women was a department head, and the other was a member of the executive staff. The case was prosecuted in federal court.

Choo Choo is the name I have given to another gang member with whom I am acquainted. In order to protect identities, the woman I call Maribel

Luna worked in a department other than education. Knowing that my research includes the collection of information that will help others understand the prison system, Choo Choo sat with me for several hours of interviews. He described his interaction with the lady whom I call Ms. Luna. Speedy, who was locked in an adjacent cell during Choo Choo's tryst with Ms. Luna, described the lieutenant's stumbling onto the event. It is from my discussions with Choo Choo and Speedy that I reconstructed dialogue to describe these alleged events.

Chapter 11

Each character in this chapter is a real person serving time in federal prison. These people spoke with me and told me their stories on condition that I would not reveal their actual identities or expose them to prosecution or disciplinary proceedings. I kept notes and journals and wrote regular articles through the years to memorialize my interactions. It is from my direct participation in conversations with the characters I call Crip Tank, Lunatic, Gangsta Pimp, Trick, Big Hoover, LaLa, Porkchop, G-Money, and Steve that I am able to reconstruct the dialogue to describe these events. All of the names in this chapter are pseudonyms.

Chapter 12

Dennis Luther is the actual name of the warden who presided over the FCI I transferred to in 1994. He allowed me to interview him in his office on three occasions as I was gathering information for my writings about prison. I based the master's thesis I wrote for my graduate degree at Hofstra University on the research I gathered from Warden Luther.

The inmate whom I call Shamrock became a close friend of mine in prison. I changed his name to protect his identity. During my many conversations with him, I frequently recorded notes to document his adjustment to prison. I base all of the reconstructed dialogue with Shamrock on the interviews I conducted with him. I changed the names of all the other characters in the chapter, including Larsen and Kramer, Swanberg, Clover, Ms. Lewis, Lieutenant Lewis, Jimmy, Smoke, Jamal, Dwayne, Dre, Red, Rabbit, Morris, and Officer O'Brian. And dialogue that includes those characters comes from my interviews with Shamrock.

Chapter 13

Fox is the prison nickname of the man who sat for several hours with me as I interviewed him specifically for this chapter. After recording notes and writing the content, I read the work back to Fox to ensure I had captured his voice, and told his story exactly as he wanted it told. The state and federal investigations of SCI Graterford are mentioned in the case of Drexel v. Vaughn, 1998 U.S. Dist. LEXIS 4294 (E.D. Pa. 1998).

Chapter 14

Prince is the prison nickname of the man who sat for several hours with me as I interviewed him specifically for this chapter. We spoke after he returned to prison from the halfway house. After recording notes and writing the content, I read the work back to Prince to ensure that I had captured his voice, and told his story as he wanted it told. I changed the name of his case manager to protect her identity, and I reconstructed the dialogue between Ms. Adams and Prince based on my interviews with him.

Chapter 15

In order to preserve identities, I have changed the names of every character in this chapter. The men whom I call Frankie and Peter are friends of mine. I was present at the table with Frankie when he saw Ms. Martin, and I listened as he told me how his relationship with her progressed. He told me about their conversations while I recorded notes. From those notes I reconstructed the dialogue as he told it to me.

Peter provided me with the complete details of his interactions with Wendy. From his discussions and descriptions, I reconstructed the dialogue between him and Wendy.

Chapter 16

In order to preserve identities, I have changed the names of every character in this chapter. The man whom I call Frank sat with me for several hours as I interviewed him specifically for this chapter. After recording notes and writing the content, I read the work back to "Frank" to ensure that I had captured his voice, and told his story exactly as he wanted it told.

Chapter 17

As an active participant in the quoted conversations of this chapter, I reconstruct my dialogue with those staff members from memory. I changed the names of Creakle, Barker, Prickster, Schreeve, and Lt. Smith. Dr. R. Bruce McPherson is the actual name of a mentor influential in guiding my life, and to whom I dedicate this book.

Chapter 18

David and Gerald are the actual first names of the people I describe in this chapter. I use those first names at the request of those participants. I changed the names of all staff members in order to protect their identities. This includes the characters to whom I gave the names Ms. Hefty, Mr. Dicker, Ms. Castro, and Officer Dagger. David sat with me for several hours of interview time in order for me to collect the information I needed for this chapter. The dialogue I quote comes from the time I spent interviewing both David and Gerald.

Chapter 19

Arnie Bengis and his former company, Haut Bay Fishing Industries, are the actual names of the subjects presented here. I sat with Arnie for several hours to interview him for this chapter. He also provided me with several legal documents and media articles about his case. After writing the content, I provided both Arnie and his wife with copies of the chapter to ensure its accuracy.

Chapter 20

After the character to whom I have given the name Crip Tank joined me in the camp, I interviewed him for several hours. Through those hours I spent with him I am able to reconstruct dialogue and describe events in which he was a direct participant. All other names in the chapter have been changed from the prison nicknames that Crip Tank gave me during the interviews.

Chapter 21

In order to preserve identities, the names mentioned in this chapter have been changed.